Earl Stanhope

The French Retreat from Moscow, and Other Historical Essays

THE FRENCH RETREAT FROM MOSCOW,

AND OTHER

HISTORICAL ESSAYS.

BY THE LATE
EARL STANHOPE.

COLLECTED FROM THE
QUARTERLY REVIEW AND FRASER'S MAGAZINE.

LONDON:
JOHN MURRAY, ALBEMARLE STREET.
1876.

(All rights reserved.)

CONTENTS.

		PAGE
1867.	THE FRENCH RETREAT FROM MOSCOW	1
1866.	LEGENDS OF CHARLEMAGNE	79
1871.	THE CHRONOLOGY OF THE GOSPELS	109
1872.	THE YEAR OF THE PASSION	139
1873.	HAROLD OF NORWAY	159
1874.	THE COUNTESS OF NITHSDALE	185
1875.	THE STATUE OF MEMNON	233

NOTICE.

THE Historical Essays which compose the following volume were written by the late Earl Stanhope between the years 1866 and 1874, having been contributed to the "Quarterly Review," with the exception of one, from "Fraser's Magazine," which is included by the permission of Messrs. Longman. It is thought by the author's nearest relatives that they may prove of interest to the public.

October, 1876.

I.

THE FRENCH RETREAT FROM MOSCOW.

THE FRENCH RETREAT FROM MOSCOW.*

WHEN Dr. Johnson composed his admirable poem on the Vanity of Human Wishes, in imitation of the no less admirable tenth Satire of Juvenal,—and we scarcely know to which of the two we should assign the palm,—we find him substituting with great felicity modern examples instead of those which Juvenal adduced. For Sejanus we have Wolsey; for Hannibal, Charles XII. of Sweden; for Servilia, Lady Vane. But when he came to the case of Xerxes, Dr. Johnson could remember no adequate parallel. Xerxes, therefore, is still the instance given in his poem, and it is the only one which he derives from ancient times.

"With half mankind embattled at his side,
Great Xerxes comes to seize the certain prey,
And starves exhausted regions in his way.

---

* 1. *Souvenirs Militaires de 1804 à 1814.* Par M. le Duc de Fezensac, Général de Division. (Journal de la Campagne de Russie, 1812, en douze chapitres.) Paris, 1863.
2. *Mémoires.* Par L. F. J. Bausset, ancien Préfet du Palais Impérial. 2 vols. Bruxelles, 1827.
3. *Itinéraire de Napoléon I. de Smorgoni à Paris.* Extrait des Mémoires du Baron Paul de Bourgoing. Paris, 1862.
4. *Leben des Feldmarschalls Grafen York von Wartenburg.* Von J. G. Droysen. 3 Bände. Berlin, 1851.

* * * * * *

The insulted sea with humbler thought he gains,
A single skiff to speed his flight remains;
The encumber'd oar scarce leaves the dreaded coast,
Through purple billows and a floating host."

But had the lot of Johnson been cast later by some scores of years, with how noble a passage might not the retreat from Moscow have supplied him! How striking the parallel between the two conquerors, each at the outset marching forward confident of victory, and at the head of many hundred thousand warriors, and each having at the close to escape almost alone, the one in a single skiff over the "insulted sea," the other in a peasant's sledge across the frozen plains!

The retreat from Moscow in 1812 is, indeed, a subject of ever new and thrilling interest. Nowhere, perhaps, does modern history display, within a compass of seven or eight weeks, so large an amount of individual suffering and national loss. Nowhere does the reckless force of the elements appear more completely victorious over all the genius, all the strength, all the resources of man. And often as we have perused the various narratives of that terrible disaster, we find ourselves ever and anon recurring to it as some fresh contributions to its story come forth from time to time. Two years since we called attention, though but very briefly, to the corresponding entries in the autobiography of Sir Robert Wilson. We now propose to resume the subject, adverting more especially to some memoirs or fragments of memoirs that we owe to France.

The judgment of the Duke of Wellington on this transaction is expressed in a short memorandum which he drew up in 1842, and which Lord Stanhope has published in his little volume of "Miscellanies." We will extract from it the following paragraphs:—

"Napoleon had made no preparation for the military retreat which he would have to make if his diplomatic efforts should fail, which they did. We see that he was distressed for want of communications even before he thought of retreat; his hospitals were not supplied nor even taken care of, and were at last carried off; and when he commenced to make a real movement of retreat, he was involved in difficulties without number. The first basis of his operations was lost; the new one not established; and he was not strong enough to force his way to the only one which could have been practicable, and by the use of which he might have saved his army—by the sacrifice, however, of all those corps which were in the northern line of operations; I mean the line through Kalouga, through the southern countries. But instead of that, he was forced to take his retreat by the line of the river Beresina, which was exhausted, and upon which he had made no preparations whatever. This is, in few words, the history of that disaster."

But besides these faults of Napoleon which our great captain has here enumerated, there was certainly another and still far more considerable error—we mean his protracted stay at Moscow. Flushed with the pride of conquest, he seems to have regarded the Russian winter as though it might be, like the Russian army, defied and overcome. Surely the near approach of that terrible season ought to have been ever before his eyes. With that prospect he should have placed no dependence on the uncertain hopes of peace, and should have remained at Moscow no longer than was absolutely necessary to rest and to re-form his troops.

Let us see whether an examination of the dates does not fully bear out this criticism. On the 7th of September Napoleon gained the battle of La Moskowa, as the French have termed it, or of Borodino, according to its Russian name—one of the hardest fought and bloodiest conflicts upon record in ancient or in modern times. On the 15th he made his entry into Moscow, and fixed his head-quarters at the Kremlin. On the very next day he left it again, driven forth by the conflagration which—we will here avoid the controversy as to its cause—had burst forth at once in various quarters of the city and enveloped the Kremlin with its lurid clouds. During three days, himself in the neighbouring château of Petrowskoi, and with his soldiers at their bivouacs around him, Napoleon might mournfully contemplate the dismal progress of the flames. At length, on the 19th, he was enabled to return to the citadel-palace. The conflagration had then almost ceased, but about four-fifths of the city were destroyed. The remaining houses, however, were sufficient to shelter the army, and there soon appeared means for its support. It is the custom in that country, owing to the length and severity of the winter, to lay in stores of provisions for several months, and thus the cellars of the burnt houses were found when laid open to contain large quantities of corn, of salted meat, of wine, and of brandy—nay, even of sugar and of tea.

Thus the soldiers could at last obtain some refreshment, and repose after all their weary marches and their murderous battles.

On the 4th of October, and not till then, Napoleon despatched one of his aides-de-camp, M. de Lauriston, with pacific overtures to General Kutusof, the Russian commander-in-chief. Now, considering the advanced position of Napoleon's army, and the close approach of the Russian winter, we hold it as incontrovertible that on this 4th of October not a single French soldier should have remained at Moscow. The march back towards Poland should have begun at latest by that day.

The Russian chiefs, on this point more far-sighted, as knowing better the extremity of cold that was near at hand, considered the gain of time as their paramount object. On this principle General Kutusof received M. de Lauriston with all courtesy and seeming frankness. But he declared that he had no powers to sign an armistice, far less to conclude a treaty. It was necessary, he said, to refer the French overtures to the Emperor Alexander at Petersburg, and to Petersburg they were referred accordingly. Some ten or twelve days would be requisite, he added, before an answer could arrive; and on M. de Lauriston's report, Napoleon determined to remain for this further period at Moscow.

Napoleon, indeed, had from the first, in common phrase, "settled down," as though resolved at all events on a considerable stay. Thus, for example, he had given orders for a series of theatrical representations, of which we learn some particulars from the amusing memoir of M. de Bausset. This was the *Préfet du Palais*—a sleek well-fed gentleman, as it becomes court officials to be. His proper post was at the Tuileries, but he had been commissioned by Maria Louisa to convey to Napoleon a full-length portrait of their son, and he had arrived at headquarters on the very day before the Borodino battle. Napoleon had at once displayed to his assembled chiefs the portrait, as he hoped, of their future sovereign, adding with much grace and dignity these words:—"*Messieurs, si mon fils avait quinze ans, croyez qu'il serait ici au milieu de tant de braves autrement qu'en peinture.*"

Subsequently M. de Bausset had attended the Emperor to Moscow, and he received from his Majesty the supreme direction of the intended theatrical representations. He found there already established a clever *directrice*, Madame Bursay, and a few good actors and actresses. Rich dresses in abundance were supplied from the Moscow stores.

"Les comédiens Français en tirèrent des robes et des habits de velours, qu'ils arrangèrent à leur taille, et sur lesquels ils appliquèrent de larges galons d'or qui étaient en abondance dans ces magasins. Réellement ils étaient vêtus avec une grande magnificence, mais leur détresse était telle que quelques-unes de nos actrices sous ces belles robes de velours avaient à peine le linge nécessaire ; du moins c'est ce que me disait Madame Bursay."

But from this comic interlude (as Madame Bursay herself might have called it) we now revert to more serious scenes. It was found by Napoleon, after long and anxious suspense, that from Petersburg there came no acceptance of his overtures. The conqueror, disappointed in his hopes of peace, wavered yet for some time in his military plans. Finally his army, then still 100,000 strong, marched from Moscow on the 19th of October, and Napoleon set out to rejoin it the next day. Even then, however, he did not relinquish his hold of the city. He left Marshal Mortier with 10,000 men to garrison the Kremlin, and the secret instructions which the head of his staff wrote to the *Intendant Général* (they bear date the 18th of October, and have been published by M. Thiers) contain these remarkable words:—"It being the Emperor's intention to return here, we shall keep the principal magazines of flour, of oats, and of brandy."

But Napoleon did not long persevere in this rash design. On the evening of the 20th, only a few hours after leaving Moscow, he sent orders to Marshal Mortier of a directly opposite tenor. The marshal was now directed to blow up the Kremlin by means of mines already prepared, to evacuate the city, and to retire with his troops and with the column of sick and wounded along the Smolensk road. On the night of the 23rd, accordingly, the Kremlin was shattered, though not destroyed, by the desired explosion, and on the next morning the marshal began his retrogade march. Thus instead of the 4th it was the 24th of October, at the verge of the Russian winter, when the last of the French troops took their departure from the Russian capital.

Meanwhile *la Grande Armée*, under Napoleon himself, was by no means marching straight to Smolensk on its way to Poland. On the contrary, it was directing its course towards Kalouga, with a view to the occupation of the southern provinces. Kutusof, however, was in its front. On the 24th one of the French *corps d'armée* gained a victory over a corresponding Russian division at Malo-Jaroslawetz. But the French had lost 4000 killed in that hard-fought combat, and it was little compensation to them to boast or to believe that the Russians had lost 6000. The Russians in the heart of their country were daily receiving reinforcements, while on the invaders, at that enormous distance even from the Polish frontier, the loss of every soldier told.

This last consideration could not fail to weigh heavy on Napoleon, when next day he found the whole army of Kutusof before him, placed in a strong position, and saw that he could only press forward to Kalouga by first giving battle. He might probably win that battle, but it would be, as at La Moskowa, after a desperate resistance and with a grievous loss of slain. Worse still, it might leave him with some 8000 or 10,000 wounded, whom he had no means of transporting, and whom when he moved onward he must leave to perish where they fell.

More than ever perplexed, Napoleon in the course of the 25th entered a barn in the little village of Gorodnia, and there held a council of his chiefs. All of them concurred in thinking an advance upon Kalouga inexpedient. Davoust alone advised an intermediate course through a not yet exhausted country. The others were for rejoining the main road from Moscow to Smolensk, and marching back to Poland by the shortest route.

The reason of Napoleon was convinced, but his pride rebelled. Retreat was a new word to him, ever since at least he raised the siege of Acre. Still undecided, he turned round, and with one of his familiar gestures seized by the ear one of his bravest officers, General Mouton Comfe de Lobau, the same who subsequently rose to political distinction in the reign of Louis Philippe. M. Thiers, who had sat with him in council and who knew him well, describes him as *soldat rude et fin, ayant l'adresse de se taire et de ne parler qu'à propos.* Napoleon, still with the general's ear in hand, asked him what he thought. The other chiefs, according to the custom at that period of the Imperial sway, had given their opinions with abundance of courtly phrases and deferential circumlocution. But Lobau, seeing the moment opportune, answered *en termes incisifs,* "I think that we ought to leave at once, and by the shortest route, a country where we have remained too long!"

This reply, and the tone of it, produced a strong effect on Napoleon. Nevertheless, as though enough of time had not been lost already, he put off his decision till the morrow. On the ensuing day, therefore, he consulted his officers again, and, finding them as decided as ever for the Smolensk road, he issued orders that the troops should next morning, the 27th, begin their march in that direction. Thus it was not till that day, the 27th of October, that at the *Grande Armée* a movement of decided retreat commenced.

It is at this point that we begin to derive many particulars from the book which we have named at the beginning of this article. M. de Fezensac, many years subsequently raised to the rank of duke, was, in 1812, a young officer of great spirit and skill. He was also son-in-law of Clarke, Duke de Feltre, at that time Minister of War. Both these circumstances may be thought to have contributed in equal degrees to his rapid advancement. When the colonel of his regiment (the 4th of the line) fell in the bloody battle of La Moskowa, Fezensac was named to the vacant post. His regiment, as we shall see, was in the rear-guard— the post of by far the greatest danger and the greatest suffering—in the worst days of the disastrous retreat; and the journal which he has written of that period is no less striking than authentic. It first appeared at Paris in a separate form, but is now embodied in the author's "Souvenirs Militaires"—the whole of which we commend, as they well deserve, to the attention of our readers.

Mojaisk—a small town on the direct road from Moscow to Smolensk—was the point to which the *Grande Armée* was directing its course from Malo-Jaroslawetz. That point would be reached in three days, which, with the eight already passed since Moscow, made eleven. But it might have been reached in four by the straight line from Moscow. Thus, then, an entire week would have been employed in unavailing marches. Nor was it merely the loss of time—time trebly precious at that season. The consumption of provisions had also to be considered. When the *Grande Armée* had left Moscow, several of its chiefs, even Napoleon himself, stood aghast at the large amount of its *impedimenta belli*. Cars and carriages, droskis and *berlines*, and every other kind of vehicle, bore along, besides the sick and wounded and the numerous officers' servants, a train of women and young children—French residents or visitors at Moscow, who were escaping from the apprehended vengeance of the Russians—and among them that company of actors and actresses of which we have already given some account. Piled on the cars were seen the munitions of war and the spoils of plunder, extending even to articles of furniture, and together with them huge bags filled with divers kinds of food. There was also an immense train, wholly out of proportion to the diminished army, of 600 pieces of artillery. All this had to be drawn along by exhausted horses—horses already more than half worn out with hard marches and insufficient food. And to this vast convoy, as it had come from Moscow, there were now to be added, as best they might, some two thousand wounded, the result of the action at Malo-Jaroslawetz.

The country around them was so poor, and so thinly peopled, as to afford little in the way of fresh supplies. Thus of the provisions brought from Moscow great part had been consumed in the week already passed, and it was calculated that scarce any would remain by the time the army reached Mojaisk. Moreover, no sooner had the army commenced its retreat than clouds of Cossacks began to hover round it with loud huzzas. They cut off all stragglers; they intercepted all supplies. By these means the French, of the rear-guard especially, were reduced to a terrible strait. If they kept close to their ranks, they could obtain no food for themselves, no forage for their horses. If, on the other hand, they wandered far to the right or left, unless in large bands, each single soldier was sure to have the lance of a Cossack at his breast.

Even while the provisions brought from Moscow lasted, much suffering prevailed. They were most unequally distributed, says M. de Fezensac, like all things which proceed from pillage. One regiment had still some oxen for slaughter, but no bread; another regiment had flour, but wanted meat. Even in the same regiment there were similar diversities. Some companies were half-starved and others lived in abundance. The chiefs enjoined an equal partition, but they were no match for individual selfishness; all means were used to blind their vigilance and elude their commands.

As if to add to the difficulties of this retreat, Napoleon, in his irritation against the Russians, issued a cruel order, which the French writers themselves have been forward to condemn. He directed that all the houses on the line of march should be burned down. Marshal Davoust, who commanded the rear-guard, and who on this occasion, as on every other, showed himself a consummate general, carried out these instructions with pitiless rigour. Detachments sent out to the right and left, as far as the pursuit of the enemy allowed them, set on fire the châteaux and the villages. The result was mainly to drive the Russian peasants to despair, and to aggravate the fate of the wounded and the prisoners who fell into their hands.

"The sight of this destruction," so writes M. de Fezensac, "was by no means the most painful of those which met our eyes. There was marching in front of us a column of Russian prisoners guarded by troops from the Confederation of the Rhine. Nothing was given out to these poor men for food except a little horseflesh; and the soldiers of the guard dashed out the brains of those who could march no further. We found their corpses lying on our route, and all with shattered heads. In justice to the soldiers of my regiment I must declare that the sight filled them with indignation. Moreover, they saw to what cruel reprisals this barbarous system might expose them."

Under these adverse circumstances we need not be surprised to find M. de Fezensac assuring us that, even in the first days, this retreat bore many symptoms of a rout. The divisions in the front pressed forward every morning, leaving their baggage to follow as it could; and thus the rear-guard had to protect and defend the whole of an enormous convoy. Bridges, which broke down under the weight, had to be repaired; obstacles, as they gathered on a narrow road, had to be cleared away. It had been designed that the cavalry, under General Grouchy, should support this covering body, but its horses were so weak for want of forage, and its numbers dwindled so fast, that it could render no active service, and Marshal Davoust sent it forward, maintaining the rear with his infantry alone. He had reason to remember the retort which General Nansouty had made to the King of Naples (Murat), when, even in the advance upon Moscow, Murat complained of some remissness in a cavalry charge—" Our horses have no patriotism. The soldiers fight without bread, but the horses insist on oats!"

Nor was it the cavalry only. Since the draught-horses also began to fail, it became necessary, hour by hour, to blow up tumbrils of artillery, or to abandon carts piled with baggage and with wounded. The soldiers of the rear-guard, who were themselves struck down, had a grievous fate before them, since in their position a wound was almost equivalent to death. It was heart-rending to hear these poor men, with loud cries, entreat their comrades at least to despatch them as they fell, rather than leave them to linger and perish, without aid, or until run through by a Cossack lance.

Napoleon himself took no heed of their calamities. Profoundly mortified at the compelled retreat, which there was no longer any side-march to conceal, he journeyed in front, surrounded by his guard, and shut up in his landau, with the chief of his staff, Marshal Berthier. He gave no personal impulse nor direction to the march, and contented himself with blaming Davoust, who, he said, was over-methodical and moved too slowly.

Amidst these growing difficulties three toilsome

marches brought the *Grande Armée* to Mojaisk. Thus far the days had continued fine, though the nights had begun to be frosty; and on their way the troops were rejoined by Mortier's division from Moscow. Mojaisk itself could yield them no resources. That ill-fated little town had been burned, and its inhabitants had fled. The troops, therefore, bivouacked in the open air, skirting, as they passed, the plain of Borodino. Several officers rode over to revisit the field of battle; they found it, indeed, a ghastly scene. In that thinly peopled region, laid waste alternately by friend and foe, scarce any peasants had remained to fulfil the duty of interment, and the slain of both armies were still lying where they had fallen, half-decomposed by the lapse of time, or half-devoured by the birds and beasts of prey. Not less dismal than the scene itself were the reflections which it could not fail to inspire. Here, then, the French army, by its own account, had lost thirty thousand men in killed and wounded. Here, then, they had perished—and all for what result? Only that their surviving comrades, after a few weeks at Moscow, should march back as they came! Only for present grief and impending ruin!

At Krasnoi, where one *corps d'armée* encamped the same night, the spectacle was still more afflicting. It was a large monastic establishment, which the French had converted into an hospital after their Borodino battle. But such was the improvidence of their chiefs as they marched onwards to Moscow, that, as M. de Fezensac assures us, they had left the sick without medicines, nay, even without food. It was with great difficulty that some scanty supplies were from time to time gleaned in the neighbourhood, and that several convoys of convalescents were despatched to Smolensk. But many more had perished, and many yet remained. "I rescued three men belonging to my own regiment," says Fezensac, "but I found it very hard to make my way to them in their neglected state, since not only the staircases and the corridors, but even the centre of the rooms, were piled up with every kind of ordure."

Energetic orders were now issued by Napoleon for the transport of all among those who could bear removal, being about fifteen hundred in number. It was directed that every baggage-cart, and even every private carriage from Moscow, should take up one at least of these disabled men. By such means their removal was in the first instance secured, but the conveyances in question were already overloaded, while the strength of the draught-horses had rapidly declined.

Smolensk was now looked to by the troops as the term of all their sufferings and losses. There it was thought they would find ample supplies; there they might expect to take up winter quarters. But from Smolensk they were still divided by eight or nine laborious marches, through a country almost destitute of resources, as having been laid waste by themselves in their advance. Nor was the Russian army at this time inactive. Marshal Kutusof had in the first instance been deceived as to the direction of the French retreat, but he was now hanging on the flank of the invaders by a side-march of his own to Medouin;

and he had, besides the Cossacks, despatched a strong division under one of his best officers, General Miloradowitch, which was well provided with artillery, and was prepared to engage the French rear-guard day by day.

It was under such adverse circumstances that the first *corps d'armée*, which still formed the French rear, resumed its harassing duties. On the 31st of October it marched half-way to Ghjat, on the 1st of November to Ghjat itself. Next morning it was again in motion towards Smolensk. Marshal Davoust, destitute of cavalry, but confiding in his veteran foot soldiers, continued to show, as they did, a truly heroic firmness. Each day they had to repel the impetuous charges of Miloradowitz, each evening to endure the privation of rest and of food. On the 1st there was a more especial accumulation at the passage of a small but slimy river and morass, where the bridge had broken down. It was necessary for the troops to maintain the conflict while the sappers re-established the bridge. All that night Marshal Davoust, with his generals and the soldiers of Gerard's division, remained on foot, without eating or sleeping, to protect the rear of the retreating army.

Next day there was a more general engagement, in which the *corps d'armée* of Prince Eugene and of Marshal Ney also took part. The French remained victorious, but with the loss of fifteen or eighteen hundred of their best veterans. And on the evening of that well-fought day what refreshment was in store for them after all their toils and dangers? Let

M. Thiers here reply :—" When they entered the town of Wiasma they found no means of subsistence. The guard and the corps which passed first had devoured everything. Of the provisions brought from Moscow, there was nothing left. In a cold and dark night these exhausted men cast themselves down at the edge of the fir forests; they lit large fires, and they roasted some horseflesh in the blaze."

Moreover, there had now begun to be in the midst of themselves—and it continued to increase through the retreat—a mingled mass of disbanded men; cavalry soldiers who had lost their horses, infantry soldiers who had flung away their muskets, men from almost every service and almost every country, now rendered desperate and callous by famine. Their sole remaining care was to provide by any means for their personal safety, and, far from continuing to protect the rearguard, they had themselves to be protected by it.

Thus beset and close pressed, the First Corps, which had 72,000 men under arms when it crossed the Niemen, which had still 28,000 when it left Moscow, had dwindled to 15,000. The other corps were also much reduced, though not as yet in the same proportion. It was obvious that the army was now drawing along three or four times more cannon than, with its diminished numbers, it could ever use in action; and Marshal Davoust applied to the Emperor for permission to leave behind the superfluous pieces of artillery, in proportion as the horses failed. But this the pride of Napoleon forbade—by no means the only instance in which his indomitable spirit proved injurious to the welfare, nay, even to the preservation of his troops. Instead of cannon, therefore, the baggage-carts with the sick and wounded had to be relinquished hour after hour, while the tumbrils of ammunition more and more frequently had to be blown into the air.

Napoleon himself saw nothing at this time of the real difficulties of the retreat. Remaining a day's march in advance, in the midst of his Guard, he was there for the most part, as M. Thiers describes him, seated in his carriage, *entre Berthier consterné et Murat éteint*. Sometimes he passed whole hours without uttering a word, absorbed in his own painful thoughts; and he commonly replied to the various representations of Marshal Davoust by a general order to march more rapidly. He persisted, says M. Thiers, in finding fault with the rear-guard, instead of going himself to direct its operations.

It was partly, then, as dissatisfied, however unreasonably, with the conduct of the First Corps, and partly as taking into account its exhausted state, that the Emperor now determined to withdraw it into the main body of his forces, committing the defence of the rear in its place to the Third Corps, under Marshal Ney. In that corps the fourth regiment of the line, commanded by Fezensac, came to occupy the post of the greatest danger and difficulty as the very last of the rear-guard.

This was on the 4th of November.

"Before the break of day next morning," says Fezensac, "the Third Corps was called to arms, and prepared to march. At that time all the soldiers who had disbanded left their bivouacs, and came to join us. Those among them who were sick or wounded lingered near the fires, imploring us not to leave them in the enemy's hands. We had no means of transport for them, and we were obliged to pretend not to hear the wailings of those we were unable to relieve. As for the troop of wretches who had deserted their standards, although still able to bear arms, I ordered them to be repulsed with the butt-ends of our muskets; and I forewarned them that, in the event of the enemy's attack, I would have them fired upon if they caused us the smallest obstruction."

On that same day, the 5th, Napoleon, with the vanguard, reached the small town of Dorogobuje. There he was assailed by cares of a different kind. He received despatches from Paris announcing the strange conspiracy of Malet—how an officer in prison could escape one night from his place of detention, could succeed in all the preliminary steps of revolution, could seize in their beds both General Savary, the Minister of Police, and General Hulin, the commandant of the city, and could seem on the point of raising the flag of a new republic. "*Mais quoi!*" exclaimed Napoleon several times after he had heard this news; "*on ne songeait donc pas à mon fils, à ma femme, aux institutions de l'Empire!*" And after each exclamation he relapsed again, says M. Thiers, into his painful thoughts, reflected and declared in his moody countenance.

The receipt of the same intelligence a few days later by some of the Emperor's suite is very graphically told by M. de Bausset. His memoirs, indeed, display a curious contrast to all others of the same place or period, coming forth with flashes of merriment in the midst of the darkest gloom. He informs us that on the morning of the 8th, still two marches from Smolensk, he found that during the night three of his carriage-horses had been stolen, and, as he supposed, already eaten by the soldiers. He bought some others to supply their place, but this operation delayed him, and he did not rejoin head-quarters till the most interesting moments of the day were passed.

"Les officiers de la Maison Impériale achevaient de dîner. Je m'étais assis, et me disposais à réparer le temps perdu, lorsque le Grand Maréchal (Duroc, Duc de Frioul), qui m'avait fait placer près de lui, me parla des nouvelles que l'estafette venait d'apporter. Mais la politique ne m'occupait guère. Il était question de la conspiration de Malet, de l'arrestation du Ministre de la Police et du Préfet de Police. Je croyais que le Grand Maréchal inventait ces nouvelles pour donner le change à la faim qui me consumait, car j'étais encore à jeûn à sept heures du soir. Je lui répondis en riant que le tonnerre tombât-il à côté de moi, je ne perdrais pas un seul instant pour me dédommager de la diète que j'avais subie toute la journée."

M. de Bausset owns, however, that when the newspapers from Paris were brought, and he saw the true state of the case, the mouthfuls began to stick in his throat.

We may add that M. de Bausset, as (in every sense) a prominent member of the Imperial household, appears to have been well cared for, even in the worst days of the retreat. Scarcely ever did he fail to find a corner at some Imperial table, or a seat at some Imperial *traineau*. By such means he could resist even a fit of the gout, which at this period most inopportunely assailed him. Thus he was enabled to return to the Tuileries in good case; and when two days afterwards he appeared at the Imperial levée—

"L'Empereur me fit beaucoup de questions sur la manière dont j'avais quitté l'armée, et me dit, en souriant avec amertume, que j'étais probablement le seul qui n'eût pas maigri dans cette longue retraite."

Meanwhile, the French *corps d'armée*, front and rear, were eagerly pressing forward to Smolensk. They had, as we have seen, suffered much from privations of food and of rest, from the burned-out peasantry, and the ever-vigilant Cossacks. But the worst of their enemies was still to come. On the 4th of November there fell the first flakes of snow. On the 5th their quantity augmented. On the 6th they grew to a storm, and the ground assumed for the season its winter robe of white. Sir Robert Wilson, then at the Russian head-quarters, describes as having first arisen on the 6th "that razor-cutting wind which hardened the snow, and made it sparkle as it fell like small diamonds, whilst the air, under the effect of its contracting action, was filled with a continual ringing sound; and the atmosphere seemed to be rarefied till it became quite brisk and brittle."

The sufferings of the French soldiers, long-tried and exhausted as they were, now became well-nigh unendurable.

"At a late hour of the 7th," says M. de Fezensac, "we reached the open plain in front of Dorogobuje. It was by far the coldest night that we had felt as yet; the snow was falling thickly, and the violence of the wind was such that no light could be kindled: besides that, the heather amidst which we lay would have afforded us but scanty materials for bivouac fires."

In this march, as in every other during this part of the retreat, Marshal Ney had set his troops the most gallant example: always among the hindmost, here the post of danger; often with a soldier's musket in his hand; and not only, like Marshal Davoust, unshaken in firmness, but unlike him, ever cheerful, light-hearted, and serene. Next morning, with the aid of another *corps d'armée*, he endeavoured to hold Dorogobuje for the day with the rear-guard, so as to allow the corps in advance some time to save their artillery and baggage. But he found himself sharply assailed by the infantry of Miloradowitch. The enemy took the bridge across the Dnieper, and forced another post of Ney in front of the church. The French, after their night without food or fire, had to maintain the conflict knee-deep in the snow. By a bold charge they recovered the lost posts, but could not maintain them, and found it necessary to continue their retreat before it was cut off by the Russians.

With all this, the long-enduring soldiers of Napoleon, for the most part, did not fail in firmness, did not fail in patience, did not fail in attachment to their chief. Sir Robert Wilson says of the French, whom he saw as captives, that they could not be induced by any temptations, by any threats, by any privations, to cast reproach on their Emperor as the cause of their misfortunes and sufferings. It was "the chance of war," "unavoidable difficulties," and "destiny," but "not the fault of Napoleon." "They famished," adds Sir Robert, "dying of hunger, refusing food rather than utter an injurious word against their chief to indulge and humour vindictive inquirers."

But how terrible the fate of these brave captives, as Sir Robert Wilson proceeds to relate it!

"All prisoners were immediately and invariably stripped stark naked and marched in columns in that state, or turned adrift to be the sport and the victims of the peasantry, who would not always let them, as they sought to do, point and hold the muzzles of the guns against their own heads or hearts to terminate their sufferings in the most certain and expeditious manner; for the peasantry thought that this mitigation of torture would be an offence against the avenging God of Russia, and deprive them of His further protection."

Sir Robert Wilson proceeds to give some particular instances, more lifelike and appalling perhaps than can be any general description, however clear and precise. One day, as he was riding forward with General Miloradowitch and his staff on the high-road, about a mile from Wiasma, they found a crowd of peasant-women, with sticks in their hands, hopping round a felled pine-tree, on each side of which lay about sixty naked prisoners prostrate, but with their heads on the tree, which these furies were striking in accompaniment to a national air or song, yelled by them in concert, while several hundred armed peasants were quietly looking on as guardians of the direful orgies. When the cavalcade approached, the sufferers uttered piercing shrieks, and kept incessantly crying, "*La mort, la mort, la mort!*"

Another afternoon, when Sir Robert was on the march with General Beningsen, they fell in with a column of 700 naked prisoners under a Cossack escort. This column, according to the certificate given on starting, had consisted of 1250 men, and the commandant stated that he had twice renewed it, as the original party dropped off, from the prisoners he collected *en route*, and that he was then about completing his number again.

The meeting with this last miserable convoy was marked by one strange act of cold-blooded ferocity which Sir Robert has related. He tells it of a Russian officer "of high titular rank," without mentioning the name, but from a note preserved among his papers we learn that it was no other than the heir presumptive to the Crown, the Grand Duke Constantine. Sir Robert says that in this group of naked prisoners was a young man who kept a little aloof from the main band, and who attracted notice by his superior appearance. The Grand Duke, after entering into some conversation with him about his country, rank, and capture, asked him if he did not, under present circumstances, wish for death? "Yes," said the unhappy man, "I do, if I cannot be rescued, for I know I must in a few hours perish by hunger or by the Cossack lance, as I have seen so many hundreds of my comrades do before me. There are those in France who will lament my fate; and for their sake I should wish to return. But if that be impossible, the sooner this ignominy and suffering are over the better." To this the Grand Duke calmly answered that from the bottom of his heart he pitied the other's fate, but that aid for his preservation was impossible; if, however, he really wished to die at once and would lie down on his back, he, the Grand Duke, to give proof of the interest he took in him, would himself inflict the death-blow on his throat!

General Beningsen was then at some little distance in front, but Sir Robert Wilson, who had stopped to hear the conversation, ventured to remonstrate with his Imperial Highness on the very peculiar proof of interest which he offered to give, urging the absolute necessity of saving the unfortunate French officer, after having excited hopes by engaging in a discourse with him. Sir Robert found, however, that the Grand Duke had no inclination to relinquish his first idea, upon which he eagerly spurred forward to overtake and bring back General Beningsen. But, happening to turn round before he could reach the general, he saw his Imperial Highness, who had dismounted, strike with his sabre a blow at the French officer that nearly severed the head from the body. Nor, adds Sir Robert, could the Grand Duke ever afterwards be made to understand that he had done a reprehensible thing. He defended it by the motive and by the relief which he had afforded to the sufferer, there being no means to save him, and, if there had been, no man daring to employ them.

Such was an early and no doubt sufficient token of

that inborn ferocity of temper which many years afterwards Constantine more clearly brought to light as Governor of Poland, and which rendered necessary even to his own perception his resignation of his hereditary rights as eventual successor to the throne.

Far different, nay, directly opposite, were the sentiments of Alexander. When he received accounts from General Wilson and others of the frequent atrocities and various modes of torture practised by the peasantry, the Emperor at once by an express courier transmitted an order forbidding all such acts under the severest threats of his displeasure and punishment. At the same time he directed that a ducat in gold should be paid for every prisoner delivered up by peasant or soldier to any civil authority for safe custody. The decree was most humane, and well worthy Alexander's just renown; yet in too many cases it remained only a dead letter. The conductors, as Sir Robert informs us, were frequently offered a higher price to surrender their charge as victims to private vengeance. Nor could the rage of the peasantry be at once restrained. How, indeed, expect mercy from men whose wives and children were at that time wandering helpless on the snow, their houses burned down perhaps by these very soldiers in consequence of Napoleon's command? Then it was that the utter impolicy of that command to set on fire all the villages in the line of retreat, its impolicy as well as its signal cruelty, grew manifest to all.

In this tremendous retreat more compassion was occasionally shown by dogs than by men:—

"Innumerable dogs," thus writes Sir Robert Wilson, "crouched on the bodies of their former masters, looking in their faces, and howling their hunger and loss. Others, on the contrary, were tearing the still living flesh from the feet, hands, and limbs of still living wretches who could not defend themselves, and whose torment was still greater as in many cases their consciousness and senses remained unimpaired."

One particular instance is added. At the commencement of the retreat, at a village near Selino, a detachment of fifty French had been surprised. The peasants resolved to bury them alive in a pit; a drummer-boy bravely led the devoted party and sprang into the grave. A dog belonging to one of the victims could not be secured. Every day this dog went to the neighbouring camp and came back with a bit of food in his mouth to sit and moan over the newly turned earth. It was a fortnight before he could be killed by the peasants, who were afraid of discovery. "They showed me the spot," adds Wilson, "and related the occurrence with exultation, as though they had performed a meritorious deed."

Ghastly, most ghastly, must have been the line of the French retreat, as the notes of Sir Robert describe it:—

"From that time the road was strewed with guns, tumbrils, equipages, men, and horses; and no foraging parties could quit the high-road in search of provisions; and consequently the debility hourly increased. Thousands of horses soon lay groaning on the route, with great pieces of flesh cut off their necks and most fleshy parts by the passing soldiery for food; whilst thousands of naked wretches were wandering like spectres who seemed to have no sight or sense, and who only kept reeling on till frost, famine, or the Cossack lance put an end to their power of motion. In that wretched state no nourishment could have saved them. There were continual instances, even amongst the Russians, of their lying down, dozing, and dying within a quarter of an hour after a little bread had been supplied."

We should observe that it was not only from want of forage or from fatigue that such numbers of French horses fell. There was also another cause pointed out with exultation by their enemy. Thus, on the morning of the 5th, on coming to the first bivouac which the French had left, some Cossacks in attendance on Sir Robert Wilson, seeing a gun and several tumbrils at the bottom of a ravine with the horses lying on the ground, dismounted, and, taking up the feet of several, hallooed, and ran to kiss Sir Robert's knees and horse, making all the while fantastic gestures like crazy men. When their ecstasy had a little subsided, they pointed to the horses' shoes, and said, "God has made Napoleon forget that there is a winter in our country. In spite of Kutusof, the enemy's bones shall remain in Russia."

It was soon ascertained that the needful precaution of *roughing* had been neglected with all the horses of the Imperial army, except only those of the Polish corps and also the Emperor's own, which Coulaincourt (Duke de Vicence), under whom was that department, had, with due foresight, always kept rough-shod according to the Russian usage.

Such is the positive statement of Sir Robert Wilson,

who was upon the spot at the time. But it is only just to observe that there are some remarks of the Duke of Wellington which point to an exactly opposite conclusion:—

"Then we are told that the loss was occasioned because the French horses were not rough-shod. . . . But the excuse is not founded in fact. Those who have followed a French army well know that their horses are always rough-shod. It is the common mode of shoeing horses in France; and in this respect a French army ought to, and would, have suffered less inconvenience than any army that ever was assembled."

As though these manifold causes of distress did not suffice, the French soldiers at this period also suffered severely from the want of warm clothes. When they had marched forward in the months of July and August the weather was extremely hot. They were glad to leave stored up in Poland their heavy capotes and their woollen trowsers. They expected that the care of their chiefs would provide them with winter necessaries before the winter came. In that expectation they found themselves deceived. No stores of comfortable clothing met them on their homeward march. They had found, indeed, fur-dresses among the spoils of the burning capital, but had for the most part sold them to their officers. Either therefore they had to wrap themselves in any garments, sometimes even female garments, which they happened to have brought from Moscow, or else to endure as best they might the growing severity of the cold. On the 9th of November Réaumur's thermometer fell in that region to

12° below zero, equivalent to 5° of Fahrenheit, and on the 12th to 17°, or according to Fahrenheit 6°, below zero. "Many men," adds Sir Robert Wilson, "were frozen to death, and great numbers had their limbs, noses, and cheeks frozen."

With two such facts before us—the neglect to rough-shoe the horses except those for the Emperor's use, and the omission of effective measures for the despatch in due time of the winter clothing—we must own ourselves unable to concur in the panegyrics on the Emperor's far-sighted policy, his close attention to details, and his provident care for his army, which are poured forth by his indiscrimate admirers even as to this campaign. That Napoleon possessed these qualities in a most eminent degree, we should be among the last persons to deny. But we must be allowed to think that he by no means evinced these qualities in the orders for his Moscow retreat. It would seem as if a long period of splendid successes and of uncontrolled authority had a tendency to perplex and unsettle even the highest faculties of mind. How else explain that Napoleon showed so little prescience of the coming Russian winter, as though by *ignoring* its approach that approach would be really delayed?

We may observe that the French eye-witnesses describe the horrors of this retreat in quite as vivid terms as either the Russians or the English. Thus speaks M. de Fezensac of the period between Dorogobuje and Smolensk:—

"Since we were at the rear-guard, all the men who left the road in quest of food fell into the hands of the enemy, whose pursuit grew day by day more active. The severity of the cold came to augment our difficulties and sufferings. Many soldiers, exhausted with fatigue, flung away their muskets to walk singly. They halted wherever they found a piece of wood for burning, by which they could cook a morsel of horseflesh or a handful of flour, if, indeed, none of their comrades came and snatched from them these their sole remaining resources. For our soldiers, dying of hunger, took by force from all the disbanded men whatever provisions they bore, and the latter might deem themselves fortunate if they were not also despoiled of their clothes. Thus, after having laid waste this entire region, we were now reduced to destroy each other; and this extreme course had become a necessity of war. It was requisite at all hazards to preserve those soldiers who had continued true to their standard, and who alone at the rear-guard sustained the enemy's assaults. As for those disbanded men who no longer belonged to any regiment, and could no longer render any service, they had no claim at all on our pity. Under these circumstances, the road along which we journeyed bore the likeness of a field of battle. Soldiers who had resisted cold and fatigue succumbed to the torments of hunger; others who had kept a few provisions found themselves too much enfeebled to follow the march, and remained in the enemy's power. Some had their limbs frozen, and expired where they had dropped down on the snow; others fell asleep in villages, and perished in the flames which their own companions had kindled. I saw at Dorogobuje a soldier of my regiment upon whom destitution had produced the same effects as drunkenness; he was close to us without knowing us again; he asked us where was his regiment; he mentioned by name other soldiers, and spoke to them as though to strangers; his gait was tottering, and his looks were wild. He disappeared at the beginning of the action, and I never saw him again. Several *cantinières* and soldiers' wives belonging to the regiments which preceded us in the line of march were in our midst. Several of these poor women had a young child to carry; and notwithstanding the egotism then so prevalent among us, every one was eager in rendering them his aid. Our drum-major bore for a long time an infant in his arms. I also during several days gave places to a woman and her baby in a small cart that I still had; but what could such feeble succour avail against so many sufferings, or could we alleviate the calamities which we were condemned to share?"

Instances like these of tenderness and kindly feeling appear, we think, doubly touching, doubly admirable, in the midst of such wide-spread and terrible woe. In a later passage of his journal, Fezensac commemorates the fate of an officer of his regiment who had married in France before the commencement of this fatal campaign. Worn out with fatigue, he was found dead one morning by the side of a bivouac fire, still holding the miniature of his wife close-pressed upon his heart.

Such, then, was the march to Smolensk. Of that city, as it appeared in 1778 and continued till 1812, a full description may be found in Coxe's Travels. He says that, though by no means the most magnificent, it was by far the most singular town he had ever seen. But to the French, in November, 1812, the name bore a fanciful charm as Eldorado in old times to the Spaniards. Smolensk! Smolensk! was now the general cry. Smolensk was to supply all their wants; Smolensk was to be the term of their retreat. Every eye was eagerly strained to catch the first glimpse of its antique towers, crowning its two irregular hills, and emerging from the vast plains of wintry snow.

But alas for these too sanguine hopes! From the difficulties which had been found of transport, and the want of precise orders as to the line of homeward march, the magazines of this city were by no means such as had been expected and announced. They would afford resources for a halt of days, but not for a sojourn of months.

Napoleon, at the head of the foremost corps, reached Smolensk on the 9th of November. He gave orders that ample distributions should be made to his Guards, and that the gates should be shut against the other divisions of his army as they came. But it was found impossible to maintain that exclusion. The late comers—some of whom had so recently fought and bled and endured every extremity of hardship for the protection of their vanguard—would not bear to be shut out. They burst through the gates, and, finding no progress made in the distributions of food that were promised them, they next broke open the magazines. "*On pille les magasins!*" was the cry that now arose in the French ranks. Every soldier rushed to the scene to secure his own part in the plunder. It was some time ere order could be restored, and the remnant of provisions be saved for the corps of Davoust and Prince Eugene. The rear under Ney was even less fortunate. Having had on the 11th another fierce conflict to sustain against the Russians, it did not appear before Smolensk till the 14th. By that time everything had been wasted or devoured. "When I went into the city," says Fezensac, "I could find nothing at all for my regiment or myself. We had to resign ourselves to our dismal prospect of continuing our march without any distribution of food."

At Smolensk, however, Napoleon roused himself from the lethargy which, as M. Thiers admits, seems to have benumbed him during the first days of the retreat. He made strenuous efforts to re-organize his army, but found the main causes of its dissolution beyond his control. The division of Prince Eugene, marching a little to the northward, had lost nearly all its artillery at the encumbered and disastrous passage of a small river, the Vop. Altogether 380 pieces of cannon had been taken or left behind. The fighting men in rank and file were now less than one-half of what they had been when the army left Moscow. On the other hand, some reinforcements appeared at Smolensk, both of horse and foot, belonging to the division of General Baraguay d'Hilliers, and these Napoleon distributed among the several corps so as in some degree to recruit their far-diminished numbers.

Besides the argument to be derived from the failing magazines, there were other strong reasons against a continued sojourn at Smolensk. Napoleon had received unfavourable accounts from both his flanks. On his right, as it became in his homeward movement, the Russian General Wittgenstein had repulsed St. Cyr, had retaken Polotsk, and was marching south. On the left the Russians had succeeded in concluding a peace with Turkey, so that Admiral Tchitchakof, who commanded their army in that quarter, had become free of his movements, and was marching north. It was not difficult to conjecture whither these two chiefs were separately tending. About half-way between Smolensk and Wilna rolls a wide river, the Beresina, so rapid in its stream as not to be readily congealed by the first frosts. The bridge across that river, in the line of the French retreat, lay at the little town of Borisow. If, then, either Wittgenstein or Tchitchakof could reach this position and seize it before Napoleon—still more if both could be combined—the French retreat would be intercepted, and the French army, including its Emperor, might be compelled to lay down its arms.

Conscious that there was no time to lose in continuing the retreat, Napoleon set out from Smolensk on the 14th at the head of his Guards; but seeing how much the other divisions which had arrived after him stood in need of rest, he gave orders that they should depart successively on the 15th and 16th, while Ney, who commanded the last, and had to complete the evacuation of the city, should remain till the morning of the 17th. By this system three days' march would intervene between the front of the army and its rear. It was a wise course so far as the refreshment of the troops was concerned, but not judicious, inasmuch as it overlooked the fact that, by the recent enormous losses of the French army, the Russians had come to exceed it in numbers. It was not hard to foresee that Kutusof, if he found his enemies thus disseminated, would endeavour to cut off their divisions in detail.

This is precisely what in fact occurred. The Russian army, moving forward while the French was taking rest, had advanced to Krasnoi, two marches beyond Smolensk, and occupied a strong position on the side of a steep ravine through which the French would have to pass. When Napoleon appeared at that defile, on the afternoon of the 15th, the Russians had not yet completed their preparations, and allowed the French to go through. But when, on the 16th, there came up the division of Prince Eugene, it was confronted by an iron wall of soldiers and by ranges of cannon ready to play. Eugene charged these obstacles with his usual gallantry, but without success; and he saw in a short time the ground strewed with two thousand of his men; dead or wounded, it was much the same, since none of the latter could be moved. He found it requisite at night to attempt a side-march to the right, avoiding the ravine by the plain along the Dnieper, and thus (his men treading softly on the snow) he was enabled, after heavy loss, to rejoin the Emperor at Krasnoi.

The difficulties of this day appear to have convinced Napoleon of the error he had committed in the dissemination of his army. Early on the 17th he marched back from Krasnoi to the ravine, and drew out the Guards in battle order ready to support the division of Davoust. By such aid Davoust, though sharply beset, was enabled to effect his junction. But both he, and Prince Eugene the day before, lost in that perilous pass the greater part of their remaining artillery and baggage.

There was no further time to lose. On the 14th the Réaumur thermometer had fallen to 20 degrees below zero, that is, to 13 below zero of Fahrenheit. Since then, however, there had been some remission of the cold, and even some commencement of a thaw. It was doubtful whether the ice upon the Dnieper would be firm enough to bear the weight of cannon and baggage, or even of horses and men. It became therefore of primary importance to secure the bridge across that river at the little town of Orcha, and in the due line of the retreat. Orcha was two marches from Krasnoi, and the Russians, of whom a large body was already in movement towards that post, would undoubtedly seize and hold it unless they were anticipated by the French.

In this exigency, Napoleon set forth in all haste at the head of his Guards, and he did succeed in reaching Orcha in sufficient time. He left to Marshal Davoust two orders: the one to keep close to Mortier, who commanded the hindmost division of the Guards; the other, to support and sustain the advance of Marshal Ney. These orders were in fact contradictory, and Napoleon must have felt that they were so, but he was unwilling to take upon himself in explicit terms the terrible responsibility of leaving to their fate Marshal Ney and the whole rear-guard. Davoust, in this choice of difficulties, deemed it—and he probably was right—the superior duty to rejoin the main body, and he accordingly marched onward to Orcha. Worse still, he was prevented, by the want of safe communication, from sending any notice to Ney of his intended departure.

Ney therefore remained entirely ignorant of the extreme peril to which he was exposed. He marched forward on the morning of the 17th, having first, according to his orders, blown up the defences of Smolensk and set the buildings on fire—orders that certainly had not in any measure consulted the welfare of the numerous French, sick and wounded, who in this very town were left in the enemy's hands. Next day he came up with the Russian army at the defile in front of Krasnoi. He made a most gallant charge, and trusted to force his way, but his division was only of six thousand men with six pieces of cannon, while the Russians had well-nigh fifty thousand men with large well-appointed batteries. Notwithstanding the intrepidity of his veterans, the result could not be doubtful. He was repulsed with heavy loss; and in the evening he received a flag of truce from General Miloradowitch, offering him a capitulation on most honourable terms. He now learnt that the other French divisions were already at or near Orcha, and that he was separated from them by the Russian army intervening, by the river Dnieper, and by more than fifteen leagues of distance. How many commanders in his place would have utterly despaired!

But the constancy of Ney was unshaken. He vouchsafed no answer at all to the flag of truce; only he retained the officer lest Miloradowitch should gather any news of his design. Towards sunset he set his troops in movement through the open fields to his right. In these critical moments, says Fezensac, his countenance showed neither irresolution nor uneasiness; all eyes were turned to him, but no one for a long time presumed to put to him any question. At length, seeing near him one of his officers—perhaps Fezensac himself—the following dialogue passed, which Fezensac relates:—

"Le Maréchal lui dit à demi-voix : '*Nous ne sommes pas bien.*' '*Qu'allez vous faire?*' répondit l'officier.—'*Passer le Dnieper.*'—'*Où est le chemin?*'—'*Nous le trouverons.*'—'*Et s'il n'est pas gelé?*'—'*Il le sera.*'—'*A la bonne heure!*' dit l'officier. Ce singulier dialogue, que je rapporte textuellement, révéla le projet du Maréchal de gagner Orcha par la rive gauche du fleuve, et assez rapidement pour y trouver encore l'armée qui faisait son mouvement par la rive gauche."

To carry out this daring design, the first object—marching in the dark and across fields—was to find the river. Marshal Ney, with the ready instinct of a good commander, that knows how to derive aid even from the most trifling circumstances, seeing some ice before him, ordered it to be broken, and observed the direction of the water that ran beneath, rightly concluding that the streamlet must be one of the Dnieper confluents. Guided by this indication he reached the river's bank, and found there a small village. Happily for his object, the river was found to be frozen—sufficiently at least to bear men, and even with great precaution some horses, though not artillery or baggage. It was also judged impossible to convey any further the wounded made in the action of that morning, who were accordingly left behind, in spite of their entreaties and cries. In that manner, towards midnight, the Dnieper was successfully passed, and the troops without further respite resumed their march. Before daylight they came to another village, where they found a party of Cossacks fast asleep; these were taken prisoners or put to the sword.

Weary as were the soldiers, their safety—and they knew it—was entirely dependent on their pushing on. They met some parties of Cossacks, who however retired before them. At mid-day they came to two more villages, upon a height, where they were happy in finding some provisions. But in the afternoon it was no longer an outpost or two of the enemy with which they had to deal; Platof and all his Cossacks were upon them. Exhausted as they were by fatigue, and inferior in numbers, it became necessary for them to quit the track, so as to avoid the risk of a cavalry charge, and to move along the pine-woods that bordered the Dnieper on that side. Darkness came, and still they struggled on beneath the trees, often separated from each other, and under circumstances when a wound might be deemed equivalent to death. M. de Fezensac has described the scene as only an eye-witness could:—

"Les Cosaques nous criaient de nous rendre, et tiraient à bout-portant au milieu de nous; ceux qui étaient frappés restaient abandonnés. Un sergent eut la jambe fracassée d'un coup de carabine. Il tomba à côté de moi, en disant froidement à ses camarades: *Voilà un homme perdu; prenez mon sac; vous en profiterez.* On prit son sac, et nous l'abandonnâmes en silence. Deux officiers blessés eurent le même sort. . . . Tel qui avait été un héros sur le champ de bataille paraissait alors inquiet et troublé."

Still more evil was their plight when the pine-woods ended, and they had to stagger onwards through the open country, painfully climbing several steep ravines, and exposed not only to the enemy's horsemen, but to his field artillery. For the greater part of the next day, Marshal Ney took position on a height and stood on the defensive. It was not till the return of darkness that he resumed his toilsome march. Meanwhile he had sent forward a Polish officer to make his way if possible to Orcha, and announce to the French chiefs his approach.

During this time, at the French head-quarters, Napoleon, having secured his passage of the Dnieper, looked back with extreme anxiety to his gallant and forsaken rear-guard. He took up his own quarters some leagues onward on the Borisow road, but instructed Prince Eugene and Davoust to remain one or two days longer at Orcha, ready, if there were still any possibility of aid, to succour Ney. Under these circumstances the two chiefs welcomed with most heartfelt delight the news which the Polish officer brought them. Prince Eugene at once led forth a part of his division to receive and welcome *le brave des braves*. Thus when, at one league from Orcha, the first men of Ney's feeble column saw close before them a body of troops, they found with inexpressible joy their cry of *Qui vive?* answered in French. Another moment and Ney and Eugene were locked in each other's arms. "One must have passed," says De Fezensac, "as we had, three days between life and death, to judge in full measure of the ecstasy which this meeting gave us."

Nor was Napoleon himself less elated. M. de Bausset was then in attendance upon him at the country house of Baranoui, some leagues beyond Orcha, and he bears witness to the pangs of suspense which the Emperor endured. At length the good news of Ney's safety came. It was brought by General Gourgaud—the same who subsequently shared the captivity of St. Helena. Napoleon, who was then sitting at breakfast, showed the most lively satisfaction. "*J'ai plus de quatre cent millions dans les caves des Tuileries; je les aurais donnés avec reconnaissance pour la rançon de mon fidèle compagnon d'armes.*" Such were the words he spoke; or, as M. de Bausset puts it, more in a lord chamberlain's style, "*Tels sont les mots que j'entendis sortir de la bouche de l'Empereur.*"

The triumph of Ney, however, was dearly bought. Of the six thousand men with whom he had marched out of Smolensk he brought less than one thousand to Orcha. But he had maintained the glory of his eagles; he had spared a French marshal and a French *corps d'armée* the dishonour of capitulation.

The losses sustained by the divers French corps at Krasnoi, and in the two marches beyond it, are computed by the French writers at ten or twelve thousand men, in killed, wounded, and prisoners. Of the whole *Grande Armée* there remained at Orcha no more than 24,000 men in rank and line, and about an equal number of disbanded soldiers partly without arms. The cavalry was almost extinct. In this extremity, Napoleon formed the greater number of the officers who still retained a horse into a body-guard, which he called *l'Escadron Sacré.* Here the captains took the part of privates and the colonels of subalterns, while the generals served as regimental chiefs.

Thus far diminished, and still diminishing, the mass pursued its dismal movement to the Beresina. There was now a thaw, and the soldiers, with worn-out shoes, and with the trees dripping down upon them, toiled painfully along through the mire. Every day was marked with some new incident, evincing, more than could any general description, the extremities that they endured. At Liady, for instance—but this was even before Orcha—some three hundred men of the First Corps, clustered together, had laid down in a barn for their night's rest. But the barn caught fire, and these poor men had become so linked and entangled one with the other that none could escape. Only one was found half dead, but still breathing, and he in mercy was despatched with two musket-balls.

Another day upon the march the troops observed some combs of honey near the summit of a lofty tree. There were no side branches, and to climb seemed a perilous venture; nevertheless some soldiers, thinking they might as well die of a fall as of famine, made the attempt and reached the place. Then they threw down the combs by morsels, on which their comrades below ravenously pounced, "like so many famished hounds," says Fezensac, who was present at this painful scene.

The Emperor was now looking forward to a junction on the Beresina with two of his *corps d'armée*—those of Marshal Oudinot and Marshal Victor—coming from the flank army on his north. The two marshals had sustained some heavy losses, but could still bring him, together, at least 25,000 excellent soldiers. On the other hand, he could no longer indulge the hope of securing without obstacle the passage of the river. The Russians under Tchitchakof had reached Borisow, routed the Polish garrison, and burnt the Beresina bridge. It would be requisite to span the river at some other point by a new bridge as rapidly as possible, and unperceived by the Russians. And here the improvidence of the arrangements for this retreat became once more apparent. There was with the army an excellent veteran officer of engineers, General Eblé. There were under his command some scores of experienced pontoniers. There was a double pontoon train (sixty in number) which was left at Orcha in the advance to Moscow, and which was found still at Orcha on the return. General Eblé earnestly pressed Napoleon to take forward at least fifteen of these pontoons, so as to secure within two or three hours the construction of a bridge, should any be found needful. But this the pride of the Emperor forbade. He preferred that the fresh draught-horses ready at Orcha for this service should be employed in dragging onward some more pieces of artillery. All that could be obtained by General Eblé was authority to transport materials for the far less expeditious *pont de chevalets*. It was almost surreptitiously that he added six tumbrils, containing the necessary tools and implements.

Yet, as it proved, it was solely on these *chevalets*— on these tools and implements—that the safety of the whole depended. There is no exaggeration in saying that but for them every man of the *Grande Armée* must have laid down his arms. For on the 24th the weather changed and the frost returned, though not in its full severity; consequently during the next few days the Beresina proved to be in the state of all others most unfavourable for a passage—not bound fast by frost, and on the other hand not free from floating ice. When with great difficulty and some good fortune a ford was discovered at Studianka, several leagues to the north of Borisow, it appeared that only men on horseback could pass, and that with extreme risk, since the huge blocks whirled along by the current would often strike down and overwhelm both horse and man.

Studianka was seized by a French detachment, while the Russians were amused by a feint of Napoleon at Borisow. Some cavalry soldiers, each taking another man behind him, rode boldly through the ford and secured the opposite bank. Then on the 25th General Eblé commenced the construction of a double bridge—the one for the artillery and baggage, the other for the horse or men on foot. The brave pontoniers, faithful to the voice of their admirable chief, plunged into the icy stream and continued at their work through the night. It was not merely the icy stream and the winter season—it was not merely the toil by night and day—but these much-enduring men had no nourishing food, no fermented drinks, to sustain them—not one ounce of bread, not one spoonful of brandy. There was only some hot broth made of horseflesh, and without salt, which was served out to them from time to time.

By unremitting exertions on the part of these devoted soldiers the bridges were completed in the course of the 26th, and the passage began. Meanwhile the Russians, at length apprised of Napoleon's real design, made some furious onsets on his rear, which, however, was well supported by the newly arrived corps of Oudinot and Victor. These two marshals here sustained a heavy loss of men, which the diminished army could ill spare. Nor could the passage be effected without further hindrance and delay. Several of the *chevalets* sank beneath the weight and were submerged. It became necessary again and again to send back into the water the heroic pontoniers, quivering as they were with cold, and faint with unsatisfied hunger. The icicles which gathered round their shoulders as they worked, and which tore their flesh, caused them cruel pain, and many were struck and maimed by the floating blocks; but still the survivors persevered.

General Eblé, in spite of his advanced years, had by no means spared himself, but plunged like his men into the fatal stream. He paid the penalty of his noble conduct a few weeks afterwards, dying in the military hospital at Königsberg of a *fièvre de congélation*—a dreadful malady, not confined to those who had suffered from frost or cold, but contagious as the plague, and in which, after grievous suffering, the limbs seem to lose their vital power and to rot away. Many of his pontoniers underwent the like or even an earlier doom. Of about one hundred who had wrought in these waters at his call, it is stated by M. Thiers that ultimately no more than twelve survived.

Such of our readers as are conversant with the

lighter literature of modern France, will no doubt remember the great skill with which M. de Balzac, in his "Médecin de Campagne," has portrayed *Gondrin*, whom he describes as the last of these Beresina pontoniers. How true to nature the complaint of the untaught man against those who have obtained promotion over his head, *les intrigans qui savent lire et écrire!* and how graphic his account of the clerks at the War Office, "*ces gens qui passent leur vie à se chauffer dans les bureaux! Ils m'ont demandé mes papiers! 'Mes papiers?' leur ai-je dit, mais c'est le vingt-neuvième bulletin.*"

We return to the Beresina. Although two days, the 27th and 28th, were devoted to the passage, it was but imperfectly effected; for, besides the occasional breaking down of the bridges and the necessity for fresh repairs, the access to them was constantly impeded by the tangled mass of carts and carriages. Many of these were upset—many others crushed together, or pushed forward into the river. It was a scene of indescribable confusion, evincing that fierce selfishness which long suffering produces. There was the explosion of tumbrils carelessly ignited—there was the stamp of horses rushing wildly through the crowd—there was the wail of women and children—there was the crash of the artillery pressed onward by the cannoniers over the living and the dead. On that last day, moreover, the French troops had to sustain, not on one bank only of the river but on both, the repeated and desperate onsets of the Russians.

The French positions however were, as usual, most

gallantly maintained. Only one division, that of General Partouneaux, missing its route and surrounded by twenty times its numbers, was compelled to lay down its arms. But Marshal Victor, who had held the effective rear-guard covering the bridges, was enabled to cross the Beresina unmolested after nightfall. Then, the whole army having passed, it became of urgent importance to destroy the bridges on the morning of the 29th, so as to prevent, or at all events delay, the Russian pursuit. There then still remained upon the eastern side a confused multitude, comprising the weakest and most helpless of the camp-followers, and numbering, it was thought, between 6000 and 8000. Napoleon had sent directions to fire the trains at seven in the morning; but the kind-hearted Eblé, anxious to save some more from that multitude beyond, who with eager efforts were now feebly struggling across the encumbered bridges, delayed the order on his own responsibility until nearly nine: then, seeing the enemy advancing and ready to pass, he—turning aside his head not to view the grievous scene—gave the fatal word. Instantly the two bridges blew up, with all the poor wretches upon them. Then, even amidst the roar of the explosion, there arose from the opposite shore the wild and despairing shriek of the people left behind. Wounded men and helpless women, and half-unconscious little children, were seen with bitter tears to stretch forth their arms in last farewell towards their countrymen, compelled by a dire necessity to leave them to their doom. Many flung themselves madly upon the fragments of the flaming bridges—others as madly dashed into the river. As to the main mass, their fate was soon decided. The hovering Cossacks, seeing them forsaken, darted down at full gallop upon them. They speared as though in playful mood the first of the crowd they came upon, and the rest they drove before them, at their lance's point, like a flock of sheep. How many may have lived through the miseries of that captivity is known to God alone; but it is believed that scarce any of the number ever again beheld their native land.

Meanwhile the French army, or rather the sad remains of it, pursued its dreary route to Wilna, still fifty-four leagues distant. It was, as usual, harassed and beset by swarms of Cossacks, but was faintly pursued on the part of the Russian generals, who must have felt reluctant to suffer further losses of their men while the elements were warring on their side. The frost had become more rigorous than ever, the thermometer of Réaumur having fallen on some occasions so low as thirty degrees below zero, equivalent to thirty-five below zero of Fahrenheit. Such extremity of cold can be ill endured by men from a milder clime, even when provided with warm beds and nourishing food. What agony, then, must it have inflicted on that famishing crowd, compelled in many cases to make their pillows of mounds of snow!

Sir Robert Wilson, who was present in the Russian camp, has well described the scene. "The sky," he says, " was generally clear, and there was a subtle, keen, razor-cutting, creeping wind, that penetrated skin, muscle, and bone to the very marrow, rendering the surface as white and the whole limb affected as fragile as alabaster. Sometimes there was a *foudroyant* seizure that benumbed at once the whole frame." It is no wonder, then, that Sir Robert should proceed to state of the French troops, "A general recklessness confounded all ranks, command ceased, and it became a *sauve qui peut* at a funeral pace."

Not at all more favourable is the account of the French themselves. M. de Fezensac declares that this period was the most disastrous of the whole retreat:—

"Let any one," he says, "conceive the sight of plains as far as the eye could extend, all covered with snow—long forests of pine-trees—villages half burned down and deserted—and in the midst of these dismal scenes an immense column of suffering wretches, nearly all without arms, marching pell-mell, and falling again and again upon the ice by the side of their dead horses and dead comrades. Their faces bore the impress of extreme dejection, nay, despair; their eyes were quenched, their features decomposed and quite black with grime and smoke. Strips of sheepskin or pieces of cloth served them instead of shoes; their heads were swathed round with tatters; and their shoulders covered with horse-cloths, women's petticoats, or half-scorched hides. All such means of warmth had their value, for, whenever any man fell from fatigue, his comrades, at once, and without waiting for his death, despoiled him of his rags for themselves to wear. Each nightly bivouac came to resemble a battle-field the next morning, and one was wont to find dead at one's side the men next to whom one had lain down the evening before."

Even the Imperial *cortège* had a share in these terrible sufferings. M. de Fezensac, who came up with it on the 3rd of December, between Ilia and Molodetschno, declares that no one who remembered its splendour at the beginning of the campaign would have known it again. The Guard was marching with disordered ranks and with sorrowing and reproachful faces. The Emperor was shut up in a carriage with the Prince de Neufchatel (Berthier). Behind him followed a small number of equipages, of led horses, and of mules—the scanty remnant from such great disasters. The aides-de-camp of Napoleon, as well as those of Berthier, walked on foot, holding by the bridle their horses, which could scarcely keep upright. Sometimes, to obtain a little rest, they sat behind the Emperor's carriage. In the midst of this sad procession feebly tottered a crowd of disabled men pell-mell from all the regiments, while the gloomy forest of pines through which it was wending appeared like a black frame around the dismal picture.

Even here the gaiety of M. de Bausset does not quite forsake him. He states that the civilians in the Emperor's train were exposed to the enemy's attack about this time, when, having once by accident outstripped their ordinary escort, they found themselves surrounded by Cossacks. But they called for aid to the brave Belliard, *Colonel-Général des Dragons*, who, though wounded, sprang from his carriage, and, gathering some soldiers round him, put "the birds of prey" to flight. The *costume* of the general, as he had assumed it for warmth, is here described. He wore over his uniform a lady's spencer of pink satin, well lined inside with fur. Before their flight the Cossacks had, however, some time for plunder; they bore away *les papiers de la Chancellerie,* and also *les provisions de bouche* secured for that day to the auditors: *C'était faire la plus grande perte possible dans la position où nous étions.* This terrible loss of his expected meal appears to have roused the lord chamberlain to a most unusual frenzy. " *C'est la seule fois dans ma vie que je me sois senti saisis de l'envie d'atteindre un ennemi!* "

A more amiable feature in M. de Bausset's character was his constant kindness to the unfortunate actors and actresses who had been under his direction at Moscow. Many of them dropped off during the retreat, and M. de Bausset never heard of them again. Madame Bursay, the *directrice,* evinced a lofty courage. She was intent on saving two things—first, a young lady and friend of her troop, Madame André; and secondly, a manuscript poem of her own, " De la Médiocrité," from which she expected future fame. M. de Bausset relates how beyond Krasnoi the wheels of the carriage that conveyed them were dashed to pieces by the enemy's cannon-balls, upon which Madame Bursay made her way on foot to the head-quarters at Liady, supporting in her arms and almost carrying her companion, who had swooned and was half dead with fear. They arrived before the bivouac fire at one in the morning, Madame Bursay still firmly clutching her poem " De la Médiocrité," *qu'elle tenait roulé dans sa main comme un Maréchal d'Empire aurait tenu son bâton de commandement.* The influence of De Bausset obtained for these ladies two remaining places in a *fourgon impérial*, and they succeeded, amidst many other dangers, in passing the Beresina and in reaching France. But the health of Madame André had failed from so much hardship, and she died within two months of her return.

Other escapes there were, as Fezensac reports them, truly marvellous amidst such scenes, and evincing in many cases the utmost sympathy and kindness from the poor perishing soldiers. One man, a drummer in the 7th, led his sick wife, a *cantinière* of the same regiment, in a small horse-car from Moscow to Smolensk. There the horse died, and the man yoked himself to the car in the horse's place. Incredible as the effort seems, he drew on his wife all the way to Wilna, and, her sickness having then increased so as to prevent any further removal, he chose, rather than proceed alone, to become a joint prisoner with her. Another poor woman, a *cantinière* of the 33rd, had set out from Moscow with her little daughter only six months old. This child, wrapped in a fur cloak taken at Moscow, she bore safely through all that famished march, feeding her only with a paste made of horse's blood. Twice she was lost by her mother, and twice was she recovered—the first time lying in a field, and the second time in a burned-down village with a mattress for her couch. At the Beresina her mother, finding both bridges at the time obstructed, passed the river on horseback with the water up to her neck, grasping with one hand the bridle, and with the other holding the child upon her head. Thus, by a succession of marvels —it might almost be said of miracles—the little girl completed the entire retreat without any accident, and did not even catch cold.

Cases of such tender care amidst such terrible sufferings—cases which do honour to the French character, and even, it may be said, to human nature itself—may, however, be contrasted with others, unavoidable we fear when human nature is so sorely tried, and when sufferings like these produce, on the contrary, a cruel selfishness. Once a general officer, worn out with fatigue, had fallen down on the road, and a soldier passing by began to pull off his boots. The general faintly gasped forth the request to wait at least till he was dead before he was despoiled. "*Mon Général,*" answered the soldier, " I would with all my heart, but if I do not take your boots, the next comer will, and therefore they may as well be mine." And so he continued to pull!

Another day an officer of the Engineers was also lying prostrate and exhausted. Seeing some soldiers pass, he called out to them for aid and told them who he was. "And are you really an officer of the Engineers?" said the soldiers stopping. "I am indeed, my friends," answered the officer, hopeful of their succour from their words. "Well, then, go on with your plans!" rejoined one of the soldiers in mockery, and they all marched on.

Amidst such scenes and sights of woe the retreat proceeded. The Emperor reached Molodetschno on the 3rd of December. There he dictated and despatched that famous bulletin—the 29th in number since the commencement of the campaign—which lifted at least in some degree the veil from the horrors of the retreat, and which, as published in the *Moniteur* of the 17th of December, diffused deep gloom in almost every family of France, since there was scarcely one perhaps unconnected in kindred or in friendship with some soldier, now most probably perished, of the *Grande Armée*. But besides this general grief, another and as strong a feeling was excited by the following words with which the bulletin concludes: "*La santé de Sa Majesté n'a jamais été meilleure.*" This phrase was introduced, as we believe, without any ill-feeling, and in defiance as it were to the strokes of adverse fortune; but it was commonly taken as evincing the insensibility of the writer to the sufferings which he beheld on every side around him, and which he in fact had caused.

This touch of the national feeling has not been left unnoticed by those Siamese twins of authorship, or rather, according to Colman's line—

"Like two single gentlemen rolled into one,"—

Erckmann and Chatrian. In their justly popular "*Conscrit*" they describe the talk as it may have passed among the peasants in the market-place at Phalsburg, when the 29th bulletin was read:—

"Les cris et les gémissemens se firent entendre. . . . Il est vrai que l'affiche ajoutait: *La santé de Sa Majesté n'a jamais été meilleure;* et c'était une grande consolation. Malheureusement cela ne pouvait pas rendre la vie aux trois cent mille hommes enterrés dans la neige."

Another phrase in this bulletin was understood in

a similar sense. It says that in this retreat the men whom Nature had endowed with superior powers still preserved their gaiety. Gaiety amidst such scenes! M. de Narbonne, who had attended the Emperor from Moscow to Smorgoni, and held the rank of his senior aide-de-camp, was thought to be foremost among the very few for whom this singular compliment was designed. When some weeks afterwards M. de Narbonne returned to Paris, one of his young friends (M. Villemain) addressed to him a question on the subject. "Were I to live thirty years longer," so writes M. Villemain in 1854, "I should never forget his keen look of displeasure as he answered, *Ah, l'Empereur peut tout dire; mais gaieté est bien fort!* And he turned aside, shedding some tears at the horrors he remembered but too well."

From Molodetschno, where this far-famed bulletin was written, the Emperor proceeded on the second day to Smorgoni, a small town still three marches from Wilna. Arriving on the afternoon of the 5th of December, he immediately summoned a council of war, which comprised Murat, Eugene, and the marshals. To these he imparted the design, upon which his mind had brooded for some days past, to quit the army and to proceed with the utmost secrecy, and also with the utmost despatch, to Paris. His return to his capital almost simultaneously with the news of his disaster would strike a salutary awe into his ill-wishers both at home and abroad, and above all would maintain the —perhaps already wavering—alliance of the German princes. At Paris also he could direct the new levies which would be requisite with the greatest promptitude and vigour, and might return in three months at the head of 300,000 men.

These were certainly, as M. Thiers admits, very powerful reasons; and yet, as the same historian proceeds to urge, there were also considerations of much weight to adduce on the opposite side. It is true that the *Grande Armée*—a term that now, alas! had become almost an irony—had dwindled, even including the Guard, to 12,000 soldiers able to bear arms, and to a mass of some 40,000 straggling and disbanded men. But if Napoleon had determined to hold fast by this ruin and to make a stand at Wilna, he would there have received some considerable reinforcements already on their march, and near at hand to join him. He might have strengthened himself with his two wings, the corps of Macdonald from the north, and of Regnier from the south; and he might further have called to his aid from the same quarters the Prussians, under York, and the Austrians, under Schwarzenberg; both of whom would certainly at that period have obeyed his call. Thus, as M. Thiers proceeds to show in some detail, he might have mustered a force fully equal to any the Russians could at the juncture in question have brought against him. There was also the proud feeling of adhering, as the commander, to an army which, under his command, had suffered the direst extremities of war.

It is remarkable that the only two familiars whose advice was sought by Napoleon before the Council at Smorgoni—namely, the Duke de Bassano and Count

Daru, the former being consulted by letter, and the second by word of mouth—both strongly urged the Emperor to remain. They alleged that the ruin of the army would become complete and irretrievable in the event of his departure; that, on the other hand, the conspiracy of Malet had left no traces in France, and that the Emperor's orders for the new armaments which he needed would be obeyed as implicitly from Wilna as from the Tuileries.

These arguments, however, did not move the Emperor from his settled design. Of the chiefs assembled at Smorgoni Napoleon asked no counsel; he merely apprised them of his will. He had resolved to name as vicegerent in his absence Murat, King of Naples, the highest among them in rank, though certainly not in knowledge and ability. Having announced to them his intentions and explained his motives, he exhorted them to unity and concord; then embracing them one by one, he bade them farewell, and set out on his journey the same evening.

The suite selected by the Emperor on this occasion consisted only of Caulaincourt (with whom he sat alone in the first carriage), Duroc, Loban, and Lefebvre Desmouettes, the Mamaluke Roustan, a *valet de chambre*, two *valets de pied*, and one *piqueur*. Beside these, there was also a young Polish officer, Count Wonsowicz, who would be of special service as interpreter during the first part of the journey. And here we would direct attention to a small booklet, "Itinéraire de Napoléon de Smorgoni à Paris," which was published at Paris in 1862, but which, as we imagine, has scarcely, if at all, reached England. It is edited by a veteran French diplomatist, Baron Paul de Bourgoing, but in fact consists of the notes which M. de Bourgoing received from Wonsowicz. This interesting little volume supplies us with some facts not hitherto known.

In commencing this journey, Count Wonsowicz and the *piqueur* went first, as explorers, in a *traineau;* at a little distance the Emperor and his remaining suite followed in three carriages. Up to the first stage, the little town of Oszmiana, they were escorted by thirty *Chasseurs à cheval de la Garde.* It was known from the outset that the expedition would be dangerous, from the swarms of Cossacks and detachments of the enemy's troops who might be in advance. But the peril proved to be much greater than had been foreseen. When the rapid *traineau* dashed into Oszmiana at past midnight, Wonsowicz was surprised to see the small French garrison, comprising three squadrons of Polish lancers, drawn up in battle order on the public square; there was, they said, a Russian force in front of them, and almost in sight; they had been attacked the day before, and expected to be attacked again. The general in command declared that there would be the greatest rashness in proceeding.

In about an hour's time Napoleon in his turn drove up, and was found to be fast asleep in his carriage; he was awakened by Wonsowicz and told the unwelcome news. He then got down and eagerly unfolded his map of Lithuania. All the chiefs in attendance pressed him to pause in the face of such imminent hazards, and wait at least till daybreak. But Napoleon, with truer wisdom, saw that promptitude alone could save him. Even a short delay might reveal the secret of his journey and quicken his enemy's pursuit. He found, moreover, that his small party need not proceed without some protection. He might take with him as an escort to the next relay, or so long as their horses' strength endured, the three squadrons of Polish lancers, amounting to 266 men. Therefore, after a few minutes' reflection, he beckoned Count Wonsowicz to his side, and spoke to him as follows:—

"'Les Lanciers Polonais sont-ils prêts?'
"'Oui, Sire; ils étaient tous là avant notre arrivée.'
"'Qu'ils montent à cheval. Il faut disposer l'escorte autour des voitures. Nous allons partir sur-le-champ; la nuit est suffisamment obscure pour que les Russes ne nous voient pas. D'ailleurs il faut toujours compter sur sa fortune; sur le bonheur; sans cela on n'arrive jamais à rien.'"

As a further measure called for by this terrible crisis, Napoleon ordered Count Wonsowicz and General Lefebvre to mount the box of his own carriage; and confiding to them a pair of pistols which he drew forth ready loaded, he addressed to them these words,—

"Dans le cas d'un danger certain, tuez moi plutôt que de me laisser prendre."

Deeply moved, Count Wonsowicz, having first asked the Emperor's permission, translated these words aloud to the Polish lancers. He was answered by a cry of enthusiasm. These gallant men declared that they would let themselves be cut to pieces sooner than allow the Emperor to be taken, or even approached.

In this guise, at two in the morning, the journey was resumed. Scarce were they out of Oszmiana when there shone forth, and above all to the left of the road, the watchfires of the Russian troops. The call of their sentinels was also distinctly heard. But the night was most intensely cold, the thermometer at twenty-eight degrees of Réaumur below zero, and, as Napoleon had foreseen, the Cossacks, couched close to their blazing logs, were reluctant to leave them in quest of an uncertain prey. Moreover, though their watchfires were seen from afar, they might themselves not distinctly see the long dark line of the carriages and horsemen which without light was wending along. In this manner the convoy, bearing Cæsar and his fortunes, passed without being assailed.

But that night of almost Siberian cold proved fatal to many of the Polish lancers. In attempting to keep pace with the carriages, their horses would slip and come down on the icy ground, frequently with broken limbs or severe wounds to the riders. Too many of these gallant men are thought to have evinced their devotion to their chief by the forfeit of their lives. When in the morning the convoy reached the relay of Rownopol, it was found that of 266 lancers who had started from Oszmiana, no more than thirty-six remained. At Rownopol, their place as escort was supplied by some fifty cavalry of the Neapolitan Royal Guard. These also suffered severely from the frost; their commander, the Duke de Rocca Romana, losing some fingers of both hands.

On arriving at Wilna, Napoleon did not enter the city, but remained for concealment in a small house of the suburb. He was thus enabled to confer for some hours with his trusted Minister, the Duke de Bassano, before he resumed his journey. At Wilna his danger from the Russians had much diminished; at Kowno and beyond the Niemen it altogether ceased. By day and night, over snow and ice, the journey was still pursued. There was only now and then a halt for meals. Such was the speed, and so frequent on the other hand the break-down of the rickety vehicles, that Napoleon left behind the greater part of his suite, which did not rejoin him till at Paris. Thus he dashed into Warsaw one afternoon with only a single carriage. Great was the amazement of the Abbé de Pradt, the French Ambassador in the Polish capital, at suddenly seeing Caulaincourt appear before him and summon him to the presence of his sovereign at *l'Hôtel d'Angleterre*. There he found Napoleon just arrived, pacing up and down a narrow room, while a servant-girl on her knees before the fire was trying in vain to blow up a flame from the damp and half-green wood. In a book published but two or three years later, M. de Pradt has given, perhaps with some exaggeration, a full account of this remarkable interview. According to him, Napoleon at each interval of the conversation repeated over and again the following phrase, since become so familiar to France: "*Du sublime au ridicule il n'y a qu'un pas!*"

At Dresden also there was a like scene, when at three in the morning Count Wonsowicz roused the good old king from his slumbers and invited him to pay a visit to the Emperor in the *Pirna Strasse*. The whole of that little Court, as Count Wonsowicz assures us, was not a little flurried at this strange event.

"Le Roi se levant au milieu de la nuit à la requête d'un inconnu, armé et vêtu d'un costume singulier; le Roi disparaissant en chaise de loange sans dire à aucune des personnes de sa Cour où il allait; c'en était assez pour donner lieu à tous les commentaires, aux plus vives inquiétudes. La Reine de Saxe, sœur du Roi Maximilien de Bavière, princesse déjà avancée en âge, fut effrayée au point d'avoir une attaque de nerfs."

Much to the same effect was the surprise in the first town within the French territory, namely, Mayence. Count Wonsowicz was again despatched with a like message to Marshal Kellerman, Duke de Valmy; and we will leave him to relate in his own words the curious conversation that ensued:—

"Lorsque l'officier Polonais arriva chez le Maréchal, il trouva ses appartements splendidement éclairés; toute la société de Mayence y était rassemblée pour un grand bal. Le Maréchal Kellerman fut appelé; mais il reçut très durement celui qui se disait envoyé par l'Empereur. Il le prit d'abord pour un porteur de fausses nouvelles.

"'Je ne vous connais pas,' lui dit-il; 'et je vais vous faire fusiller comme un imposteur.'

"'Vous en aurez toujours le temps, Monsieur le Maréchal,' répondit sans s'émouvoir l'officier Polonais; 'mais avant d'en venir là, veuillez-vous assurer de la vérité de ce que je vous annonce?'

"'Comment,' réprit le Maréchal, 'comment est-il possible que l'Empereur soit à Mayence, et que je n'ai pas été prévenu de son arrivée?'

"'Veuillez aller le lui demander, Monsieur le Maréchal; moi je ne suis chargé que de vous annoncer son passage.'

"Le costume très en désordre de l'envoyé Impérial avait au premier abord indisposé le Gouverneur. Il n'y voyait qu'un déguisement pour le tromper. Il se rendit enfin, et partit pour aller trouver l'Empereur, tout en faisant garder à vue le Comte Wonsowicz, ne lui permettant de communiquer avec personne, et l'emmenant avec lui, flanqué de deux gendarmes. Mais cet incident et cette méprise furent de courte durée.

"L'Empereur, voyant arriver le Duc de Valmy, lui dit, après quelques phrases très affectueuses:

"'Mon armée est perdue en grande partie; mais soyez tranquille, d'ici à quelques mois j'aurai sous mes ordres huit cent mille baïonnettes, et je prouverai à mes ennemis que les éléments seuls pouvaient nous vaincre. J'ai eu tort, je l'avoue, d'exposer mes pauvres soldats à un climat pareil. Mais qui ne fait pas de fautes en ce monde? Quand on les reconnait il faut tâcher de les réparer.'"

In proceeding onwards, even through his own dominions, the Emperor maintained the same incognito. On the 18th, when he expected to reach Paris, he stopped to dine at Château Thierry; and there also *il fit une grande toilette afin de se présenter convenablement à l'Impératrice.* But his mischances were not yet at an end. Some miles further his carriage broke down, and Napoleon had to enter *une de ces disgracieuses voitures de voyage à deux immenses roues et à brancard, qu'on nommait alors une chaise de poste.* At Meaux it was found that the sum assigned for the travelling expenses had come to an end. The Emperor, the Duke de Vicence, the Count Wonsowicz, and the Mameluke Roustan, who since Warsaw had formed the entire party, gave what money they had about them, but the total amounted to less than eighty francs. The Duke de Vicence could only apply to the postmaster for an advance, which fortunately was not refused him.

At half-past eleven the same night the rustic vehicle — *cet affreux équipage,* as Count Wonsowicz terms it—appeared at the *Grille du Carrousel.* Naturally enough, it was denied admittance. But Count Wonsowicz, dismounting, led the officer on guard close to the carriage-window.

"L'officier de garde reconnut son Souverain, et s'inclina avec une profonde émotion. La grille s'ouvrit alors. On peut se figurer quelle sensation produisit dans le palais des Tuileries cette arrivée inespérée. L'Empereur, une fois entré dans le château, défendit expressément qu'on fît aucun bruit qui pût éveiller l'Impératrice; il se rendit sur-le-champ à son appartement."

In this guise then did he, so lately the conqueror and arbiter of Europe, re-enter his palace, and resume the government of his empire. The account of his disasters, as comprised in the 29th bulletin, had been published by the *Moniteur* only the day before.

If we ask the effects produced by the departure of Napoleon on the melancholy remnant of his troops, which continued its retreat from Smorgoni to Wilna, we shall find them described by M. de Fezensac in few but expressive words:—

"Dans la situation de l'armée ce départ était pour elle une nouvelle calamité. L'opinion que l'on avait du génie de l'Empereur donnait de la confiance; la crainte qu'il inspirait retenait dans le devoir. Après son départ chacun fit à sa tête; et les ordres que donna le Roi de Naples ne servirent qu'à compromettre son autorité."

Murat, indeed, could not direct; and under such a chief the marshals would not obey. The large and rich city of Wilna, the ancient capital of Lithuania, had been looked to by the suffering soldiers as the probable term of their calamities. They counted every step, says M. de Fezensac, that brought them nearer to this long-desired haven of rest. But, alas, how empty the hope, how evanescent the dream! How sharply were they roused from their illusion, the last to which they clung, when they appeared before Wilna, in part on the 8th, and in part on the 9th of December! Expected though they were, no due measures had been taken for their reception and relief. Rushing up pell-mell as they came to the narrow gateway, there was soon an amount of obstruction and confusion comparable to that on the Beresina bridges. Yet while the multitudes were thus pressing on each other with cries and yells, with bruises and with blows, while, in fact, great numbers had to remain the whole night without the city—there were all the while, to the right and left, open gaps through the walls, which no one had been stationed to point out!

Within the city it was much the same. There were ample magazines, both of provisions and of clothing, but no order had been made for their right use. The perishing soldiers would not be denied, and thus, for lack of distribution, there was plunder. Moreover, it was found that the city could not be maintained. Several divisions of the hostile army were close at hand, and the sound of their artillery boomed nearer and nearer. Under these circumstances Murat made a precipitate retreat, at four in the morning, with the remains of the Old Guard. In his hurry he appears to have given no directions for the guidance of the rest. Marshal Mortier heard of his departure only by chance, and then followed with the Young Guard, or what was left of it. Marshal Ney, with a handful of heroic men, again forming the rear, undertook to maintain the city a few hours more. Immediately on his departure the Russian troops poured in. Of the French, several generals, a great number of officers, and more than twenty thousand soldiers, nearly all sick or wounded, remained at Wilna, utterly exhausted and unable to move farther. They became, therefore, prisoners in the enemy's hands.

The ruin of the army, however, was completed a few miles from Wilna, at a steep hill forming the left bank of the Wilna valley. That hill had become one slippery sheet of ice. The horses—for there were still some horses undevoured—were urged to drag up the remaining cannon or carriages, but they were urged in vain. Not one piece of artillery, and scarce any of the lighter vehicles, could be saved. Here, then, were relinquished the last resources of the army, its military chests, carried from Wilna, and containing ten millions of francs in gold and silver coin. The soldiers passing by were permitted to take what they could, and it was a strange spectacle, writes De Fezensac, to see men heavily laden with gold, and yet half-dead with hunger. Here, too, were left "the trophies of

Moscow," as they were termed, which had been conveyed safely thus far amidst so many dangers and disasters—above all, the great cross of Ivan, taken down from the highest spire of Moscow, and designed, in memorial of the conquest, for the ornament of the Invalides at Paris.

At Kowno, as at Wilna, no stand could be made. The French army, now reduced to scattered bands, fled, band by band, across the Niemen. There were now only hundreds of armed and effective men upon the same ground where there had been hundreds of thousands the summer before. At Königsberg they found a short respite, but no permanent halting-place until on the line of the Vistula—behind the ramparts of Dantzic and Elbing.

The aspect of Wilna and Kowno, just before they were thronged with the mass of the retreating French, is well portrayed in a book which has had but little circulation in Germany, and none at all, we believe, in England. We allude to M. Droysen's biography of General York, published at Berlin in 1851. York, as is well known, was, at the close of 1812, commander of the Prussian force in Courland, which acted as an auxiliary to France, and had Marshal Macdonald as immediate chief. Perplexed at the ominous rumours which began to prevail as to the fate of the *Grande Armée*, York secretly despatched one of his young officers, Baron Canitz, on an exploring mission to Wilna. The memoir of the Baron, as drawn up on his return, now lies before us in its native German, being given by M. Droysen in the appendix to his first volume; and we are here tempted to translate, and sometimes abridge, several of its graphic details:—

"On the afternoon of the 4th of December I reached Kowno. Till then I had met scarce any one upon my route, and seen no traces of the war. But at Kowno the ruins of demolished houses, the remains of bivouac fires, and the dead horses on the roadside, spoke but too plainly of an army's line of march. The town was full of scattered soldiers, many sick or wounded, derived from every possible corps, and decked with all varieties of uniform. The first of whom I asked my way to the post-station was a half-frozen Portuguese, who could speak of nothing but the cold. I found it almost impossible to obtain post-horses, but lighted, by good fortune, on a French courier charged with despatches, who offered to take me with him on my paying one-half his expenses. I gladly accepted his proposal, and we were off in half an hour.

"The places we passed through were half demolished, and the inhabitants had fled, so that besides the French soldiery there was no creature to be seen. A few miles from Kowno we overtook a body of some hundred cavalry —cuirassiers and lancers—proceeding as a reinforcement to the *Grande Armée*. The horses not being rough-shod were constantly slipping and falling on the icy ground. So the men had for the most part to proceed on foot, leading their steeds by the bridle, and expressing their dislike of this mode of march by a myriad of execrations. My courier called out without ceasing, "*Agauche, mes camarades; c'est un courier de l'Empereur qui doit passer;*" and in this manner we went through the devoted band, which, as I compute it, must have arrived at Wilna just in time to share in the general destruction.

"Wilna, like most cities in Poland, is a strange assemblage of splendid palaces and miserable huts mingled with each other. Its streets bore a most variegated aspect, as comprising samples and specimens of all the different corps which had formed *la Grande Armée*. Still there was a certain order preserved; the Guards of the King of Naples, who stood sentinels at the principal doors, were not only trim but splendid in attire; and there were only the ghastly figures of the *revenants des hôpitaux*, as they were termed, to remind us of the coming catastrophe. French ballets and comedies had been acted in the evening; and French shops were open in every direction, several for jewelry or other *articles de luxe*, and all with huge French signs.

"From General Knesemark I learnt the latest news. He told me that according to his reports the French cavalry and artillery were utterly destroyed—that there was little hope of a stand being made at or near Wilna—that the Emperor was on the point of taking his departure, and committing the command to the King of Naples. It was to be the general's last day at Kowno. He had been summoned by the Duke de Bassano, in common with his brethren of the *corps diplomatique*, to proceed at once to Warsaw, so that he would not be able to judge with his own eyes of the retreating army.

"In company with a friend, Major Schenk, whom I found at Wilna, I repaired to a *restaurateur*, at the sign of the *Aigle Impérial*—a visit of which I stood greatly in need, since meals do not abound in a Polish journey. Never, perhaps, did any cook deserve more thoroughly this name of *restaurateur*. How many men did I see come in who were feeble and famished, and to all appearance crest-fallen and heart-broken, but who, after the long unwonted comfort of a good repast, could sally forth again with a firm step and a cheerful mien! Of those I spoke with, none made any secret of the enormous losses sustained on the retreat. But they expressed their belief that the Russian army was almost as much ruined as their own, and that no serious resistance would be offered to the attempt of ceasing the retreat, and making a rally at Wilna.

"This was on the 5th. On the morning of the 6th the agitation in the city was visibly increased; and all who could find a conveyance had set out. Our host of the *Aigle Impérial* was already gone. We went to another *restaurateur* to breakfast, at the sign of *La Couronne Impériale* He, too, was packing up. Several officers represented to him that there was no sort of danger, and that he had better stay. '*On a des nouvelles très consolantes de l'armée*,' answered he; '*je n'en doute pas, mais je partirai demain à la pointe de jour*.' Napoleon may perhaps have taken exactly the same view when he stepped into his carriage at Smorgoni, and bad the King of Naples lead his army into winter quarters.

"All through the day I saw *revenants* from the army pour in. Forms so gaunt, so ghastly, that even the direst dream could scarcely image them, arrived in almost an unbroken line, some on sledges, and some on foot. Out of many hundreds hardly one carried a musket or a weapon of any kind. Many fell down exhausted in the streets, and lay helpless, while the rest passed them heedlessly by. To see a man dying, after so many other scenes of woe, seemed to induce no more impression than to see a man drunk in a Polish fair.

"I was assured that the Guard was expected on the morrow—reduced to a mere handful, and marching in utter disarray; and I should have wished to judge with my own eyes the actual state of that proud band which I had beheld last June, in all its splendour, passing through my native land. But the officer at the post-station told me that he could give me no horses if I lingered; and so I set out on my return that very night."

In concluding the slight sketch of these terrible disasters it seems natural to inquire the total loss which the French sustained. M. Thiers computes that, of the soldiers who had crossed the Niemen, about 100,000 became prisoners of war, and about 300,000 were either slain in action or died of their wounds, or perished from famine and cold. Vast as are these numbers, they appear to be fully borne out by specific details. Thus M. de Fezensac gives us the particulars of his own regiment. It had 2150 men when it passed the Rhine, it received a reinforcement of 400 men at Moscow, one more to the same amount at Smolensk, and another of only 50 men at Wilna, making 3000 in all. "Now, of these 3000 men," adds De Fezensac, "only 200 returned with me to the Vistula, and about 100 subsequently came back from captivity, so that our loss was 2700 out of 3000, that is, nine-tenths." And even of these 200 who remained in arms upon the Vistula, how many may have belonged to the detachments that joined at Smolensk or at Wilna, and that never saw Moscow!

The causes of this great catastrophe are by no means difficult to trace. Of course the rigour of the season forms the first. But the closer we inquire, the more fully shall we find confirmed the opinion of the Duke of Wellington, which we quoted at the commencement of this article, that the arrangements of Napoleon were short-sighted and defective. That opinion will be found developed with more details, and fortified by numerous instances, in another essay or rather series of remarks by the Duke—some notes which he drew up in 1826 on M. de Ségur's recently published history of the Russian campaign. Those notes have hitherto remained in MS., but they will appear in the forthcoming volume of the "Wellington Papers," and meanwhile we have been enabled by the favour of the present duke to peruse them in the *proofs*.

The Duke here observes:—

"This chapter (the second) affords another proof of Napoleon's extraordinary character. He had taken the utmost pains to ascertain the difficulty and danger of the enterprise which he was about to undertake; these difficulties and dangers are represented to him from all quarters and in all forms. He is sensible of them, yet he is determined to persevere. He wants a military success, and he must seek for it; he is blind to every difficulty, or rather will not see any; and will take no measures to insure his success (excepting to collect a large French army), and most particularly none which can check for a moment the gratification of his hatred of Bernadotte.

"It is certainly true that this young empire had all the disorders of old age. Here are officers making false reports, and a Minister concealing the truth, lest the truth should displease the Emperor!"

On the whole, then, in discussing the events of 1812, we may presume to say that Napoleon had made no preparations for a military retreat. In his other campaigns, both before and after, that extraordinary man evinced a genius for the organization of an army, little inferior to his genius in the field. It was far otherwise in the Moscow episode. There the Emperor appears to have confided in his star—to have supposed that his former course of uninterrupted triumphs must be uninterrupted still, even though he should neglect the provident care by which, among other qualities, these triumphs were achieved.

We would observe, however, as a fact that may explain—and not only explain but in a great measure excuse—his deficiency of arrangements at this time, that all through the advance from Witepsk to Moscow, and probably at Moscow also, Napoleon appears to have been in a state of feverish excitement and great mental disquietude. Of this curious fact there has recently appeared some remarkable testimony. Duroc, who during so long a period was admitted to his daily intercourse and familiar conversation, and who beyond all other men deserved the title of his personal friend, dotted down at the time, in great secrecy and only for himself, some notes upon the subject. Forty years later these notes, having come into the hands of M. Villemain, were published by him in the first part of his "Souvenirs Contemporains." We shall conclude this essay by transcribing them, thinking that they form perhaps a key to no small part of what ensued:—

"4 Août, deux heures du matin. A pris le bain : grande agitation. Il faut marcher, réparer vite le temps perdu ; nous ne pouvons pas bivouaquer éternellement dans cette bicoque du palais du Duc de Wittemberg.

"5 Août, un heure du matin. Dictée sur les mouvemens des corps. . . . . Que servirait de prendre Riga ? Il faut une immense victoire, une bataille devant Moscou, une prise de Moscou, qui étonne le monde.

"L'Empereur a dormi deux heures ; il m'a montré le jour déjà clair à l'horizon. 'Nous avons encore,' m'a-t-il dit, 'du beau temps pour près de trois mois; il m'en a fallu moins pour Austerlitz et Tilsit.'

"7 Août. L'Empereur a été physiquement très souffrant; il a pris de l'opium préparé par Methivier. Duroc, il faut marcher ou mourir. Un Empereur meurt debout; et alors il ne meurt point. Vous avez peur des Prussiens entre Moscou et la France; souvenez-vous d'Iena, et croyez encore plus à leur crainte qu'à leur haine; mais pour cela il faut marcher; il faut agir. L'Empereur a souffert encore. Il faut finir cette fièvre du doute."

We may sum up the whole, perhaps, with a forcible exclamation of the Duke of Wellington, as we find it in his Ségur notes:—"It is that which strikes one as most extraordinary in the history of the transaction of our times—how much of the fate of the world depends upon the temper and passions of one man!"

II.

LEGENDS OF CHARLEMAGNE.

LEGENDS OF CHARLEMAGNE.*

LEGENDS and mythical stories of various kinds have often in the progress of time gathered around the memories of remarkable men. But there is one curious fact respecting them, which has only of late years been, I might, perhaps, say discovered,—certainly, at least, acknowledged. They were formerly thought to have proceeded, like any other falsehoods, from a deliberate purpose to deceive. Now, on the contrary, it seems to be admitted by most persons that they spring up almost unconsciously, and in many cases with a full conviction of their truth by those who first composed them.

The explanation of this the later, and, as I should say, the sounder, view is to be found in the following train of thought which we may assume to have passed in the mind of the credulous fabulist. The thing must have been so and so; therefore the thing was so and so. Such a man was a great hero—of course

---

* Reprinted by permission from *Fraser's Magazine* of July, 1866.

then he was eight feet high. Such a man was very learned—of course then he had studied the Black Art. Such a man was a Saint—of course then we cannot be wrong in ascribing to him any virtue or any marvel. A process of reasoning like this in the darker ages has sufficed to transform Attila into a giant, Virgil into a magician, and Mahomet into what he certainly never claimed to be, a worker of miracles. Thus does wonder crowd on wonder, each succeeding writer adding a new circumstance, until at last the true historical personage is obscured, and well-nigh lost to sight in a cloud of legendary lore.

On no period of history however have these legends settled more closely or in greater numbers than on the era of Charlemagne. That great Sovereign might well make a powerful impression on the popular mind. His dominion was as extensive as that of Napoleon, and indeed almost conterminous with it, while the duration of his reign was about three-fold. The excellence of his civil institutions enhanced the glory of his military exploits; and he looms high above the series both of his predecessors and of his descendants.

The life and character of Charlemagne have been described with full authority by Eginhard, an accomplished man of letters, who knew him well, and who filled an office at his Court. This is in truth the only quite accurate and trustworthy record. But on the other hand, it is rather brief and summary, and might well appear to the next age incommensurate to the extent of his conquests and the lustre of his reign.

In order to supply this popular craving there came forth in the eleventh century a fabulous history of Charlemagne, falsely ascribed to Turpin, who in the days of the great Emperor had been Archbishop of Rheims. To the same effect, but in divers forms, and in every variety of language, has started up a whole host of ballads and romances.

Eginhard—who by the way was not in truth Eginhard at all, for he always called himself and his contemporaries always called him Einhard or Einhardus—tells us that Charlemagne gave orders to put in writing "the barbaric and most ancient poems in which the deeds and wars of the old Kings were sung." The object of the great Emperor was that these poems might be safely transmitted to posterity; and the encouragement which he thus afforded to such compositions was, though unconsciously, conducive to his own renown. Other poems in celebration of himself sprung up within the next two centuries; and although the great fame of Charlemagne might fairly rest on his authentic and admitted deeds; yet certainly, in the eyes of our forefathers, and perhaps even in our own, his figure has seemed enormously enhanced and magnified when contemplated through the haze of fiction.

On no point I think has that fiction been so rife as on the many legends relating to the twelve peers of Charlemagne, or, as they are sometimes called, his Paladins. But Charlemagne in real fact had no peers at all. The idea is quite imaginary. It appears to take its rise from the supposition that every man of might ought to be attended by certain followers of commensurate renown; and the gospel history may perhaps have suggested the number twelve as especially solemn and sacred. Thus, in like manner, the Spaniards have an epic on Alexander the Great which dates from the thirteenth century, and which represents the Macedonian conqueror also as having around him his twelve peers.*

As to the name of Paladin it has been, like so many others, elucidated by the skill and learning of Ducange. He shows from quotations that the *d* in the word is a later corruption of *t*, and that the original term was "Palatin," not "Paladin;" the signification being "one that belongs to the palace;" a chosen champion, or, if you prefer it, a guardsman of the Sovereign.

Charlemagne himself in some legends is raised to the stature of a giant. His life by the pseudo-Turpin declares that he was at least eight feet high. In other legends he is exalted to the dignity of a Saint. Such at all events was the idea entertained of him by Joan of Arc. She said to Charles VII., at Chinon: —"I tell you, gentle Dauphin, that God has pity on you, your realm, and your people, for St. Louis and St. Charlemagne are on their knees before Him, and offer supplications for you."

But the event of this reign in which all the poetry, all the legends, all the pseudo-histories, may be said

---

* This is the "Alexandro" of Juan Lorenzo Segura, a poem of above ten thousand lines. See Mr. Ticknor's "History," vol. i. p. 54.

to culminate is the retreat of the French from Spain, attended by the rout of Roncesvalles and the fall of Roland. The real facts are to be gathered from two passages of Eginhard; the one in his "Life of Charlemagne," and the other in his "Annals" under the date 778. It appears then that Charlemagne being invited to Spain by Ibn Araby, one of his Moorish allies, marched over the Pyrenees, took Pamplona, and advanced to the Ebro, under the walls of Saragoza. There he received hostages in token of submission from several of the Saracen princes, and so far had been successful in his object. But on his march homewards his rearguard was assailed and put to the sword in one of the Pyrenean passes by an armed body of Spanish Basques. "In which conflict," adds Eginhard, "there fell, with very many others, Anselm, Count of the Palace, and Roland, Præfect of the Marches of Brittany." * I may remark that the name of Roland is here given in the truly barbaric form of *Hruodlandus*. Much more important is the note here appended by M. Teulet, the latest and best editor of Eginhard. "This passage," he says, "is the only one among the early historians in which any mention is made of the famous Roland who plays so great a part in all the Carlovingian romances."

On this scanty groundwork then has arisen, as I may term it, an air-built and fantastic castle. In the first place Roland is made the nephew of Charlemagne —a relationship which would certainly not be un-

---

* Eginhard, "Opera," vol. i. p. 32, ed. Teulet.

noticed by Eginhard if it had been real. Next he is invested with the trusty sword Durandal, with which he not only demolishes his enemies, but on one occasion, when pursuing the Moslem, cleaves a pass through the Pyrenees which towers above *le Cirque de Gavarni*, and is still called *la brèche de Roland*. Moreover he had a horn scarcely less tremendous, which he sounded in the rout of Roncesvalles to apprise Charlemagne of his danger, and which was heard by the Emperor at a wonderful distance. Further still the romancers are so obliging as to provide him with a bride, the Lady Alda, who remains at Paris, and is awaiting his return from Spain.

As it appears to me, there is here a striking similarity between the Roland of France and the William Wallace of Scotland. The exploits of both are unrecorded in the meagre chronicles of the time. These exploits live only in tradition and in song. But taken as a whole they have, in my judgment, a just claim to be believed. All that tradition has done is to confound the dates and exaggerate the circumstances. We may be sure that so great and so general a fame could not in either case have arisen had not the living hero impressed his image on the public mind. I should therefore entirely agree with Sismondi, who in the second volume of the "History of France" contends, that although Roland may not have been pre-eminent at Roncesvalles, he must have performed achievements and acquired renown in former years, when warring against the Saracens of Spain.

Many other characters of Roncesvalles, though

familiar to the minstrel, are wholly unknown to the historian. Such are Oliver and other Paladins in the French romances. Such are Durandarte and Calaynos in the Spanish ballads. But above all in frequency of mention stands Ganelon, the arch-traitor, who misled Roland in the mountain passes and caused the "dolorous rout." M. Génin, a high authority on the Carlovingian period, has discussed the subject of this name,[*] conceiving it to be derived from an Archbishop of Sens, also called Ganelon, who in 859 was guilty of gross ingratitude to his Sovereign and benefactor Charles the Bald. This seems to me a wholly unfounded idea. The ingratitude of Archbishop Ganelon did not lead to any such striking or fatal action as would at all impress itself on the popular imagination; and moreover it appears that the Emperor and the prelate were reconciled together before the close of the same year. Nor is the sacerdotal character preserved in the legendary Ganelon, as one would expect it to be if an Archbishop had been in truth its prototype.

I consider it therefore very far more probable that Ganelon may have been the real appellation of the treacherous chief of the Navarrese or Spanish Basques who assailed the rear-guard of Charlemagne. Nor does it seems to me at all surprising that Eginhard in his very summary account of the transaction, and omitting even the name of Roncesvalles, should omit also the name of any leader on the enemy's side.

Be this as it may, however, there is no doubt

---

[*] "Chanson de Roland," Introduction, p. xxv.

that within two centuries and a half from the death of Charlemagne the songs and ballads founded on the tragical tale of Roncesvalles had grown popular in France. One proof of this—connected also with the history of England—is given by Robert Wace in his "Roman de Rou." He tells us that as the Normans of William the Conqueror marched onwards to the battle of Hastings they had in their front ranks a valiant minstrel who from his deeds of arms was surnamed *Taillefer*, "the hewer of iron." Taillefer then in the front ranks went singing, as the old French rhymes declare it—

> "De Carlemaigne et de Rolant,
> Et d'Olivier et des vassaus,
> Qui morurent en Rainscevaux."

Or,

> "Of Charlemagne and of Roland,
> And of Oliver and the vassals,
> Who died in Roncevaux." *

Nor were the ballads of Roncevaux less in vogue among the Spaniards. Of this I may give a striking example, though of a later period, derived from the very masterpiece of Spanish genius.

There is a passage in the second part of "Don Quixote," † where the knight of La Mancha and his squire repair to Toboso in quest of the peerless Dulcinea. There—

"a country labourer passed them going out before daybreak to plough, and as he came along he was singing the old ballad which says—

---

* See Génin, "Introduction à la Chanson de Roland," p. lxiv.
† Part ii. chap. ix.

'Ill ye fared, ye Frenchmen,
In the chace of Ronceval.'

"'Let me die,' said Don Quixote, hearing the ballad, 'if we have any good success to-night; dost thou hear what the peasant sings, Sancho?'"

The ballad thus quoted by Cervantes as sung by a clown in La Mancha, is given by him (so far as regards the opening lines), with some slight verbal differences from its printed form in the "Romancero"—differences which, arising, as of course, from traditionary recitation, are of no particular account. It has been rendered into English verses by Mr. Lockhart, under the title of "The Admiral Guarinos." And here I cannot but pause for a moment to commemorate the admirable spirit and brilliancy with which Mr. Lockhart has translated—or rather in many cases not exactly translated but rather paraphrased and new-formed—these ancient Spanish ballads. My own warmth of feeling may indeed mislead me when I mention a friend of great intimacy and of cherished memory, now passed away. But I would desire you to consider how strong on this point is the testimony of an American gentleman, Mr. Ticknor. In his excellent book—"The History of Spanish Literature"—Mr. Ticknor observes of these translations of Lockhart, that in his judgment they form "a work of genius beyond any of the sort known to me in any language." *

If indeed I may be permitted to adduce a single instance in proof of this great superiority I shall be content with one, the concluding stanza of this very

---

* "History of Spanish Literature," vol. i. p. 115, ed. 1863.

ballad on the Admiral Guarinos. It relates how Guarinos—not a Moslem as you might imagine from his title, but one of Charlemagne's captains, and made a prisoner at Roncesvalles—after seven years' durance being by a fortunate accident mounted once more on his favourite war-horse, and grasping once more his ancient lance, makes his way from Spain. I will give you first a translation as literal as I can make it of the Spanish lines, and next Mr. Lockhart's version.

Here is a literal translation of the concluding Spanish lines:

> "The Moors who looked upon this
> All with one accord sought to slay him;
> But Guarinos, as became a brave man,
> Began forthwith to fight
> With the Moors, who were so many
> That they might have darkened the sun.
> In such guise then did he fight
> That he was able to set himself free,
> And to reach once again his own land,
> His native soil of France.
> Great honour there they showed him,
> When they thus saw him return."

How incomparably finer, how far more abounding in life and fire, is the corresponding stanza of Mr. Lockhart:

"With that Guarinos, lance in rest, against the scoffer rode,
Pierced at one thrust his envious breast, and down his turban trode.
Now ride, now ride, Guarinos, nor lance nor rowel spare,
Slay, slay, and gallop for thy life, the land of France lies *there!*"

But let me make myself clearly understood. While I think that the Spanish lines which close "The Admiral Guarinos" are extremely poor and tame, I am far indeed from applying that character in general to the Spanish ballads, or other lyric pieces. On the contrary, many amongst them possess a natural charm, an inborn simplicity and grace, and sometimes also an exquisite tenderness which cannot be too highly praised, and which seem almost to defy the power of translation. As combining all these qualities I might mention, for instance, the little poem beginning "En los tiempos que me vi," which is the original of Lockhart's "Valladolid," and one other, "La niña Morena," which is the original of "Zara's Ear-rings." In some of these cases, however, the Spanish poem is marred by later interpolations, as Depping considers them, or, as I should rather say, by an original defect in the *couleur locale*, as the French term it. Thus, in "Zara's Ear-rings," the Moorish maiden speaks of herself attending mass, a rite of course, peculiar to the Christians; and also of admiring the rich brocade of a marquis, a title never known among her countrymen.

Excellent as are undoubtedly these translations by Lockhart, taken as a whole, there are yet some few cases in which they have been even surpassed. Thus there is another fine ballad derived from the age of Charlemagne, "Lady Alda's Dream," Lady Alda being the fabulous bride of the scarcely less fabulous Roland. Of this, Mr. Ticknor observes that in its English dress Lockhart must yield the palm to another most accomplished man who is still preserved to us; I mean the former Governor of Canada, Sir Edmund Head. In this ballad Lady Alda, being left at Paris with her train, has a dream of a falcon overpowered by an eagle. One of her damsels seeks to interpret this dream in an auspicious sense. But I will leave Sir Edmund Head to continue the tale:

"'Thou art the falcon, and thy knight is the eagle in his pride,
As he comes in triumph from the wars, and pounces on his bride.'
The maidens laughed, but Alda sighed and gravely shook her head:
'Full rich,' quoth she, 'shall thy guerdon be, if thou the truth hast said.'
'Tis morn; her letters stained with blood the truth too plainly tell,
How in the chace of Ronceval Sir Roland fought and fell."*

But I have not yet done with the Admiral Guarinos. In the passage which I read to you from "Don Quixote," you will observe how Cervantes makes his hero declare that he can expect no good fortune that day, since it had begun by the singing of a ballad upon Roncesvalles. It appears then that the singing of a ballad upon Roncesvalles was deemed of ill augury among Spaniards. On the other hand, since, as I have lately shown you, the soldiers of William the Conqueror marched forward to the battle of

---

* The Lady Alda reappears in one at least of the *Chansons de Geste*, where she is mentioned as the sister of Sir Oliver:

"Et si vient belle Aude, la soreur Olivier."

"Gui de Bourgogne," p. 39, ed. 1859.

Hastings singing another of these ballads upon Roncesvalles, we may conclude that it was deemed of good augury among Frenchmen. Is not this a strange fact? —I think not hitherto noticed. Here are the songs on the rout of Roncesvalles held to be ill augury among the supposed descendants of the victors, and of good augury among the supposed descendants of the vanquished! Surely this is the very reverse of what on any pre-conceived idea we might expect to find.

In English poetry we find the rout of Roncesvalles not unfrequently mentioned. There is in the first book of "Paradise Lost" a reminiscence—no doubt high-toned and sonorous, but a little misty—in which Milton ranks not only the famous Roland, but the great Emperor himself among the slain:

"When Charlemagne with all his peerage fell by Fontarabia."

Coming to later times, we find a pathetic ballad by Matthew Gregory Lewis, entitled "Durandate and Belerma," for which he is only in some part indebted to the Spanish. It begins as follows:

"Sad and fearful is the story
Of the Roncevalles fight;
On that fatal field of glory
Perished many a gallant knight."

Nor can you have forgotten the beautiful opening of that poem, one of the very finest of its class, which commemorates the death of the Black Prince at Bordeaux, and which Sir Walter Scott has interwoven with the novel of "Rob Roy:"

> "O for the voice of that wild horn
> On Fontarabian echoes borne,
> The dying hero's call;
> That told imperial Charlemagne
> How Paynim sons of swarthy Spain
> Had wrought his champion's fall."

Pass we to Italian. Dante has a passage very similar to Milton's, in which he refers to "the dolorous rout," *la dolorosa rotta,* and to the sounding of the terrible horn.* It is remarkable that in the same place Dante calls the enterprise of Charlemagne "the saintly deed," *la santa gesta*—a phrase derived, as I conceive, from a later period—the Crusades—when the recovery of the Holy Sepulchre suggested the idea of every conflict with the Moslem as a holy war.

But in Italy the legends of Charlemagne did not merely, as in England, give rise to some passing allusion or to some imitative song. On the contrary they produced two great epic poems, the epic of Boyardo and the epic of Ariosto, both having for their hero the brave Roland, or as the Italians call him, Orlando.

The poem of Boyardo, founded on an imaginary siege of Paris by the Saracens, is now very little read, at least beyond his own country. But the few among us who are qualified to judge, have judged him very favourably. Thus speaks Mr. Hallam:

"The 'Orlando Inamorato' of Boyardo has hitherto not received that share of renown which seems to be its due, overpowered by the splendour of Ariosto's poem." †

---

* "Inferno," canto xxxi.
† "Introduction to the Literature of Europe," vol. i. p. 313.

Ariosto's poem has indeed cast into the shade nearly all other poems of romantic fiction on his side the Alps. So much was it read and relished by the Italians as to reflect a share of its own popularity on the older Carlovingian legends, out of which it sprung.

This Italian appreciation, from whatever cause arising, of the Carlovingian legends, may be proved by some slight but significant examples. Thus is it not curious that the common Italian word which means "to deceive," *ingannare*, is held to be derived from the name of Ganelon, or shortly, Gan, the arch-traitor at Roncesvalles?

Thus, again, many a wayfarer on the old and beautiful post-road—seldom, I fear, to be re-travelled—from Florence to Rome, by way of Terni, may have noticed to his left, perched on one of the summits of the Apennines, the decaying town of Spello. One of its gates bears, it seems, a piece of mediæval sculpture, with an inscription in honour of Orlando. They are marked by the grossness of a less cultivated age; and I cannot fully explain them. It may suffice for my purpose to say that they are intended to commemorate the hero's gigantic size and warlike prowess.[*]

In France, the poems belonging to the Carlovingian cycle are very numerous, and some of considerable length. They were called "Chansons de Geste," an old French word derived from the Latin *Gesta*, so that the meaning is: "Songs of heroic deeds." One of the chief of these is the "Chanson de Roland," having

---

[*] They are described at length by M. Génin, "Chanson de Roland," Introduction, p. xxi.

for its author Turold or Théroulde, and for its date, as is probable, the eleventh century. The last and best edition of it was in the year 1851, by M. Génin, who prefixed an ably written and interesting introduction, to which in my present essay I am much beholden.

M. Génin, in the true spirit of a commentator, ascribes great poetical merit and beauty to the work which he has edited. Such is also the opinion of a gentleman in this country, Mr. Ludlow, who in 1865 published two volumes of the "Popular Epics of the Middle Ages." Mr. Ludlow there says that he considers the *Song of Roland* "the masterpiece of French epic poetry." * For my own part, I cannot concur in these praises. So far as I have read in the *Song of Roland*, I have found it very tiresome reading, and discovered no trace of poetical beauties. Its value, as it seems to me, is as illustrating the temper and the manners of the time; and of these I shall now proceed to offer one or two examples.

In the fifth book of the "Chanson de Roland" is an account of the final conflict under the walls of Saragoza. We find the "Amiralz" or Emir before it commences invoking his false gods, calling in one breath upon Apollo and Mahomet, and vowing to each an image in fine gold. And after the city is taken the poet continues in a passage which may serve to show the idea of liberty of conscience as current in that age:

---

* See vol. i. p. 363.

" The Emperor has Saragoza taken;
A thousand Frenchmen search through the city,
Its synagogues, and its Mahoundries (*Mahumeries*);
Holding mallets of iron and hatchets,
They break the images and the idols.
The Bishops meanwhile bless the waters,
And lead the pagans to the baptistery.
If any one should gainsay great Charles,
He is hanged, or burned, or slain.
More than one hundred thousand are baptized
And made good Christians; all but the Queen—
She is led away a captive to fair France,
That she may be converted by love."

The authors of these poems were disposed to follow a good old Oriental precedent. When in the East one of the "Arabian Nights" or some other tale of wonder is recited, it is usual for the reciter to stop short at the most interesting period, and declare that he will not finish the story unless a piece of money be put down by every person present. Just so in these "Chansons de Geste." Thus in "Huon de Bordeaux," there is a pause after five thousand lines, when Huon is just about to encounter the giant in his castle, and the minstrel says—I will translate the lines:

" Oh mighty *Segnors*, I am sure you see full plain
That it is near vespers, and that I am weary.
* * * * * *
Let me then go and drink, for such is my desire.
* * * * * *
But do you return to-morrow, after dinner,
And let me pray each of you to bring with him
A *maille* (a halfpenny) tied up in a fold of his shirt,

For there is little liberality in these *Poitevines;*
Miserly and mean was he who first had them made,
Or who first gave them to the courteous minstrel!" *

Poitevines, let me explain, are a very small French coin, so called because they were first coined in Poitou. Small as they were, however, it was found worth while to counterfeit them, for we find in old French the word *Poitevineur* as applied to the maker of false *Poitevines.*†

But I come back to the minstrel in "Huon de Bordeaux." It would seem that his hearers on the morrow had neglected to bring in their shirts the much-desired *mailles.* Therefore after some five hundred lines of further recitation, the minstrel breaks forth again:

"Take you notice, so may God give me health,
I will at once put an end to my song:
I will excommunicate on my own authority,
Also by the power of Auberon and his rank,
All those who shall not open their purses and give to my
 wife!" ‡

Auberon, I need not say, is the old French form of the German or the English *Oberon.* But I may add that in the course of my reading I have met with this name Auberon in the French form upon only two occasions, first in the legend of the Fairies, and next in the pedigree of the Earls of Carnarvon.

The story in this "Chanson de Geste," "Huon de Bordeaux," is substantially the same as that in the

---

* "Huon de Bordeaux," p. 148, ed. 1860.
† Roquefort, "Glossaire de la Langue Romane" (*sub voce*).
‡ "Huon de Bordeaux," p. 164.

romantic poem the "Oberon" of Wieland. But its recital is extremely rude and bold, and it seems still more so when contrasted with the masterpiece of the graceful German.

One of its peculiarities is as to the parentage of Oberon, which it states at the outset in some lines as follows:

> "Know ye that Auberon was son of Julius Cæsar,
> Who reigned in Hungary, a savage land,
> Who held Austria also, and its inheritance.
> Moreover, he held court in Constantinople,
> And there built walls seven leagues in length,
> Which are standing at this very day.
> * * * * * *
> His son, then, was Auberon, the noble knight,
> Who was only three feet in his stature,
> But was a fairy, as you ought to know."

A publication of these "Chansons de Geste," under the name of "Les Anciens Poètes de la France," was begun in 1859, with the liberal patronage of the Imperial Government, and under the able direction of M. Guessard. In 1859, and the subsequent year, there were five volumes of this series published belonging to the Carlovingian cycle. Several more have more recently appeared, and it is announced on the flyleaf that to complete that cycle no less than forty volumes in all will be required. I hope, however, that this only too liberal promise may not be carried out. The few volumes already given to the world seem to me sufficient to satisfy even the most craving curiosity. There is little variety in the stories, and none at all in the style. The poetical beauties, if indeed any exist, are at all events but thinly scattered; and the sole value of these works lies as I conceive in the glimpses which they now and then afford of the manners and feelings of the age of chivalry during which they were composed.

Those glimpses are not very favourable. The knights and Paladins, though properly held forth as fearless, appear in at least an equal degree ferocious. Moderation in conquest, and mercy to the vanquished, are seldom to be ranked among their virtues. The prelates are represented not as ministers of the God of Peace, but rather as doughty champions, seeking to kill as many Saracens as possible. For example, we find in "Gaufrey," a French chief, Berart, address the Archbishop of Rheims as follows:

" ' Turpin, Sir Archbishop, be a knight to-day;
It is a trade in which you are already skilled.
Let you and me try our might against the pagans!'
And Turpin made answer: 'So let it be,
I shall read them a very dolorous psalm-book,
One cannot every day be reading texts and versicles;
Times come when one should strike with one's trusty steel!'"

So then Berart and the Archbishop rushing forward deal fierce blows upon the enemy:

" Of Saracens they made more than one hundred fall,
Who will not stand up again either in March or in February."*

---

* "Gaufrey," p. 196, ed. 1859.

As to the ladies, I may cite also from "Gaufrey" the description of Flordespine, who is represented as a pattern princess:

"Her age was but fourteen years and a half:
She knew well how to speak Latin, and she understood Romane;
She knew well how to play at tables (or draughts) and chess;
And as to the course of the stars and shining moon,
She knew more than any woman living in this age." *

The princesses were no credit to this excellent training. Not only did they on occasion bear arms and strike blows like the Bradamant of Ariosto, but they too frequently appear both treacherous and cruel. Thus, in "Fierabras," one young lady dreading some evil machinations from her aged governess, lures her close to a palace window, and then makes a sign to her chamberlain behind, who flings the matron out of window into the sea, where she is drowned. The same princess, the beautiful Floripas, is afterwards consulted by her father, the Emir, as to the disposal of some French knights, his prisoners:

"'So tell me then, my daughter, what counsel you give me.'
'Sir,' said Floripas, 'hearken to my words:
Have their feet and their limbs cut off,
And burn them in a fire outside the city.'
'Daughter,' said the Emir, 'you have spoken right well.'" †

---

* "Gaufrey," p. 55. † "Fierabras," pp. 67, 83.

These *gentes pucelles* cannot by any means be accused of carrying to excess their feelings of maiden reserve. When Floripas becomes enamoured of Gui de Bourgogne, she does not scruple to ask his hand in marriage. Gui at first objects, saying, that he will take no wife except from the choice of Charlemagne. But Floripas rejoins:

"I swear by Mahomet, that if you will not take me
I will have you all hanged and waving in the wind."

And upon this Gui very naturally yields.*

In view of this auspicious event we find that Floripas consents to adopt the Christian faith. We cannot say, however, that her ideas of female propriety are in consequence very much improved. She has to undergo a siege in one of her castles with the knights who were recently her father's prisoners; and although they have no fear that the donjon will be taken, they apprehend a wearisome blockade. Upon this Floripas has an expedient for beguiling the time:

"I have with me five maidens of right noble birth,
What can I say more? Let each knight take a paramour,
Then so long as we are here, we shall lead a joyous life."

This proposal finds great favour among the five knights:

"'Certes,' answered Roland, 'you have spoken courtesy,
Never yet saw I a maiden of such noble behaviour.'" †

The devotion expressed in these "Chansons de

---

* "Fierabras," p. 85.
† Ibid. p. 118. Nearly the same words are ascribed to Floripas in an earlier passage, p. 69

Geste" is indeed of the most grovelling kind, and worthy of the darkest ages. It scarcely soars above the worship of the negro on the coast of Guinea for his fetish, adoring it when he is prosperous, and threatening or even maltreating it when he thinks that it does not yield him due protection. I will give two instances from this same poem of "Fierabras," the one as applied to a Mahometan, and the other to a Christian prince. First, then, of the Emir with whom we have already made acquaintance as the father of Floripas. Being worsted in battle, he exclaims:

"Ah, Mahomet! Sir, how you have forgotten me!
Ill love have you shown me this day.
If ever I return in safety to Spain,
You shall be so beaten in the ribs and sides
That there is no man in the world but will pity you;
And I shall hold you more vile than any dead dog."

Let us come next to the mighty Emperor Charlemagne himself:

"'St. Mary, our Lady,' said Charles of the haughty aspect,
'Protect Oliver, so that he may not be killed or taken;
For, by my father's sword, if he were slain,
In no monastery of France nor yet of other lands
Should priest or clerk be any more ordained:
I would cast down both crucifix and altar!'"*

Charlemagne himself appears wholly transfigured in these "Chansons de Geste." First he is represented as in extreme old age. Thus in the opening passage of "Huon de Bordeaux," he is made to say that he was a hundred years old at the birth of his eldest son

---

* See these two passages in the "Fierabras," pp. 175, 28.

Charlot, who is already grown up to manhood. Thus, again, in "Doon de Mayence," we are told that Doon and Charlemagne were born on the same day,* and yet Charlemagne survived to be also the contemporary of a grandson of Doon, no other than the traitor Ganelon.

In conformity with the idea of decrepid age, the "Chansons de Geste" no longer hold forth Charlemagne as the wise and mighty sovereign, such as he is shown both in the earlier fictions, and in authentic history. On the contrary, he is represented as feeble and fretful, timorous and wavering, and bearded even to his face by his bolder Paladins. There is among several others, one curious dialogue of this kind in "Gui de Bourgogne," the scene being laid in Spain. The great Emperor is so nettled by a taunt from Roland, that he nearly, says the poet, struck him with his glove across the nose:

> "'Sir,' so spoke Oliver, 'you are much to blame,
> And I swear that I will not let seven days pass by
> Before I begin my march homewards to France.'
> * * * * * * *
> 'By my head,' quoth Roland, 'I will do the same.
> Let us leave this old man, who is wholly besotted,
> And may a hundred thousand devils possess him!'" †

The constant and as it were systematic depreciation of Charlemagne in these later poems might well surprise us. Perhaps it is best explained by remembering how, since the time of Charlemagne, the great feuda-

---

* "Doon de Mayence," p. 162.   † "Gui de Bourgogne," p. 33.

tories of the Crown had succeeded in depressing both his own descendants and the first kings of the succeeding dynasty. A feeble monarch surrounded by powerful and overbearing vassals, might seem, at least to the dependents of the latter, the most eligible form of government. Hence it would be natural for them to suppose that in the time of the far-famed Emperor also a like system had prevailed. The poet makes Roland address to Charles the Great the same terms as the Comte de Vermandois may really have addressed to Charles the Simple.

Besides the "Chansons de Geste" there exists a wholly separate class of poems relative to Charlemagne, which is made known to us in some detail by M. Louis Moland in his "Origines Littéraires de la France." These poems belong to the literature and were prompted by the spirit of the first Crusades. Assuming a pilgrimage to the Holy Land as amongst the highest of earthly duties, and taking for granted that the mighty Charlemagne could not have neglected that sacred obligation, they represent him as visiting both Constantinople and Jerusalem in company with his twelve peers. The principal composition of this class, extending to nearly nine hundred lines, dates from the twelfth century. There is a transcript of it in the fifteenth, which is preserved at the British Museum, and which is illustrated with admirable skill. It contains for example, on the *verso* of one of the first folio pages, a superb miniature representing John Talbot, the first and famous Earl of Shrewsbury, who, on his knees, is supposed to present this very volume to Queen Margaret of Anjou.*

It was from this transcript at the British Museum that the poem was published for the first time in 1836, by a French gentleman well known in antiquarian literature, M. Francisque Michel. Fully sufficient extracts, however, will be found in the work of M. Moland.

I will here translate the lines describing what Charlemagne found in the temple of Jerusalem,

"He entered a church of marble, richly painted.
There stood an altar of renowned sanctity:
At this Christ had chaunted the Mass, and His Apostles
  also.
And the twelve stalls are still there entire,
The thirteenth in the midst, sealed and closed.
Charles came in, rejoicing at his heart.
The twelve peers took their seats on both sides,
But Charles took his seat in the midst.
No man ever sat there before him!" †

Such then were the legends of Charlemagne. I certainly cannot commend them to my hearers as a rich and fertile field from which an abundant harvest may be gathered in. They rather, on the contrary, resemble some rude moorland, or some thicket full of briars, upon which, nevertheless, a few berries may be found. Dropping metaphors, I would say that while I am unable to discern in these poems any of

---

* At the British Museum, marked "Bibl. Reg," 15, E. vi. It was published by Mr. Pickering in 1836—not 1846, as M. Moland erroneously states.

† See this passage in the "Origines Littéraires," p. 104.

the beauties ascribed to them by their more ardent commentators, and while I think that their stories are for the most part ill-contrived and destitute of interest, I yet conceive that they afford very striking illustrations—and the more striking because wholly undesigned—of the customs and the feelings in the "age of chivalry"—which was never very chivalrous in the modern sense of the term.

III.

THE CHRONOLOGY OF THE GOSPELS.

THE CHRONOLOGY OF THE GOSPELS.*

ALL Biblical students have long since been aware that the Common Era, computing events from the Nativity of Christ, and fixed in the 753rd year from the foundation of Rome, is altogether untrustworthy. It was first devised by Dionysius, an abbot of the sixth century, and first brought into general use under the Carlovingian Kings. But, however well it might pass muster in an uncritical age, a very slight examination sufficed to show that it was wholly at variance with the first chapters of St. Matthew's Gospel. This a very few words will make plain. We may deduce from Josephus that Herod the Great died in the spring of the year 4 before Christ according to the Dionysian Era.† Taking then into account the Flight into Egypt, and the Massacre of

---

* 1. *Das Geburtsjahr Christi; geschichtlich-chronologische Untersuchungen* von A. W. Zumpt. Leipzig, 1869.
2. *Fasti Sacri, or a Key to the Chronology of the New Testament.* By Thomas Lewin, Esq., of Trinity College, Oxford, M.A., F.S.A. London, 1865.
† "Ant. Jud.," lib. xvii. c. 8. See the Essay by M. Freret in the "Mémoires de l'Académie des Inscriptions," vol. xxi. p. 278.

the Innocents, as recorded by St. Matthew, it is impossible to place the Nativity of Christ later than five years before the period that is commonly assigned.

Thus far there is no difficulty. Nor is there any other connected with chronology in the whole first Gospel. But on passing to the third, we find ourselves greatly perplexed. St. Luke tells us at his outset that his narrative begins "in the days of Herod, the King of Judæa." When, however, he comes to the taxing of the Roman empire, or at least of the province of Judæa, which brought Joseph and Mary to be taxed at Bethlehem, he makes mention of Cyrenius, more properly according to the Roman form Quirinius, or, if we desire to be most accurate of all, Quirinus. The words of St. Luke in this passage are rendered as follows in our Authorized Version:—"And this taxing was first made when Cyrenius was Governor of Syria."

It is at this point that our perplexities begin. We learn from St. Matthew that, upon the death of Herod, his son Archelaus was appointed to reign in Judæa in his room.[*] We learn from Josephus that, after ruling for not quite ten years, Archelaus was deposed and banished by the Emperor Augustus.[†] Then, and then only, that is, in the year 6 of the Common Era, Judæa was reduced to a Roman province, and Publius Quirinus, who was sent over as Governor of Syria, proceeded to take in hand the business of the census. Or, as Josephus states it, "Moreover, Quirinus came himself into Judæa, which was now added to Syria

---

[*] Matt., c. ii. verse 22.
[†] "Ant. Jud.," lib. xvii. c. 15; and "Bell. Jud.," lib. ii. c. 7.

to take an account of their substance and dispose of Archelaus's money." *

It would seem, then, at first sight, as though St. Luke had placed the birth of our Lord some ten or twelve years later than the date which other and equal authorities compel us to assign.

But supposing this difficulty solved—and we will presently show how many attempts have been made to solve it—there is still a subsequent text which is far from being clear. St. Luke goes on to give a precise date—the only precise date, we may observe in passing, that is given by any one of the four Evangelists. He adduces "the fifteenth year of the reign of Tiberius Cæsar, Pontius Pilate being Governor of Judæa." Now, Augustus, having died in his own month of August, A.D. 14 of the Common Era, the fifteenth year of Tiberias may be taken to point to A.D. 29. In that year, continues St. Luke, "the word of God came unto John, the son of Zacharias, in the wilderness." A period somewhat later, by a few months at least, must be ascribed to our Lord's own baptism and the commencement of His ministry. At that time, says St. Luke, "Jesus Himself began to be about thirty years of age." So it stands in our Authorized Version, but, perhaps, more accurately, as follows, in the note to Tischendorf's edition: "And Jesus Himself, when He began, was about thirty years of age." Now, then, taking His Nativity, for the reasons already given, not later than the year 5 before the Common

---

* "Ant. Jud.," lib. xviii. c. 1. We give the words from Whiston's version.

Era, it would follow that at the commencement of His ministry he must have been, not as St. Luke states, "about thirty"—ὡσεὶ ἐτῶν τριάκοντα—but at least thirty-four or thirty-five years of age.

These difficulties—and above all those connected with the "taxing" of Quirinus—have exercised in no small degree the ingenuity of commentators. Most various have been their expedients. Some have declared the whole parenthesis about Quirinus to be an early gloss and interpolation of the text. Others, observing that Sentius Saturninus had been Governor of Syria some time before the death of Herod, desired, although with no authority from manuscripts, to substitute his name for that of Cyrenius in St. Luke. This, it appears, no less an authority than Tertullian was willing to do.* Other changes in the text were proposed by others. Some, without tampering with the words, attempted to construe πρώτη in the sense of προτέρα; the meaning of St. Luke being, as they alleged, to explain that the census which caused the journey to Bethlehem differed from and was earlier than the census of Quirinus. There seems, however, no adequate motive for such a reflection on the part of the Evangelist, and that construction would be, moreover, a force upon the Greek.

Leaving the words as they stand, there has also been more recently an ingenious but fanciful theory. There was only one census, it is said, but that interrupted in its progress. As commanded by Augustus,

---

* "Advers. Marcion.," lib. iv. c. 19.

and as commenced, we may suppose, in the year 5 before Christ according to the Common Era, it may have proceeded so far that Joseph and Mary, and many more, went down to their own city to be taxed. But Augustus, in his indulgence, having perhaps relented, the new taxation may have been laid aside and not resumed till twelve years afterwards, when Judæa was reduced to a province and Quirinus sent out as governor. By this theory the first chronological difficulty might perhaps be explained away; but then this theory rests only on conjecture, without one shred of evidence or corroborative testimony.

On the whole, then, this parenthesis of St. Luke about Cyrenius has remained obscure. Strauss, in his "Life of Jesus," points to it with exultation as to one of those points in which he desires to convict the Gospels of contradiction or inaccuracy. On the other side the ablest commentators have been willing to allow that the passage is difficult, and has not yet received that full elucidation of which it would doubtless admit.

It is therefore with especial pleasure that we welcome this publication of Dr. Zumpt. We gather from the dedication that the author was a favourite pupil of Dr. Twesten, the eminent Professor of Theology in the University of Berlin; and we are informed that, as a classic scholar and exponent of Roman history, he enjoys a very high reputation in Germany. This gentleman has devoted a whole volume to the point at issue, and propounded a careful and consistent theory upon it.

That theory, indeed, is not altogether new. It was first propounded by Dr. Zumpt, in a Latin essay which appeared at Berlin in 1854: "Commentatio de Syriâ Romanorum provinciâ ab Cæsare Augusto ad T. Vespasianum." Since that time it has been most favourably noticed in this country. Mr. Lewin has adopted it in his able and comprehensive, though not always convincing, work on the New Testament Chronology which we have named second in the heading of this article.* Dr. Alford, Dean of Canterbury, whose untimely death, even while these pages are passing through the press, we observe with deep concern, has on two occasions given to the theory of Dr. Zumpt the sanction of his high authority; first, in 1860, in the article "Cyrenius," which he contributed to Dr. Smith's "Dictionary of the Bible," and again, in 1863, in the corresponding passage of his own excellent Commentary on the Greek Testament.

On neither occasion, however, has the dean gone into the case at all fully. "Zumpt," he says in his Commentary, " by arguments too long to be reproduced here, but very striking and satisfactory ——."

But this Latin dissertation of Dr. Zumpt—only known, as we imagine, to the highest class of Biblical scholars—has been recently succeeded by a book from the same hand in a living language. Here the theory in question is both more fully stated and more forcibly defended. As it stands before us in its full proportions, we cannot but acknowledge its force and power.

---

* "Fasti Sacri," p. 132, ed. 1865.

Proceeding, as it does, by the way, not of vague conjecture, but of sound historical deduction, it seems to us to explain the entire difficulty, and to establish the accuracy of the Gospel narrative on this point beyond the reach of future cavil.

It is not, however, the date of the Nativity that is alone concerned. Dr. Zumpt, in this volume, points out that, on his first theory, combined with another which he urges, the exact date of the Passion also may be probably deduced. Under these circumstances, it has seemed to us that a fuller exposition of the case than has hitherto been afforded in this country might perhaps be welcome to many English readers.

In this attempt we do not propose, however, to follow through every wandering the footsteps of Dr. Zumpt. So great—so very great—are his stores of learning and his powers of research, that they have sometimes led him into collateral narratives or illustrations not at all essential to his argument. We, neither possessing his vast erudition nor inclined to make so unmerciful a use of it, shall confine ourselves to the main proofs by which his positions are defended. We hope, therefore, while giving an account of his "discovery," as Dean Alford has justly termed it, to be able to present it to the public in a plainer and more popular form.

At the very outset the word "first" (or $\pi\rho\omega\tau\eta$) in the text is perhaps sufficient to afford a clue, or at least to suggest an inquiry. Might not Quirinus have held the office of Governor of Syria, not once only, but on two occasions—first, in the year 4 before the Christian Era, when Judæa, after some previous preparations and announcements, was taxed according to the Jewish manner, each man repairing to his own city for that purpose; and secondly, in the year 6 after the Christian Era, when Judæa, reduced to a Roman province, was taxed according to the Roman fashion, and when Quirinus was sent out for the second time to the same post? Were such the case, the words of St. Luke, in strict grammatical construction, would mean only that the census preceding the birth of Christ was the first census taken under Quirinus, as distinguished from the second.

Such, then, briefly stated, is the theory that Dr. Zumpt and Mr. Lewin desire to maintain. But was the fact really so? Did indeed Quirinus fill his Syrian office at an earlier date? Now, for the events of this epoch in the East we have, in general, two separate and trustworthy authorities, the one Roman, and the other Jewish, Dion Cassius and Josephus. It so happens, however, by a singular coincidence, that both of these fail us at this particular point, exactly for the same period of time. There is an interval in the history of Dion Cassius, arising from a break in the manuscript, from the year 6 before Christ till the year 4 after, according to the Common Era. Josephus relates very fully the reign of Herod the Great, and also the first events in the reign of his successor, but breaks off abruptly at the marriage of Archelaus to his brother's widow, and does not resume his narrative until the accusation brought against this prince in the tenth year of his reign, when he was summoned to

Rome by Augustus, and deposed. For the fact, then, which we are seeking we have no direct historical testimony, either in proof or disproof. We can only proceed by historical inference, which, as all students of history know, is sometimes quite as convincing as the former.

The Governor or "Legatus" of Syria was at this time one of the most important officers of the Roman empire—representing the person of the emperor, not merely in the province, but in any adjacent and dependent kingdom. To fill this post, a previous consulship was a necessary qualification; and such, we may observe in passing, was possessed by Quirinus, even at the earlier period, since he had been consul in the year 12 before Christ.

We find that Caius Sentius Saturninus, a man also of consular rank, administered Syria from the year 9 to the year 6 before Christ. In the latter year, he was succeeded by Publius Quinctilius Varus, another *consularis*, so well known subsequently from his terrible disaster in the German forests. Owing to the break in the established histories, as already explained, we lose sight of Varus in his Eastern course after the summer of the year 4. Our next direct evidence as to this succession of chiefs is derived from a coin which was struck at Antioch eight years later, that is, in the autumn of the year 4 after Christ, and which names Lucius Volusius Saturninus as the Roman Governor of Syria.

It does not seem probable that Varus continued in Syria much beyond the autumn of B.C. 4, when all trace of him ceases. It was a maxim laid down under Augustus, for the better administration of the Roman empire, that no governor having command of an army in a province should, as far as was possible to apply one uniform rule, be left at his post for less than three years or for more than five;* by the former limitation obtaining the benefit of some experience, and by the latter guarding against ambitious hopes and schemes of independent authority. In practice, however, it will be found from the instances adduced during this reign, that the period of three years was much more frequent than the term of five, although occasionally, and after an interval, the term of office was renewed. It is thought by Dr. Zumpt and Mr. Lewin that Varus was called away from Syria soon after the term when he is last named in connection with that province, and that he was immediately succeeded by Quirinus.

We come now to the proofs. Quirinus survived till the year 21 of the Christian Era, and Tacitus, while recording his death, has rapidly sketched his career.

"Quirinus," he says, "was born at Lanuvium, a municipal town; and he was in no wise related to the ancient patrician family of the Sulpicii; but, being a brave soldier, was for his vigorous military services rewarded with the consulship by the Divine Augustus; and soon after with triumphal honours for having stormed the strongholds of the Homonadenses in Cilicia. Next, when Caius Cæsar was sent to bear sway in Armenia, Quirinus was appointed his guardian, and at the same time paid court to Tiberius, then in exile at Rhodes." †

---

* Dion Cassius, lib. lii. c. 23.
† "Nihil ad veterem et patriciam Sulpiciorum familiam Quirinus

Tacitus goes on to state, in a passage which does not so immediately concern us, that Tiberius, on account of former friendship, pleaded warmly for the honour of a public funeral to Quirinus, which the senate accordingly decreed as the emperor desired. To others, adds the historian, the memory of Quirinus was far from grateful, on account of the dangers to which, as elsewhere explained by Tacitus, his wife Lepida had through his means been exposed, and also on account of his own avaricious and overbearing old age.

It is to be observed that Tacitus, in the passages which we have quoted, does not give, or profess to give, all the main incidents of this statesman's career. He says nothing, for example, of the government of Syria, which Quirinus held in the year 6 after Christ, or of the memorable census, as recorded by Josephus, which he then enforced on his province. It is very natural that the first government in the year 4 before Christ should, in express mention, be omitted also. But still the few facts which the Roman historian does allege are of the highest value for the question now before us.

We have first to consider the Caius Cæsar to whom Tacitus is here referring. This was the grandson and presumptive heir of Augustus. In the first year of the Christian Era he was despatched by the emperor to Syria, proceeding from thence to Armenia to wage war

---

pertinuit, ortus apud municipium Lanuvium, sed impiger militiæ et acribus ministeriis consulatum sub Divo Augusto, mox expugnatis per Ciliciam Homonadensium castellis, insignia triumphi adeptus, datusque rector Caio Cæsari Armeniam obtinenti, Tiberium quoque Rhodi agentem coluerat." (Tacit. "Annal.," lib. iii. c. 48.)

against the Parthians. To this young prince, then, as Tacitus tells us, Quirinus was appointed guide or guardian (*rector*). It appears, however, that for some reason not explained, Quirinus did not long hold that office. We find Suetonius name another man of consular rank, by name Marcus Lollius, as acting in the same capacity to Caius (*comes et rector*) as the war proceeded.* It proved disastrous both to chief and adviser. Caius received a wound before the town of Artagera, of which he never recovered, and he expired in the year 4 of our Era. Lollius was suspected of treacherous communication with the enemy, and died, it is said, of poison administered by his own hand.

Lollius, as we learn from another historian, was succeeded by Censorinus,†—Caius Marcius Censorinus, that is, who had also filled the consulship in former years. The question then arises, whom Augustus, on sending his grandson into Syria, was likely to select as his guide and guardian. Dr. Zumpt maintains that it must have been some man already conversant with Eastern affairs, and that in all probability it was the governor of this very province and the chief of the army stationed there. He holds, then, that Quirinus was at this time Governor of Syria, as were also, in succession to him, first Lollius and then Censorinus.

Dr. Zumpt has certainly one strong instance to allege, so far as analogy can guide us. In the year 17 after Christ, Tiberius, then emperor, sent on a mission to the East his adopted son Germanicus, who, as regards

---

* Suetonius, "Tib.," c. 12.
† Velleius Paterculus, lib. ii. c. 102.

the heirship of the empire, stood in much the same relation to him as Caius Cæsar had done to Augustus. There was this difference, however, that while Caius was young and untried, Germanicus had experience in war. He required, therefore, not a guardian (*rector*), but only a helper (*adjutor*). Tiberius, desiring to appoint as such a man on whom he could thoroughly rely, recalled Creticus Silanus from the government of Syria, and set in his place Cnæus Piso, who was directed at the same time to attend upon and assist the prince.*

This argument does no more, we admit, than make the earlier government of Quirinus probable. But by another train of reasoning it becomes very nearly certain. Tacitus tells us that Quirinus obtained the emblems of a triumph from his expedition against the Homonadenses in Cilicia. Some readers may feel surprise that we should here be eagerly discussing the affairs of an obscure tribe with an interminable name. Yet it is perhaps with this obscure tribe that lies the clue to the whole system of Gospel chronology. And first, When did this expedition occur? It is placed by Tacitus after the consulship of Quirinus, and before his attendance on the grandson of Augustus. It must therefore have been some time previous to the year 1 of the Christian Era. Next, In what capacity did Quirinus obtain his triumph? It can only have been as governor of the province to which this savage tribe was considered to belong. In the system of the pro-

---

* Tacit. "Annal.," lib. ii. c. 43.

vinces under the dominion of Rome, there was never any severance of civil government from military leadership. The same chief who conducted a war had at the same time the supreme administration of the province which was the scene, or had been the starting-point, of that war. It was not till the third century of our Era that a change was made in this respect. So fixed was this rule, says Dr. Zumpt, that not even one single exception can be found to it up to the period which he names.

With this result to spur us, we may be willing, in company with Dr. Zumpt, to explore the scanty records of this robber tribe—for such the Homonadenses were. The sovereignty over them had been claimed by Amyntas, King of Galatia, who was slain by treachery in the year 25 before Christ, while attempting to subdue them.* At his death, Galatia became a Roman province, its first prætor being that same Marcus Lollius who subsequently became the *comes et rector* of Caius Cæsar. The mountainous district of Cilicia—the rugged Cilicia, *Cilicia Aspera*, as the Romans termed it—had also formed part of the dominion of Amyntas, and it fell, at his decease, to Archelaus, King of Cappadocia. It is probable that the little robber-land shared at this time the fate of Rugged Cilicia, and was afterwards with it embodied in the empire. Certain it is that the predatory habits of this people roused at no distant date the resentment of Rome, and gave rise to the victorious expedition of Quirinus.

---

* Strabo, "Geogr.," lib. xii. c. 6.

We have further to observe of the Homonadenses that they dwelt so near the confines of Cilicia as sometimes to be called its inhabitants, and sometimes only its neighbours.* It is quite clear, however, from the express words of Tacitus, *per Ciliciam*, that, in the time the conquest of Quirinus was achieved, the Homonadenses were taken as within the Cilician borders. *Per Ciliciam*, we admit, is not exactly the same phrase as *in Ciliciâ*: it implies that these robber-fastnesses were scattered up and down the province, but it implies also as conclusively that they were not beyond or outside it. Now, as to Cilicia, there seems to be no doubt that all through that age, after it came under the dominion of the empire, it was held to be a portion or dependency of the Syrian province. Of this there are several proofs, which we may state as follows:—

In the year 16 after Christ, Vonones, expelled from his kingdom of Parthia, sought refuge with Creticus Silanus, Præfect or Governor of Syria. This governor confined him in Pompeiopolis, *Ciliciæ maritimæ urbem*, as in a city subject to his Syrian jurisdiction.

In the year 19 after Christ, Cnæus Piso,† seeking to recover his province of Syria, sent to the petty chiefs (the *reguli*) of Cilicia, as though dependent on that province, to levy men for him.‡

The Clitæ, as we learn from Tacitus, were among the

---

* "Est contermina illi gens Homonadum quorum intus oppidum Homona." (Plin. "Hist. Nat.," lib. v. c. 23, not 94 as we find it in Zumpt.) On the other hand, an expression of Strabo indicates that he reckoned them as Cilicians. ("Geograph.," lib. xii. c. 6.)
† Tacit. "Annal.," lib. ii. c. 4 and 58.
‡ Ibid., lib. ii. c. 78.

tribes of Cilicia.* We find that, in the year 36 after Christ, Vitellius, as Governor of Syria, sent his legate, with four thousand legionaries, to reduce that tribe.†

Again, in the year 52 after Christ, we find another Præfect of Syria, Curtius Severus, march with his cavalry against the Clitæ.‡

Thus also, in the year 72 after Christ, Antiochus, King of Commagene, being at Tarsus, a principal city of Cilicia, Cæsennius Pætus, then Governor of Syria, despatched a centurion to that city to arrest him and send him in bonds to Rome, thus treating Tarsus as a part of his own territory.§

It follows, then, that when Quirinus commenced his expedition against these mountaineers, he did not outstep the bounds of his appointed jurisdiction, and was dealing with a dependency of the Syrian province.

The same conclusion as to his government at that time of this particular province is also arrived at by Dr. Zumpt through a different process—the process of exhaustion. He inquires what province, if not Syria, Quirinus could have held in this campaign. Bithynia, Galatia, and Pontus are eliminated by him, as not being consular provinces, or, in other words, not territories which had invariably for their governor some chief, as was Quirinus, of consular rank. There remain in the East only the province of Asia Proper and the province of Syria. But in Asia Proper, there

---

* "Agrestium Cilicium nationes quibus Clitarum cognomentum." (Tacit. "Annal.," lib xii. c. 55.)
† Tacit. "Annal.," lib. vi. c. 41.   ‡ Ibid., lib. xii. c. 55.
§ Josephus, "Bell. Jud.," lib. vii. c. 7.

were no troops;* while in Syria four legions were stationed. From the latter province alone could have proceeded such warfare as would entitle the successful chief to triumphal honours.

It will be observed that these separate trains of argument all tend to one result. They render all but certain a former government of Quirinus in Syria—that government commencing probably in the latter months of the year 4 before Christ, and continuing till the year 1 after Christ. Five years would then elapse before his re-appointment, and during these five years it might very well be that he held the other consular province in the East, the province of Asia Proper, as seems to be stated in the ancient inscription to which we shall presently refer.

The list of the Governors of Syria at this period, with the dates at which they entered upon office, is accordingly established by Dr. Zumpt as follows:—

C. Sentius Saturninus from the year	9 before Christ.
P. Quinctilius Varus	6 ,,
P. Sulpicius Quirinus	4 ,,
M. Lollius	1 after Christ.
C. Marcius Censorinus	2 ,,
L. Volusius Saturninus	4 ,,
P. Sulpicius Quirinus	6 ,,
Q. Creticus Silanus	11 ,,

It is true that this succession which Dr. Zumpt establishes does not at first sight solve the entire difficulty caused by the words of St. Luke. For, as we cannot place the Nativity of Christ later than the

---

* Tacit. "Annal.," lib. iv. c. 5.

year 5 before the Common Era, so we can as little place the first governorship of Quirinus earlier than the year 4. But this remaining difficulty is apparent only. It is easy to conceive that a general census, more especially according to the Jewish method of division into tribes, must have taken a considerable time for its completion. It is easy to conceive how Joseph and Mary might go "to be taxed" at Bethlehem in the year 5, under the government of Syria by Saturninus or Quinctilius Varus, and yet not be called upon to pay, nor find the taxing finally ordered, till two or three years later, under the government of Quirinus. In this manner all ground for cavil disappears.

There might yet be another source of information on this subject. No scholar but is well aware of the great value for historical researches of the ancient inscriptions. Collected they were, in great part, even two centuries ago, but it is only of late years that they have been completed and classified and provided with classical notes by the skill of such men as Orelli. On this path, however, it behoves us to tread warily, for the ground is strewed with pitfalls. Forgeries, of modern date, though in Ciceronian Latin, are very frequent. Thus, many years since, we had occasion, in the pages of this Review, to show that the famous epitaph on Julia Alpinula, so much admired by Lord Byron, and so familiar to the readers of Childe Harold, is, in fact, the work of a modern hand.* It is strange how few scruples were felt, and how lightly such falsi-

---

* "Childe Harold," canto iii., stanza 66. *Quarterly Review*, No. clv., June, 1846.

fications were regarded. Thus Mr. Surtees, of Mainsforth, the historian of Durham, a man of the highest character, and wholly incapable of falsehood or deception on any other subject, sent to Sir Walter Scott a Northumbrian ballad which was, every line of it, his own handiwork, but which, as he alleged, was taken down from the recitation of a woman, eighty years of age, mother of one of the miners in Alston Moor. "She had not," she said, "heard it for many years; but when she was a girl it used to be sung at merry-making till the roof rung again." No wonder that a tale so circumstantial was implicitly believed. Sir Walter received the gift with pleasure, and inserted it without suspicion in his "Border Minstrelsy" as an authentic record of the olden time.*

It so happened that, long before any idea was raised of an earlier term of office for Quirinus, some surprise was expressed that, considering the importance of his government of Syria in the year 6 after Christ, when Judæa was first reduced to a Roman province, no record of him should remain on any known inscription. As though to meet this want, it was ere long announced that a monument in his commemoration had been discovered in the Venetian territory. This was first published at Padua in 1719. It refers to the proceedings of Quirinus, intending by that reference the year 6 of our Era, and it goes on to state that one of his lieutenants, Æmilius Secundus by name, had by his orders taken the census at

---

* Note 12 to first canto of "Marmion;" and "Life of Robert Surtees," published by the Surtees Society.

Apamea, where he found 117,000 citizens. Since this inscription deals only with the government of the year 6, it would be, even though of unquestionable authenticity, wholly immaterial to our present object. But it is in truth a mere modern forgery. First, as in the case of Julia Alpinula, the original stone could never be produced. Next, there are some slips in the lapidary Latin. "I hold it to be fictitious," says the sagacious Orelli.* "Only those," says Dr. Zumpt, "who are not conversant with such inscriptions could give any credit to this."

There is, however, another inscription which is thought to refer to Quirinus, and of which the authenticity has never been disputed. It is on a sepulchral tablet discovered near Tivoli. Several copies, the first in 1765, have been with more or less correctness taken from it; but, unhappily, the first part has altogether perished, while the second is much mutilated. We will give it as it stands in the last and most authentic copy, as taken by Mommsen and inserted by Orelli†:—

* * * * * * * *
. . . EGEM QUA REDACTA IN POT . . .
AUGUSTI POPULIQUE ROMANI SENATU . . .
SUPPLICATIONES BINAS OB RES PROSP . . .
IPSI ORNAMENTA TRIUMPH . . . .
PRO CONSUL ASIAM PROVINCIAM OP . . .
DIVI AUGUSTI . . TERUM SYRIAM ET PH. . .

---

* "Inscriptionum Latinarum Collectio." No. 623, ed. Turici, 1828.
† No. 5366 in the third and supplemental volume, published 1856. The stone itself is now *in horreis Vaticanis*. *Litteræ magnæ sunt et pulchræ.*

Mr. Lewin, who has taken great pains and shown great sagacity in discussing this inscription, has no doubt of its application to Quirinus. He observes that the two lines previous to the first that now remain might perhaps be restored as follows:—

CIVITATEM SUBEGIT HOMONADENSIUM QUI
INTERFECERANT AMYNTAM RE—

And he gives as an alternative of the second line—

ADFLIXERANT LATROCINIIS ARCHELAUM RE—

Of these two alternatives we must say that we greatly prefer the latter. The slaughter of King Amyntas could not be stated as the motive for the expedition of Quirinus, since an interval of some five and twenty years elapsed between these events.

On the first line of all, did it still remain, we might expect to find the name and titles of Quirinus; and the following would be the most probable restoration of the rest:—

* * * * * * * *

[CIVITATEM SUBEGIT HOMONADENSIUM QUI
ADFLIXERANT LATROCINIIS ARCHELAUM RE]
GEM QUÀ REDACTÀ IN POT[ESTATEM DIVI]
AUGUSTI POPULIQUE ROMANI SENATU[S]
SUPPLICATIONES BINAS OB RES PROSP[ERE GESTAS ET]
IPSI ORNAMENTA TRIUMPH[ALIA DECREVIT]
PROCONSUL ASIAM PROVINCIAM OP[TINUIT LEGATUS]
DIVI AUGUSTI ITERUM SYRIAM ET [PHOENICIAM].

Our readers will observe how exactly the *Ornamenta triumphalia* of this inscription tally with the *insignia triumphi* of Tacitus, as distinguished from an actual triumph. Nor will they fail to observe the *iterum Syrium* stating distinctly that twofold term of government which our argument has been striving to establish.

But Dr. Zumpt demurs. Writing, as is his wont, with perfect fairness, he does not adopt any argument merely because it points to his own conclusion. In this case he has a strong doubt whether, in fact, this inscription refers to Quirinus; and he thinks that Sentius Saturninus is more probably the person implied. His main reason is founded on a passage in the "Epitome of Roman History" by Julius Florus. Thence, as he thinks, we may deduce that Quirinus, in the period between his two governments of Syria, had subdued certain African tribes, the Marmaridæ and the Garamantes, which, if he did at all, he could have done only as Proconsul of Africa or Cyrene. During that period, therefore, he could not have been proconsul also of Asia, as the inscription declares. Mr. Lewin argues on the contrary side, but appears to overlook the strongest of all the pleas that can be urged against this text of Florus, namely, the uncertainty of the right reading. It is well known to students of Roman history that the copies of Florus differ much from one another. Professor William Ramsay says of it: "As might be expected in a work which was extensively employed in the Middle Ages as a school-book, the text is found in most manuscripts under a very corrupt form."* In the particular

---

* Article "Florus" in Dr. Smith's "Dictionary of Greek and Roman Biography."

passage which we are now discussing, several manuscripts give the name, not of Quirinus, but of Furnius. So it is, for instance, in the edition which is now before us, printed by Hall at Oxford in 1650, and enriched by the commentary of Stadius, Professor of History at Louvain.* The Furnius here referred to was, like Quirinus, of consular rank, having been consul in the year 17 before Christ. He is commemorated in a passage of Seneca for a graceful saying of his to Augustus, when he obtained his father's pardon in the Civil Wars.†

If, then, we are willing—as we may, on adequate authority—to read Furnius in this passage of the "Epitome," we shall have no further difficulty with the tablet from Tivoli. We may, then, be fully justified if we ascribe it to Quirinus, and please ourselves with the *iterum Syriam*—a phrase, indeed, which on any other supposition remains wholly unexplained. Should there be, however, any doubts remaining, we would by no means allege this inscription or lay any stress upon its terms, conceiving as we do that the argument of Dr. Zumpt is thoroughly convincing without it.

We must observe, however, that, as regards the

---

* This edition gives the passage as follows :—[Augustus] " Marmaridas atque Garamantas Furnio subigendos dedit. Potuit et ille redire Marmaricus sed modestior in æstimandâ victoriâ fuit" (Florus, lib. iv. p. 133).

† "Nullo magis Cæsarem Augustum demeruit et ad alia impetranda facilem sibi reddidit Furnius quam quod, cum patri Antonianas partes secuto veniam impetrasset, dixit; *Hanc unam Cæsar habeo injuriam tuam; effecisti ut viverem et morerer ingratus.*" (Seneca, "De Benef.," lib. ii. c. 25.)

exact year of the Nativity, we are not altogether in accord with Dr. Zumpt. He is not quite satisfied with fixing it at the year 5 before the Common Era, and would rather choose the year 7. His principal motive is, that in the last-named year there was a thrice-repeated conjunction of the planets Jupiter and Saturn in the sign of the Fish, corresponding, as he thinks, to the "star in the east" which is recorded by St. Matthew, and which led the "wise men" from their country to Bethlehem. This is a suggestion which, under various forms and dates, has been not unfrequently debated of late years. But, as is well observed by the present Archbishop of York, "the words of St. Matthew are extremely hard to reconcile with a conjunction of planets." At all events, this is a wholly different order of ideas, into which we decline on this occasion to follow Dr. Zumpt. We take him for our guide only so far as he treads on historical ground.

Adhering, then, to that ground, we continue to maintain that the first difficulty which we have stated as arising from the text of St. Luke—his mention, namely, of the census of Quirinus—is most fully cleared up. There remains the second difficulty, from the age of about thirty years ascribed to our Lord at the commencement of His ministry. Let it be observed that this difficulty will still exist, whatever view we may take of Quirinus. For in any case, knowing as we do the exact date of Herod's death, we cannot place Christ's birth at an earlier date than 5 before the Common Era. Assuming, then, the 15th year of Tiberius to be equivalent with 29 after Christ, there would still remain at the latter period an age of at least thirty-four years.

With this difficulty, also, Dr. Zumpt proceeds to deal in the second portion of his book. He shows, with a vast extent of erudition and alleging many cases of analogy, that St. Luke appears to have computed his 15th year of Tiberius not from the year 14, when Augustus died, but from the year 11, when Augustus, by formal decree, associated Tiberius with himself as co-regent of the provinces and joint *imperator* of the troops. On this basis, the commencement of Christ's ministry would fall in the year 26, Christ being then between thirty and thirty-one years of age. His Passion would ensue in the year 29, under the consulship of the two Gemini, the very date assigned to it by the constant and uniform tradition of the early Church.

This explanation, which Dr. Zumpt has so ably vindicated, was, as he informs us, first propounded by an Englishman almost a century and a half ago,— Nicholas Mann, whose Latin Essay bears date 1743.[*] In our own time it has been countenanced by the high authority of the present Archbishop of York. "The rule of Tiberius," he says, "may be calculated either from the beginning of his sole reign, after the death of Augustus, in the year of Rome 767, or from

---

[*] We learn, however, from that excellent and most useful book, Allibone's "Dictionary of English Literature," that this Latin Essay was only a translation of the author's earlier work in English, published 1733. Mann was master of the Charterhouse. Both his treatises—the Latin and the English—are in the library of the British Museum.

his joint government with Augustus, that is, from the beginning of the year 765. In the latter case, the 15th year would correspond with the year of Rome 779, which goes to confirm the rest of the calculations relied on in this article." *

We do not, however, propose to follow Dr. Zumpt into this, the second part, of his book. It is wholly distinct from the former in its line of argument, and might form the subject of a separate essay. We desire only, in adverting once again to Dr. Zumpt's complete success (for so we deem it) in the first part of his researches, to point out how encouraging is the example it affords. Here is a difficulty which but some thirty years ago Dr. Strauss was gloating over and declaring to be entirely insoluble—and now we behold it solved. Here we have another proof that Biblical studies are not, as they were once regarded, a stationary science, but, like all other sciences, admit of progression and increase.

It was certainly too often the custom of English divines, during the whole of the last century, and during also a part of the present, to put all thorny questions as much out of sight as possible, or, if compelled to deal with them, to be content with what the Germans call *Gerede*—an array of high-flown words that convey no definite meaning. It was not felt how much more danger there is to faith in leaving every student to discover these difficulties for himself, with-

---

* Smith's "Dictionary of the Bible," article "Jesus Christ." The archbishop was then, as Dr. Thomson, Provost of Queen's College, Oxford.

out any clue to guide him through them. It was not felt how far more earnest and high-minded would be the system that has now succeeded—frankly to admit the lack of clearness whenever the explanation is imperfect: not as owning the objection to be valid, but only as inviting further thought and inquiry to resolve it. Did we desire to show an instance of the practical result of either system, we might select, on the one side, the annotated edition of the English Bible compiled by Bishop Mant and Dr. Doyly, and, on the other part, the recent Commentary on the Greek Testament by Dean Alford. Without intending any disrespect to the first two theologians, we must say that a student who refers to them in any perplexity will derive from them very little satisfaction. He will never find the depth to be fathomed, but only the surface smoothed over. In Dean Alford's book, on the contrary, the tone is manly and outspoken; the object is not to bind up the eyes of the inquirer, but rather to direct and invigorate his sight. It is only, we are convinced, in the latter spirit that the Church of England can continue to prevail in the coming contests. Thus, and thus alone, as we conceive, in the anxious time that is now before us, can the Christian cause be worthily professed and efficiently defended.

IV.

THE YEAR OF THE PASSION.

THE YEAR OF THE PASSION.*

IN a former number of this Review we dwelt upon the chronological difficulties that attend the Gospel narrative of our Lord's Nativity; and we explained the ingenious discovery of Dr. Zumpt, by which, as we think, these difficulties are most successfully surmounted. We also on that occasion, though only in one or two sentences, touched upon the separate train of argument by which, as it seemed to us, the year of the Passion also might be with great probability established. It is our present purpose to resume the latter subject and to treat it in detail, taking for our text a recent publication of Canon Norris. This is but a brief compendium, yet it shows the candour as well as the ability and learning of the author, stating its points in the clearest manner, and exciting its readers to a more minute investigation than its own limits would allow. We are of course the better pleased with

---

* *A Key to the Narrative of the Four Gospels.* By John Pilkington Norris, M.A., Canon of Bristol, and formerly one of her Majesty's Inspectors of Schools. London, 1870.

it, since we find it come to the same conclusion as we had formed.

To those who would explore the chronology of the Gospels, the true sheet-anchor is the date of King Herod's death. With so renowned a tyrant this has not been hard to trace. We do not indeed derive any light from the statement of Josephus, that he was in his seventieth year when he expired, since we are nowhere told the time when he was born. But Josephus goes on to say that he reigned thirty-four years since he caused Antigonus to be slain, and thirty-seven since he was declared king by the Romans. Now, the decree of the senate, which named Herod king of the Jews, was passed in the second consulship of Domitius Calvinus, that is, in the year 40 before Christ, according to the Common Era. And the taking of Jerusalem by Sosius, and the slaughter of Antigonus, the last king of the Asmonean line, took place during the consulships of Marcus Agrippa and Canidius Gallus, that is, in the year 37. Both these indications, therefore, combine in fixing for the death of Herod the year 4 before the common but faulty Christian Era.

It is possible, however, to be still more precise. Josephus commemorates an eclipse of the moon as having occurred during Herod's final illness; and the calculation of modern astronomers has assigned this eclipse to the 13th of March in that year. But, as another passage of the Jewish chronicler informs us, Herod had died before the Passover which ensued. A controversy has indeed arisen whether that Passover took place in regular course at the full moon of the first Nisan, which would make it the 12th of April, or whether there might not be in that year the intercalation of a second Nisan month, by which the Passover would be delayed until the 10th of May. But in either case it is clear that the date of Herod's death is confined to narrow bounds.*

The inference is equally plain. Accepting as we do in its full extent the narrative in St. Matthew's Gospel of the visit of the Magi, the flight into Egypt, and the Massacre of the Innocents, it follows that the date of Herod's death must govern the date of Christ's Nativity. Under these circumstances it seems that we can scarcely fix the period of the Nativity later than the closing months of the year 5 before the Common Era—before the date, that is, which in the Middle Ages was assigned to it. This error in the old computation has been long since a well-known and admitted fact, and we only advert to it here as giving more completion and clearness to our subsequent case.

The next note of time which we obtain is derived from the Gospel of St. Luke. He relates to us how John commenced his preaching in the wilderness, and how shortly afterwards Christ Himself was baptised. These events he fixes "in the fifteenth year of the reign of Tiberius Cæsar;" and he adds, according to the improved translation which we find in Tischendorf's New

---

* The passages of Josephus here referred to are to be found in the "Jewish Antiquities," lib. xvii. chaps. 6, 8, and 9. So far back as 1748 these were ably drawn out and discussed by M. Freret, whose essay may still be consulted with advantage: "Mémoires de l'Académie des Inscriptions," vol. xxi. p. 278.

Testament, "And Jesus Himself, when He began, was about thirty years of age." To this important text we shall presently return.

As regards the third great event in the Gospel history—namely, the Passion—the Gospels give us no chronological clue. It is natural, however, to suppose that the date of year would be preserved by tradition in the early Church. Here was a public and judicial act, witnessed by thousands of spectators, and in recording the year of which there could be no chance of error. Here was an event that formed the very keystone of the newly founded faith. Can it then be doubted that the first Christians, even though unversed in literature, would consider its date as a matter of deep interest, and carefully hand it down among themselves?

This reasonable presumption is fully borne out by the actual fact. So early as we can trace the Christian records on this point, we find them state, without a shade of hesitation, that Jesus suffered under the consulship of the two Gemini. This was in the year 782 from the foundation of Rome, and corresponds to the year 29 of the Common Era as fixed five centuries later. Tacitus, at the commencement of his fifth book of Annals, speaks of it as follows:—"Rubellius and Fufius were then consuls, each of whom bore the surname of Geminus." Brotier adds, in a note, "There is a common agreement among ancient writers (*consentit antiquitas*) that the Passion of Christ took place when the Gemini were consuls;" and in his supplement to the lost books he places that event accordingly.

It may further be said, as we think, that the occurrence—so rare in the consular annals—of both the magistrates bearing the same surname must have greatly tended to distinguish that year from others and impress it on the popular mind.

Looking, then, to some of the main authorities for early Christian history, we find them all concur in the date of year. It is mentioned as a certain fact by Tertullian. Lactantius records it in two separate passages. Augustine, in his great work, "De Civitate Dei," bears witness to the same fact;[*] and though Augustine lived so many years later, great weight is certainly due to his deliberate testimony, not only from the penetrating genius which he brought to the study of the Scriptures, but as showing that the early tradition was still accepted and alive.

It seems, indeed, scarcely too much to say that if the uniform tradition of the Church is to be set aside in a case like this, we do not see how it can be sustained in any other. There are, nevertheless, two difficulties in the way. First, the writers we have named, and some others also, undertake to give not only the date of the year but also the date of the day, and in this last they do not quite agree. Tertullian, after telling us that the Passion took place in the consulship of the two Gemini, goes on to say that it was *mense Martio, temporibus Paschæ, die VIII. Calendarum Aprilium.* Lactantius, in the former of his two pas-

---

[*] Tertullian, "Advers. Judæos," c. 8. Lactantius, "Instit. Div.," lib. v. c. 10. "De Mort. Persec.," c. 2. Augustin. "De Civit, Dei." lib. xviii. c. 54.

sages, fixes it *ante diem decimum Kalendarum Aprilium;* while in the latter he says, *post diem decimum Kal. Aprilis.* The question is further perplexed by modern astronomers, who seek to give us year by year the exact days of the Paschal full moon, but who are not entitled to speak with any confidence on this point from the irregularity of the Jews at that time in their mode of reckoning and their occasional intercalation of an entire month in their year. So acute a critic as Wieseler, after all his laborious researches, is obliged at last to own that at the period of our Lord it is almost impossible to show what exact day in the Julian Calendar corresponds with a day in the Jewish.*

This irregularity in the old Jewish Calendar will go far to explain the difference of opinion in the ecclesiastical writers as to the precise day of the Passion. Moreover, it should be borne in mind—as indeed we may still observe—how very varying from year to year are the days of the Easter celebration. It would be far from easy, before the time of almanacs, to recollect precisely which had been the date only a few years before; nor would any importance be ascribed to such exactness, as compared at least with the importance of being accurate as to the year of that great event. Under these circumstances, we can well understand how, within certain small limits, some uncertainty, some contradiction, might arise as to the day; and we cannot admit that such doubts afford

---

* "Chronologische Synopse," ed. 1843. See especially p. 439. "According to Ideler the calendar of feasts now in use among the Jews was not established till the fourth century of our Era."

any valid argument to discredit the strong testimonies as to the year.

But there is yet another difficulty, although at the outset not so regarded. During the second and third centuries of our Era the Christian writers, while accepting the tradition of the two Gemini as the date of Christ's Passion, were no less bound by the words of St. Luke, which fix the fifteenth year of the reign of Tiberius as the date of His baptism. Now, since Augustus died in the month of August of the year 14 of the Common Era, these words would seem to point to the same year 29. Pressed in this manner between the tradition and the text, some of these writers concluded that the ministry of Christ on earth had endured only for one twelvemonth, or less: and this they called ὁ ἐνιαυτὸς τοῦ Κυρίου, " the year of the Lord."

Such an idea, however, could not stand the test of any critical examination. Those who have been accustomed to weigh the facts of history will certainly agree that such manifold acts and teachings as are recorded of Christ could not be compressed within so narrow bounds. Still more important is it to observe that, since the Gospel of St. John enumerates or implies three Passovers as occurring during the term of our Lord's ministry, it follows that, according to St. John, His ministry must have continued for at least two years and some months; and such may be taken as at present the common and received opinion.

This conclusion, as derived from the fourth Gospel, was well known to some at least of the ancient Fathers.

It is given by Jerome in nearly the same words as we have used.* With such a conclusion, derived from such authority, the idea of a single "year of the Lord" could strike no lasting root. Yet still the perplexity as to the dates remained. Still was it desired to combine, if possible, the tradition and the text. Sometimes the tradition was sacrificed; sometimes the text was explained away; but much more frequently, perhaps, the two statements were left without elucidation, though standing as it were side by side.

It was an English divine who first proposed what we take to be the true solution. Nicholas Mann, Master of the Charterhouse, published in 1733 a treatise "Of the true years of the Birth and Death of Christ." The name of the author does not stand upon the title-page, but it appears as signature of the dedication to the Bishop of Chichester; and there followed in 1743, for the benefit of foreign scholars, a Latin version of the work.

The object of Mann is to show that we should compute the fifteenth year of Tiberius in the passage of St. Luke not from the year 14 of the Common Era, when Augustus died, but from the formal decree issued three years before, which named Tiberius co-regent of the provinces, and joint commander of the armies. In this well-devised explanation Mann is, no doubt, entitled to the honour of priority. But in

---

* "Scriptum est in Evangelio secundum Joannem per tria Pascha Dominum venisse in Jerusalem, quæ duos annos efficiunt."—Hieron. "Comm. in Isaiam," chap. xxix. ver. 1, Op. vol. iii. p. 245, ed. 1704.

all other respects—in argument, in learning, in powers of illustration—his treatise is far inferior to that of Dr. Zumpt, which appeared in 1869, and which, in connection with another subject, was discussed last year in the pages of this Review. It is mainly, therefore, by the aid of the latter work that we shall now proceed to state the case.

It appears, then, that Augustus, finding the infirmities of age advance upon him, and having already adopted Tiberius as his heir, resolved to associate that young chief, without any restriction, in the government of the empire. For this purpose, as Velleius Paterculus tells us, he obtained a decree giving to Tiberius co-equal powers with himself over all the provinces and armies. This decree, it should be noted, was passed in most solemn form, not by the senate only, but in the name of the senate and the people.* Its exact date is not recorded, but it is placed by Velleius just before the return of Tiberius from his German expedition, and his triumph over the hostile tribes. Now, this triumph was celebrated January 16, A.D. 12, and we may therefore fix the date of the decree towards the close of the preceding year. Reckoning the fifteenth year of the reign of Tiberius from that period, we shall come to the last weeks of A.D. 26.

It should be observed that in this passage of St. Luke the word "reign," as our Authorized Version gives it, rather exceeds the meaning of ἡγεμονία in

---

* Velleius Paterculus, "Hist.," lib. ii. c. 121.

the Greek original. The word "reign," it is obvious, can be used only of a sovereign, and in general a sovereign ruling singly, while the Greek term may serve for any case of high authority. In this very text the Evangelist does not merely apply it to Tiberius, but gives the same epithet (as ἡγεμονεύων) to Pontius Pilate, and this, in an earlier passage, he does likewise to Publius Quirinus, as Governor of Syria. The exact meaning of St. Luke might be rather thus expressed: "in the fifteenth year since Tiberius first bore sway."

The joint rule of Augustus and Tiberius is attested by two ancient inscriptions, both of which Orelli has inserted.* The first was found in Dalmatia. It is of P. Cornelius Dolabella, who held an office at this period. The words referring to this are as follows:—

"PRO. PR. DIVI AVGVSTI ET TI. CAESARIS AUGUSTI."

As its date, Orelli gives in his note 10 A.D.,—at least a twelvemonth too soon.

The second of these inscriptions is, or was, at the monastery of Monte Cassino. It commemorates one Caius Ummidius, who under Claudius became Governor of Illyria, and under Nero Governor of Lusitania, but who under the joint emperors held the office of Quæstor in Cyprus. Here are the words upon the last-named post:—

"PROVINC. CYPRI Q. DIVI AVG. ET TI. CAESARIS AVG."

Considering the high title here ascribed to the

---

* "Inscript. Latin. Collectio," ed. Orelli, Nos. 2365 et 3128.

young emperor, and the co-equal obedience implied on the part of the officers of state, it seems difficult to doubt that, if the writers of these inscriptions had been asked at a later period to name the first year of the reign of Tiberius, they would have named the year 11 A.D., rather than the year 14 A.D.

It is certainly true that not only Tacitus and Suetonius, but Josephus also, date the reign of Tiberius from the death of Augustus. Such, it appears, was the practice of historians who wrote for the great world at Rome. But the case might be far otherwise with local and provincial writers, who looked to the realities of power rather than to its due transmission and descent. They could distinguish between the radiance of the rising and the dimness of the setting sun; they saw from whom the orders came, and to whom the petitions were addressed; and where they saw the authority wielded they would deem the reign to have commenced.

There is a striking analogy to this case in the one that immediately precedes it—the sole sway of Augustus. However historians and annalists at Rome might concur as to the date of his sovereignty, there was no such agreement elsewhere. From the coins or the inscriptions engraved in various cities, we find that no less than eight different dates were assigned as the commencement of his reign.* Thus in the East, some reckoned it from the battle of Actium, others from the

---

* Marquardt-Becker, "Handbuch der Römischen Alterthümer," vol. ii. 3, 229, as cited by Dr. Zumpt. Clinton, in his "Fasti Hellenici" (vol. iii. p. 276, ed. 1834), enumerates only five of these dates.

taking of Alexandria. In other provinces, further removed from such local impressions, some computed from the time when the title of Augustus, and some from the time when the office of Imperator, was bestowed. Since, then, we have to admit eight such dates as current for the commencement of the reign of Augustus, it does not seem unreasonable to infer that two might be in vogue for the commencement of the reign of Tiberius,—the one reckoned from his joint authority, the second from his undivided sway.

It seems natural, however, to inquire whether any light can be brought to bear upon this controversy from the other notes of time in St. Luke. Let us, in the first place, transcribe the two verses in question:—

"Now in the fifteenth year of the reign of Tiberius Cæsar, Pontius Pilate being governor of Judæa, and Herod being tetrarch of Galilee, and his brother Philip tetrarch of Ituræa and of the region of Trachonitis, and Lysanias the tetrarch of Abilene,

"Annas and Caiaphas being the high priests, the word of God came unto John the son of Zacharias in the wilderness."

There is no chronological point to be established from the mention of Annas and Caiaphas as the high priests; nor does Lysanias of Abilene yield us any further information. The name was borne, it would seem, in succession by two chiefs at least of that little state. Of Herod's two sons, as we learn from Josephus, Philip died A.D. 34, after ruling thirty-seven years; and Antipas was deposed and banished by Caligula A.D. 37, after ruling thirty-five.* It is plain that these dates apply equally well to either theory, whether we fix the Tiberius era at A.D. 11 or A.D. 14.

There remains, then, the case of Pontius Pilate; and here again we have Josephus for a guide. We learn from him that, near the close of Tiberius's reign, Pilate was accused of grievous cruelty to the people of Samaria, and was sent home by Vitellius, then Governor of Syria, to answer for his conduct. On arriving at Rome, however, he found that the emperor had already expired.† Now, the death of Tiberius took place on the 16th of March, A.D. 37, and we may fix the recall of Pilate in the month of January preceding. Josephus says that he had been ten years in Judæa. But here, as elsewhere, the Jewish historian speaks only in round numbers as to years, and takes no account as to months; and we have strong grounds to conclude that several months must, in this case, be added. For the predecessor of Pilate in office —namely, Valerius Gratus—had been recalled at the close of the year A.D. 25, and it seems in the highest degree improbable that for the space of an entire twelvemonth the Romans would have left so turbulent a province without a chief.‡ If, then, we take the government of Pilate as commencing in mid-summer, A.D. 26, and ending in mid-winter, A.D. 36, we shall find that it consists as well with the theory of Mann as with that more commonly received.

---

* " Ant. Jud.," lib. xviii. c. 4 and 7. † Ibid. c. 5.
‡ See this conclusion more fully established by Dr. Zumpt, " Des Geburtsjahr Christi," p. 297, ed 1869.

But there is another passage in the Gospels which is, as we think, entirely and without any doubt decisive in favour of Mann's theory. We would refer to the second chapter of St. John, where it is related how, shortly after the first miracle of Jesus in Cana of Galilee, and how being then at Jerusalem for the approaching feast of Passover, He was engaged in controversy with certain of the Jews:—

"Then answered the Jews and said unto Him, What sign shewest thou unto us, seeing that thou doest these things?

"Jesus answered and said unto them, Destroy this temple, and in three days I will raise it up.

"Then said the Jews, Forty and six years was this temple in building, and wilt thou rear it up in three days?"

Here the first question that arises is, whether at this time the building of the temple was completed. If it were, it might have been so for some time previous; and the Jews might still, very fairly for their argument, allege the number of years that its building had required. But if it were not completed then, the Jews could speak only of its progress up to the time at which they spoke; and in that case, by determining the date when the construction of the temple was commenced, we could also determine the date of the discussion which the Evangelist records.

Now, in both these cases our information is precise and clear. The main body of the temple was closed in and in use for the Jewish services for a long time before the ministry of Jesus, but the edifice was not brought to a completion until a long time afterwards. It was not finished till the year A.D. 63, in the reign of the Emperor Nero. On the other hand, we learn that Herod began the construction of the temple in the eighteenth year of his reign. Both these facts, with their dates, stand on the high authority of Josephus.*

But when did Herod's reign begin? We have already had occasion to show that, as in the case of Tiberius, there were two different computations for it; the one reckoning from the decree of the Roman senate, which named him king; and the other from his actual acquisition of the kingdom by the taking of Jerusalem and the death of the last Asmonean prince. The first of these events was in the year B.C. 40, the second in 37. However, we are left in no doubt as to which date Josephus here designed. For after telling us that the building of the temple was commenced in the eighteenth year of the king's reign, he goes on to say that it was "after the acts already mentioned" (μετὰ τὰς προειρημένας πράξεις). Now, the acts just before related by Josephus were the visit of Augustus in the spring to Syria, and his return in the autumn to Samos; and this visit, as we learn from other sources, took place in the year B.C. 20. We may therefore fix the foundation of this, the third temple of Jerusalem, towards the close of B.C. 20 or the beginning of 19. If the Jews, as appears to have been their common practice with days, reckoned the broken year at the commencement as entire, the forty-six years stated from

---

* "Ant. Jud.," lib. xx. c. 9, and lib. xv. c. 11.

the first building would bring us to the early months of A.D. 27, and this is the more probable time. If, however, the broken year be not so included, we come then to the early months of A.D. 28; but by no possibility can this computation allow a later date. Those, therefore, who place the first appearance of our Lord in the year 29, do so in the very teeth of the deductions which the statement of the Jews in the fourth Gospel enables us to make.

There is another argument which we have reserved to the last, and which, as we hope, will have much weight with a large majority of our readers. It is only by the theory of Mann and Zumpt that we can fully vindicate the accuracy of St. Luke. If in our Biblical chronology we desire to postpone the first public appearance of Jesus till the year A.D. 29, and if we bear in mind that it is incumbent upon us to place His Nativity some months before the death of Herod, we must admit that He was thirty-four or thirty-five years of age at the commencement of His ministry. Now, St. Luke has told us that He was then "about thirty;" and this, were it really brought home to him, would in an Evangelist be a considerable error—above all, in one who speaks of himself as "having had perfect understanding of all things from the very first."

We have now brought to a close our argument on the year of the Passion, which we have endeavoured to state as briefly as clearness would allow. But, before we conclude, we desire to express the wish and hope which we have formed that some scholar worthy of the task—Dean Stanley, perhaps, or Mr. Grove—might consent to undertake a local history of Jerusalem, similar to those which we already possess of Rome. From the excavations and researches that are even now in progress, he might compare to great advantage the descriptions in the Old Testament with the traces of foundation that still remain. The essay of M. Jacob Bernays, as published at Berlin in 1861, has with singular ingenuity brought to bear some facts, hitherto unnoticed, on the memorable siege of Titus—facts that any future writer would certainly not neglect. The Arabic manuscripts might—more doubtfully—afford him some new details as to the edifices in the Moslem period, and above all, as to the mosque of Omar. From that era of servitude the spirit of the annalist would kindle, and his materials, far from failing, would gather in masses round him, as he came to the days of the great deliverance—when, after contests fierce and dire, the Holy City was regained by Christian arms under auspices that even Gibbon can scarcely record without a thrill of enthusiasm—when in his own words, —" on a Friday, at three in the afternoon, the day and hour of the Passion, Godfrey of Bouillon stood victorious on the walls of Jerusalem." *

---

* " Decline and Fall," vol. vii. p. 227. Dr. Smith's edition.

V.

HAROLD OF NORWAY.

HAROLD OF NORWAY.*

MR. DASENT'S book, which we have named first on our title-page, seems to us to have considerable merit. We can laugh with his "Jest," and learn a great deal from his "Earnest." As to the first we must, however, except from our commendation two political squibs of great personal acerbity and very questionable taste, which we think Mr. Dasent would have done well in not producing. We can with far more pleasure join him in his lightsome trips to the Faroe Islands and the Wildbad waters. As regards his "Earnest," all persons, we think, must admit that he employs to great advantage the large stock of ancient Scandinavian lore, of which, in several former publications, he has shown himself most fully possessed. We have found him all through that rugged region an able and sure-footed guide.

---

* 1. *Jest and Earnest, a Collection of Essays and Reviews.* By George Webbe Dasent, Esq., D.C.L. 2 vols. London, 1873.

2. *Inscription Runique du Pirée*, par C. C. Rafn à Copenhague, 1856.

3. *Historia Haraldi Severi, ex vetere Sermone Latine reddita, operâ et studio Sveinbjornis Egilsonii in Islandiâ.* (In the sixth volume of the "Scripta Historica Islandorum," Hafniæ, 1835.)

M

Of the several grim trans-Baltic heroes with whom Mr. Dasent makes us better acquainted, there is certainly none so striking—more especially remembering his close connection with our own history—as the Harold of Norway, whom his contemporaries surnamed Hafi, that is "the Tall;" but whom his chroniclers call Hardrada—or, as the English historians have made it, Harfager, that is "the Severe." We design with our author's aid to offer to our readers a sketch of his remarkable career. But here at the outset we have a fault to find with Mr. Dasent, not indeed for what he tells, but for what he has left untold. To our mind there is no point in Harold's life so curious as his unexpected connection with one of the monuments of ancient Greece; and yet this story is dismissed by Mr. Dasent in only half a sentence. We, on the contrary, shall endeavour to detail it at full length, deriving our information from other sources, and, above all, from the learned and excellent work which we have named as second at the head of the present article.

When literature and learning first revived among the Western nations of Europe, little or nothing was known of the actual state of Athens. It was not till the year 1573 that Martin Kraus or Crusius, a professor at Tübingen, showed some curiosity on the subject. He contrived to open a communication with two Greeks residing at Constantinople, and believed to be men of learning. In his own letters he says that Athens had been described to him as totally destroyed, and occupied only by a few fishermen's huts; and he desires to learn whether such was the real fact. He had little cause to congratulate himself on the answers he received. One of his correspondents, Zygomalas by name, told him that being a native of Nauplia he had often visited Athens, and admired an edifice on the Acropolis, which surpassed all other edifices, and this edifice, he said, was the Pantheon! His second instructor, Simeon Kavasila, referred in like manner to the Parthenon; but called it the Temple of the Unknown God which St. Paul had mentioned!* If such were the learned men of Greece at this period, we confess that we should have liked to see a sample of the ignorant.

In the next century this ignorance as to the ruins of Athens was in part dispelled by some visitors from Western Europe, though few and far between. Chief among them were the fellow-travellers Spon and Wheler, the one a physician from Lyons, the other an English gentlemen. They not only speak of the Parthenon under its right name, and with its historical antecedents, but have given us a good description of it as it was in 1675—a description the more valuable since, in little more than ten years from that time, the glorious building was shattered and in part subverted by the explosion of a bomb in the Venetian siege.

But it was not merely the Parthenon that Spon and Wheler describe. Their published travels notice

---

* Mart. Crusius, "Turco-Græciæ," lib. vii. ep. 10 et 18, ed. 1854.

many other objects of antiquity; among others two colossal lions of Pentelic marble. Better judges have since pronounced these statues admirable works, in the highest style of Attic art. The one, in a sitting posture and ten feet in height, stood on the inner shore of the Piræus harbour, which it seemed to guard. From that statue the harbour itself derived the name of Porto Leone, which it bore among the Franks all through the Middle Ages and down to our own times. As such it is mentioned by Lord Byron in "The Giaour." The Greek fisherman, he says—

> "Though worn and weary with his toil
> And cumber'd with his scaly spoil,
> Slowly yet strongly plies the oar
> Till Port Leone's safer shore
> Receives him by the lovely light
> That best becomes an Eastern night."

The second statue, also of Pentelic marble, was nearly equal to the first in point of art, but far less good in point of preservation. The travellers of 1675 saw it on its original base, a little outside the city, near the ancient "Sacred Way." The animal is represented as couching and at rest; and Spon says that he felt inclined to address it in the following words: "Sleep on, Lion of Athens, since the Lion of the Harbour watches for thee." *

Twelve years later, after the successful but destructive siege, it came to pass that Morosini at the head of the Venetians found it requisite to retire from the

---

* "Voyages de Spon et Wheler," vol. ii. pp. 145 et 177, ed. 1679.

city. Before he went, however, he resolved that he would bear away with him some memorial of his conquest. First he turned his thoughts to a magnificent piece of sculpture on the western pediment of the Parthenon, representing the car of Victory with horses of the natural size, and this he gave orders to remove. But so careless or so clumsy were his workmen, that the whole group was thrown down in the act of lowering it, and shivered almost into dust. *Si ruppero non solo, ma si difecero in polvere*, writes a Venetian captain, who was present.*

Foiled in his first object, this worthy precursor of Lord Elgin—

"Cold as the crags upon his native coast
His mind as barren and his heart as hard,"

—next betook himself to the separate statues of lions, in and about the city. Of these he carried off three to adorn the Arsenal at Venice, and from the spoils of Corinth a fourth was subsequently added.† That and one of the others also are of lesser size and inferior merit, and need not be further mentioned. But the remaining two—the lion *séjant* from the Piræus, and the lion *couchant* from the Sacred Way—as placed before the gate of the Arsenal, command to this day the admiration of all lovers or connoisseurs of art.

If it were not for the three centuries that separate the life of Dante from the removal of these monuments to Venice, we should certainly have assumed

---

* Leake's "Topography of Athens," vol. ii. p. 87.
† Ibid. vol. i. p. 371.

that the great Italian poet had in his mind the Lion of the Piræus, when he describes in lofty strains the majestic repose of the Mantuan Sordello:—

> "O anima Lombarda,
> Come ti stavi altera e disdegnosa;
> E nel muover degli occhi onesta e tarda!
> Ella non ci diceva alcuna cosa,
> Ma lasciavane gir, solo guardando
> A guisa di leon quando si posa." *

Close observers at Venice must, however, from the first have noticed with great surprise that the statue of the sitting lion bore around each of its shoulders, and in serpentine folds, the remains of barbaric inscriptions. These strange characters were after a time recognized as Norwegian Runes. Still, with every effort they could not be deciphered. They had been much defaced, and flattened at the edges, in great part it would seem by the effect of musket balls, the inscriptions having probably been used as marks in firing by some of the soldiery in Greece. Many wild conjectures were put forth during tens of years to explain how the Runes of Norway could have come to the Piræus or appear on monuments of Hellenic art. It was not till our own day, however, that the mystery was solved.

The merit of this remarkable discovery belongs wholly to the late M. Rafn, an antiquary of Copenhagen, distinguished by profound learning and many ingenious researches. When at Venice he tried in vain, like all his predecessors, to decipher the battered

---

* "Purgatorio," canto vi. verse 61.

Runes. He could, indeed, make out separate letters here and there, but not a connected word, or still less a connected sentence. He had given up the attempt in despair and had returned to his native country, when as it chanced a large stone was laid bare at the village of Harrenstrup, in the Isle of Zealand, which had on its surface some ancient sculpture, or rather scratches, representing ships. M. Rafn went forth with several friends to view these rude engravings, but found them so nearly effaced that no drawings of them could be made. The visitors after some hours of noonday examination relinquished the object. Still, however, they lingered near the spot till sunset, when, previous to departure, one of the party walked back to take a last look at the stone. How great was his surprise to find that the lengthening shadows had brought into relief the slight irregularities left upon the surface by the effaced designs, and enabled their outline to be correctly traced.

This experience was not lost on M. Rafn. It occurred to him that the like method, if applied to the Runes from the Piræus, might be attended with the like success. In the first place, however, he obtained a cast in plaster from the original marble, as also copies of the best designs that had been taken. These he kept by him for the purpose of comparison with the shadows to be observed both at sunrise and sunset upon the statue. This was in December, 1855. M. de Bertouch, a Danish gentleman, was at that time residing at Venice. He undertook to observe and note the shadows, not only at various hours of the day, but also at several seasons of the year. Selecting the most favourable of these views, M. de Bertouch despatched to Copenhagen two large photographs of the double inscription, in which, to the great delight of M. Rafn, many of the vanished letters, and some quite clearly, reappeared. Thus did M. Rafn find himself enabled to decipher nearly all the words, and it was with especial pleasure that he remarked among them the name of a chief so renowned in Northern story as was Harold the Tall.

To complete or to correct the observations of his friend, and the ideas upon the subject which he had already formed, M. Rafn once more repaired to Venice. "At last," he says, "I have attained my object, and can offer to the public an almost certain interpretation of the Runes,—a result which at the outset I was far from expecting." Both the inscriptions are in serpentine folds, as is common with the ancient Runes, but if reduced to straight lines, that on the lion's left shoulder is as follows. We transcribe it from M. Rafn's book, with this explanation, that where there are but faint traces of a letter he has printed it in small capitals, while on the other hand he uses common type in the few places where he had nothing beyond conjecture to guide him.

: HAKUN : VAN : ÞIR: ULFR : ᴀUK : ASMᴜDʀ : ᴀUK : AᴜRN : HAFN : ÞESA : ÞIR : MeN : LᴀɢÞU : A : Uᴋ : HARADʀ : HAfI : UF IABUTA : UPRᴀɪStar : Vegna : GRIᴋIAÞIÞIS : VARÞ : DALKr . NaUþᴜGR : I : FɪᴀʀI : LAÞUM : EGIL : VAR : ɪ : FARU : miþ : RAGNARɪ : ᴛɪʟ : RUmanIU . . . . auk : ᴀRMENIU :

We will now present to our readers this inscription literally rendered, observing only that in our English version, as in M. Rafn's French, the names are given in accordance with the common spelling,—

"Hakon, combined with Ulf, with Asmund, and with Örn, conquered this port [the Piræus]. These men and Harold the Tall imposed [on the inhabitants] large fines, on account of the revolt of the Greek people. Dalk has been detained in distant lands. Egil was waging war, together with Ragnar, in Roumania and Armenia."

We may notice that these chiefs in the Varangian Guard (as we shall presently show them to be) who possessed themselves of the Piræus were desirous to explain in this inscription the absence of their comrades. The one was detained, perhaps as a prisoner, in a foreign country; the two others were in active service on the frontiers of the empire.

We will now give the inscription from the right shoulder of the lion,—

: ASMUDR : HJU : ruNAR : Þ̄ISAR : Þ̄AIR :
ISKir : auk : ÞuRLIFR : ÞURÞIR : AUK : IVAr :
at : BON : HARADS : HAFa : ÞUAT : GRIKiAR :
uf : hUGSAÞu : auk : bAnaÞu :

Or, in English,—

"Asmund engraved these Runes in combination with Asgeir, Thorleif, Thord, and Ivar, by desire of Harold the Tall, although the Greeks on reflection opposed it."

It is worthy of note in this last paragraph how the people of Athens, fallen as they were from their high estate, still, where they could, resented the defacing of their ancient monuments. The same feeling may be traced more than seven centuries later, during Lord Elgin's depredations. Thus wrote Dr. Clarke to Lord Byron in a note subsequently published:—

"When the last of the Metopes was taken from the Parthenon, and in moving of it great part of the superstructure, with one of the triglyphs, was thrown down by the workmen whom Lord Elgin employed, the Disdar, who beheld the injury done to the building, took his pipe from his mouth, dropped a tear, and in a supplicating tone of voice said to Lusieri, τέλος! I was present."

Having thus interpreted the Runes from the Piræus, we will proceed to sketch the career of Harold and explain his connection with the revolt of the Athenians. Our chief materials are derived from those Sagas of Iceland which, in their Latin version, we have named as third on our title-page.

Harold, the son of Sigurd, was born in the year 1015; half-brother of Olaf the Saint, King of Norway. Even in his boyhood his heroic spirit is extolled by the Iceland Saga. He was but fifteen years of age when King Olaf was about to engage in the decisive battle of Stiklastad. "Let my brother keep aloof," said Olaf, "he is but a child." Not such was the choice of the young prince himself. "I will not keep aloof," he cried; "if I am thought too weak as yet and unable to wield a sword, I know the remedy; let my hand be tied fast to the hilt, and I shall be found amongst the foremost!" In the battle which ensued he showed all the valour he had promised; but the result was most disastrous: King Olaf was defeated and slain.

Young Harold, grievously wounded, was borne from the field by some trusty followers, and kept concealed in a cottage until his strength returned. Next spring he sought refuge in Gardarika, as Russia was at that time called by the Norwegians. He was kindly received by the Grand Duke Jaroslav; and in due time became enamoured of Elizabeth, daughter of his host. But when he pressed his suit Jaroslav proved as flinty-hearted as any father in a modern novel. "Not yet," he said; "you must first do some high deeds in warfare, and lay the foundations both of wealth and fame."

The path of fortune in that age was clear and open to any aspiring youth of Northern race. It was to seek service at Constantinople in the emperor's body-guard—the far-famed Varangians. Of these Varangians but a very brief account is to be found in Gibbon. Of their name, which perplexed the early critics, Mr. Dasent says: "*Var*, Anglo-Saxon, *woer*, from which the word arose, had nothing to do with war. It meant oath, or a promise sanctioned by an oath, and from this point of view might be considered only as a translation of the Latin *Sacramentum*—the oath taken to their colours by the Roman soldiers."

The Varangians of the emperors at Constantinople might be compared on some points with the Swiss Guard of the Popes at Rome. They were exclusively Northern, recruited by Norwegians, Danes, and English, and their numbers are computed by Mr. Dasent as varying from 1000 to 2400 men. The south-western wing of the palace was reserved for their head-quarters, and bore the Latin title of *Excubitum*. Whenever the emperor went forth, on any occasion of business or state, it was their special duty to attend him, armed with their two-edged Norwegian battle-axes. To them also was assigned the important post in that land of domestic conspiracies, to keep watch at the door of the emperor's bedchamber.

But it was not only with the emperor that their sphere of duty lay; a band of them was frequently despatched to the armies on the frontier, even in the emperor's absence, there to act as a *Corps d'Elite*, and set an example to the degenerate Greeks engaged in the same service. The best proof perhaps of their prowess lies in the present extension of their name. Thus writes Mr. Mounsey, a recent traveller in Persia, and the author of a very pleasant book thereon.* The scene is at Tabreez :—

"Riding through the bazaar on the morning after my arrival, ever and anon as I passed along, I heard amongst the Babel of sounds and street-cries the words 'Feringhee, Feringhee;' and as the term seemed connected with my person, and was the only one which, in my ignorance of the language of the country, had the definite form of a word to my ear, I naturally asked my companion, the consul, what it meant. 'Stranger,' was the reply. 'All Europeans are included in the term.' As I afterwards found, this is the case all over Persia. The educated man has, indeed, some vague ideas that there are other countries and nations in the world besides his beloved and glorious Iran; he knows something of Turkey, of India, and Arabia, and if his studies have been deep, even of

---

* "A Journey through the Caucasus and the Interior of Persia." By Augustus H. Mounsey, F.R.G.S., Second Consul to H.B.M. Embassy at Vienna. London, 1872.

Yengidunya—'the young world'—America; but for the masses there is in Europe, or rather westwards of Constantinople, but one land—'Feringhistan,' and one race, that of the 'Feringhee.' The Varangians came from that land, and their prowess or notoriety was so great that in this ultra-conservative of countries all foreigners are still designated by a corruption of their name."

Harold, who had set out from Russia, and whom we have left too long on his way, reached Constantinople in 1033, being then eighteen years of age. He had shot up to a giant's—or at least a hero's—size, seven feet in height at the very lowest computation. After some brief interval, he and his attendants enrolled themselves in the Varangian Guard. For some reason, not quite clear, but probably to conceal his connection with Jaroslav, he suppressed his real name, and, as the Saga tells us, took that of "Nordbrikt," which he continued to bear through the whole of his Eastern career. No wonder if an appellation so dissonant to Southern ears should not be commemorated by the Byzantine writers, who, indeed—and we suppose for the same reason—scarcely ever mention a Varangian by name. The Varangians, on their part, made strange havoc with the Southern appellations. Thus, the great church of St. Sophia, the "Hagia Sophia" of the Greeks, became with them "Aegisif," and the Hippodrome "Padrein." Their own quarter, the Excubitum, or, as the common people at Constantinople called it, "Skuviton," was in their mouths contracted to "Skift."

The stalwart form of Harold, his undaunted courage, and perhaps also some knowledge or suspicion of his princely rank, gained him almost from the first a lead among his comrades in arms. He appeared to no less advantage in the games of football and wrestling, the favourite pastimes of the North, which the Varangians were wont to practise after their musters and reviews; and on one of these occasions he attracted in an especial manner the notice of the Empress Zoe. We will leave the story to Mr. Dasent to tell in part, and in part only.

"Then when the games were at their height, and some played, while others sat round in a triple ring, and amongst them Harold 'Nordbrikt,' it happened that the empress and her ladies came that way, and stopped to gaze on their manly forms. After admiring for a while their strength and skill, the empress cast her eyes on Harold, and going straight up to him said, 'Listen, Northman! give me a lock of thy hair.' Harold's answer it is impossible to give . . . but the reply, though coarse and rude, was witty and quick, and all laughed that heard it, though they wondered at the boldness of the youth who thus dared to turn the tables on the empress, and did not spare her with his biting words. Zoe herself, whose taste could not have been over-nice, seems to have been little shocked, and went on her way, smiling at Harold's words."

It may well be supposed that this tale is not recorded by the Byzantine historian of the period, the courtly Cedrenus; but the Northern Saga states it in all its native rudeness.

But it was not at Constantinople that Harold was commonly found. We read of him as leading forth bands of the brave Varangians, sometimes to quell the revolt of an inland province, and sometimes to combat an enemy upon the frontier. Several of his campaigns and sieges against the Saracens in Sicily are related in the Saga, but with too manifest an admixture of legend and of fable. In other years, we find him warring with the wild tribes in Syria or Armenia. By the spoils which he won, and the contributions which he exacted, he soon amassed considerable treasure, and this from time to time he transmitted for safe custody to his Russian friends, who hoarded it faithfully for him.

As the constant companion and the chief lieutenant of Harold in his various campaigns, the Saga commemorates Ulf—a word equivalent to Wolf—the same whose name appears on the Runes of the Piræus. Harold had also with him—perhaps even in the East, but more probably after his return to Norway—one of the Northern *Skalds*, Thiodolf by name, who sings his praises in the barbaric spirit of that age. Here is one of his strains:—

> "Let all men know that Harold
> Was engaged in eighteen fierce fights
> * * * * *
> Great King! thou hast stained with gore
> The hungry beak of the eagle,
> And the wolf that followed in thy track
> Has ever been gorged with prey."

The year 1040, as M. Rafn thinks, may be fixed as the time when Harold and his followers overcame the Athenian insurgents, and caused the Runes of the Piræus to be engraved.

Harold was at Constantinople in the spring of 1042, when there occurred one of those revolutions of the palace, so frequent in the Byzantine story. The Emperor Michael, consort of Zoe, had died three months before, and Zoe, in compliance with his last request, had raised to the purple his nephew, another Michael. The new sovereign showed his gratitude by an early plot against his benefactress. In the night of the 19th of April he caused Zoe to be seized, shaved her head, and shut her up in a convent. But next day, the multitude being apprised of the event, rose in arms, shouting aloud for "Zoe! our mother, Zoe!" Harold and his Varangians also took her side. A desperate struggle ensued, in which three thousand people are said to have fallen. Their cause, however, at last prevailed. The Varangians broke into the palace to search for the emperor, and plundered all the treasure they could find. Michael himself fled to a monastery, and disguised himself in a monk's cowl; while Zoe and her sister Theodora were proclaimed joint empresses. A sentence was passed that the fallen emperor should be deprived of sight; accordingly he was torn from his hiding-place, and dragged to the place called Sigma, where his eyes were at once plucked out.

The Skalds, or Court poets of Harold, and of course his constant panegyrists, could sing in after years how "the mighty leader tore away both the emperor's eyes," or, in another place, how "the prince (Harold) won yet more gold, but the King of the Greeks went stone blind from his sore wounds." It seems from such expressions—this is Mr. Dasent's just remark—as if the bloody deed had been done with Harold's own hand.

Other things are related by the Saga of Harold at Constantinople. We have that inevitable scene in all the High North legends of an encounter with a gigantic snake or dragon in a cave. We have some love passages of Harold with a certain Maria, called the niece of the Empress Zoe, though that descent ill accords with the Byzantine pedigrees. All these tales are so largely intermingled with fable, that the slight foundation of fact, if any, can scarcely be discerned.

In 1044 Harold, having completed eleven years of service in the East, obtained his discharge and went back to Russia with a band of faithful followers. Embarking at Constantinople, they steered up the Black Sea, and thence up the Sea of Azof and the Don. As they sailed along Harold was moodily brooding over the reception that might await him at the Court of Jaroslav—how, in all probability, the young princess had forgotten and would reject him. Full of these thoughts he composed a poem, in sixteen stanzas, some of which are still preserved. They are all on the same model, and all in eight lines, the first six recounting his exploits and accomplishments, and the last two as a *refrain* anticipating the failure of his love. Here is one as a sample:—

> "There are eight things that I know:
> I can write a poem;
> I have experience in riding;
> I have often practised to swim;

> I know how to wield the long pole;
> Not unskilled to throw the spear, or to row:
> Yet the Maid who dwells in Gardarika,
> Adorned with golden rings, disdains me."

Why, when Harold began by boasting of his eight accomplishments, he should, in fact, enumerate no more than six, we cannot undertake to explain. We can only suppose it to arise from the cruel necessities of the metre, which limited his enumeration to six lines.

Here is another stanza of much greater interest, since it seems to bear upon the question that we just now discussed. These lines we derive from the later and most careful translation of M. Rafn:—

> " Neither the Maid nor the Matron
> Can deny that we have been
> One morn at the burgh in the south,
> Then how we brandished the steel!
> By our swords we laid open a track;
> A memorial is there to record it;
> Yet the Maid who dwells in Gardarika,
> Adorned with golden rings, disdains me."

This phrase "burgh, or borg, in the south," is explained by M. Rafn as denoting Athens, which the Norwegian writers call "Athenuborg." M. Rafn adduces some other passages to show that even in the dark ages they regarded Athens with respect, and declared it the first of all Grecian towns. In like manner M. Rafn contends that the word *merki*, which we have translated "memorial," and which we take to be closely allied to the German *merkmal*, refers, in all probability, to the Runes engraved upon the sides of the lion.

To the same effect as Harold's stanza, is one by his Court poet, the constant extoller of his exploits, Thiodolf:—

> "The greed of the wolves was appeased
> By the valiant Chief of the hosts,
> At the time when the lances were brandished
> And the vanquished sued for peace.
> Oft has he gathered great spoil
> From the south of the sea by his sword,
> While faint-hearted men kept aloof:
> A memorial of this still remains."

Here the Norwegian word is not *merki*, but *minni*, which, however, is said to bear exactly the same meaning. It may be applied not only to monuments, strictly so called, but to any form of record, whether fixed or movable. Thus in the Saga the word is used of a great bell which Harold, when reigning in Norway, presented, in memory of St. Olaf, to the church at Thingvall.

We may add that if Harold and his comrades designed on taking the Piræus to leave behind them some permanent memorial of their conquest, there was scarce any other course open to them than the engraving of Runes. Sculpture was out of the question in an age when the art had not merely declined, but had, it may be said, expired.

On reaching Kieff, where the Russian sovereign then held Court, Harold found that his apprehensions had been vain. He was warmly welcomed by Jaroslav, and perhaps more warmly still by his first love, the Princess Elizabeth, whom he now espoused. With all his exploits he was still but twenty-nine years of age. Henceforth his thoughts reverted to his paternal realm of Norway, where was peaceably reigning his nephew Magnus, the son of St. Olaf, and himself surnamed the Good.

But Magnus the Good was no match for Harold the Dauntless. The latter landed in Sweden, gathered around him a band of followers, and presented so formidable an appearance that the pacific Magnus quickly came to terms. An equal partition was agreed upon. The two young princes were to be joint kings of Norway, and Magnus was to receive one-half of Harold's treasures. It seems doubtful whether in any case that compact could have long endured. But an accident brought it to a speedy close. King Magnus, while riding at full speed, was thrown from his horse, and in falling struck his head against the root of a tree, and from the wounds which he then received he died.

By the decease of Magnus Harold became sole sovereign of Norway, and reigned as such for twenty years. The harshness of his rule may be sufficiently inferred from the surname that he gained of "Hardrada," the Severe. He was still upon the throne when there came the year 1066, so memorable in the annals of England. The Crown being grasped by Harold the Saxon at the death of Edward the Confessor, a confederacy gathered against the new king. His own brother, Tosti, fled to Flanders and implored the alliance of Norway, while William of Normandy was preparing his forces on the coasts of France.*

Harold Hardrada, ever warlike and ambitious, eagerly closed with the overtures of Tosti. The two chiefs made common cause. Early in September Harold appeared at the mouth of the Tyne with a formidable armament of three hundred ships of war. He was joined by some sixty sail from Flanders, under the command of Tosti, who thereupon did homage to Harold as to his liege lord. Ascending the Humber with their fleets combined, they landed their troops with little or no resistance, and in a battle which ensued utterly routed the two great earls, Edwin and Mercer, the brothers-in-law of King Harold the Saxon.

But scarcely was this victory achieved than the tidings came that King Harold the Saxon, at the head of considerable forces, was marching from the south against them. Tosti, as arrayed in arms against his brother, felt by this time some scruple of conscience, or more probably perhaps some mistrust of success. He sent a message to King Harold inquiring what might be the conditions of a peace. The result has been told by Sir Walter Scott in a passage of "Ivanhoe" as follows. It is condensed from the ancient chronicles with admirable grace and spirit:—

---

* It is beside the purpose of the present sketch of Harold's career to narrate at length his invasion of England, or to enter into a critical examination of the commonly received story. We must refer our readers, for these points, to Mr. Freeman's exhaustive account in his "History of the Norman Conquest" (vol. iii. pp. 327, foll.)—a work of which we hope to give, at some future time, the detailed notice which its importance deserves.

"'Yes,' said Cedric, 'it was in this very hall that my father feasted with Torquil Wolfganger when he entertained the valiant and unfortunate Harold. It was in this hall that Harold returned the magnanimous answer to the ambassador of his rebel brother. Oft have I heard my father kindle as he told the tale. The envoy of Tosti was admitted when this ample room could scarce contain the crowd of noble Saxon leaders who were quaffing the blood-red wine around their monarch.'

"The envoy of Tosti moved up the hall, undismayed by the frowning countenances of all around him, until he made his obeisance before the throne of King Harold.

"'What terms,' he said, 'lord king, hath thy brother Tosti to hope if he should lay down his arms and crave peace at thy hands?'

"'A brother's love,' cried the generous Harold, 'and the fair earldom of Northumberland.'

"'But should Tosti accept those terms,' continued the envoy, 'what lands shall be assigned to his faithful ally, Hardrada, King of Norway?'

"'Seven feet of English ground,' answered Harold, fiercely; 'or as Hardrada is said to be a giant, perhaps we may allow him twelve inches more.'

"The hall rang with acclamations, and cup and horn was filled to the Norwegian who should be speedily in possession of his English territory.

"The baffled envoy retreated to carry to Tosti and his ally the ominous answer of his injured brother. It was then that the walls of Stamford, and the fatal Welland renowned in prophecy, beheld that direful conflict in which, after displaying the most undaunted valour, the King of Norway and Tosti both fell, with ten thousand of their bravest followers. Who would have thought that upon the proud day when this battle was won, the very gale which waved the Saxon banners in triumph was filling the Norman sails, and impelling them to the fatal shores of Sussex?"

We are loth to mar the effect of this fine passage by any criticism of its historical accuracy. Yet we cannot well refrain from observing that Sir Walter was not quite so good an antiquary upon English as upon Scottish ground. He has here confounded Stamford Town, in a corner of Lincolnshire and on the river Welland, with Stamford Bridge, about seven miles east of York, and on the river Derwent. It was at the latter place, beyond all question, and on the 25th of September, that the battle was fought. The result was long undecided. Both the Harolds performed prodigies of valour; and it was perhaps the fall of the one that decided the fortune of the day. Harold, King of Norway, was standing firm among the foremost—wielding, we may suppose, his redoubtable two-edged battle-axe—when, as Mr. Dasent relates it, a stray arrow smote him in the throat under the chin. The giant frame tottered; a rush of blood spirted out of his mouth, and Harold Hardrada fell dead. Tosti also was among the slain.

How vast was then the vicissitude produced by so few weeks! The Saxon banner supreme at Stamford Bridge on the 25th of September, and struck down for ever at Hastings on the 14th of the next month!

VI.

THE COUNTESS OF NITHSDALE.

THE COUNTESS OF NITHSDALE.*

COLLECTIONS of family papers have of late years much increased in both size and numbers. Even where no one of the name has risen to historical importance there are chests full of documents and letters that are lavishly poured forth. At present it not unfrequently happens that the records of a single not always very eminent house take up as many printed pages as would have been deemed sufficient thirty years ago to instruct a young student in the whole history of England or almost of Europe.

We are far, however, from complaining of this abundance. Even when a man was not himself distinguished, he may have had companionship or common action with those who were. By such means a thousand little traits of character may come unexpectedly to light. Still oftener there may, nay, there must, be reference to the domestic economies, the modes of living, and the manners and customs of

---

* *The Book of Carlaverock.* 2 vols., large quarto. Edinburgh, 1873 (not published).

past times. Thus, when family papers are selected with care and edited with judgment—as was eminently the case, for example, with the "Caldwell Collection," comprised in three quarto volumes, and printed for the Maitland Club in 1854—they scarcely ever fail to yield fruit of price to the historian.

In the collection now before us are contained the records of the Maxwell family, belonging to Lord Herries, the present head of that ancient house, and confided by him to Mr. William Fraser for arrangement and annotation. The result has been a truly splendid work. These are two quarto volumes of the largest size, almost, indeed, rising to the dignity—as they certainly exceed the usual weight—of folios. The one volume is of 604 pages, the other of 590:—

> "Vix illud lecti bis sex cervice subirent,
> Qualia nunc hominum producit corpora tellus."

No expense, we may add, has been spared in the beautiful types, in the facsimiles of ancient autographs, and the engravings of family portraits or family seats. The book is not for sale; and the impression, we observe, has been limited to 150 copies, so that we should consider it beyond our sphere, and printed only for private circulation, had not Lord Herries made it *publici juris* by presenting a copy in July last year to the library of the British Museum.

Mr. Fraser, as editor of this collection, seems to us to have done his part with—we may say at least—perspicuity and candour. We have only to complain that, in the first half, at all events, of the eighteenth century, to which in these volumes our attention has been exclusively directed, he has made himself but very slightly acquainted with the other writers of the time. From this cause, as we conceive, he has left in obscurity some points which a wider reading would have enabled him to clear. To give only one instance —for we should take no pleasure in any long list of minute omissions—Mr. Fraser, in Lady Traquair's letter of January, 1724, has failed to see, or certainly, at least, has failed to explain, that the "Sir John" therein mentioned was one of the cant names for the Chevalier de St. George, or the Pretender, as we used to call him. Nor has he observed that the document there discussed is a letter of that prince, dated August 20, 1723, and printed by Mr. Fraser in one of his preceding pages.

Of the many personages who in these volumes are presented to us, there is only one that we shall here produce. We desire to give our readers some account of that lady who saved her husband's life from the extremest peril, by the rare combination of high courage and inventive skill, a determined constancy of purpose, and a prompt versatility of means.

Lady Winifred Herbert was the fifth and youngest daughter of the Marquis of Powis; himself descended from the second son of the first Herbert Earl of Pembroke. The exact year of her birth is nowhere to be found recorded. The marquis, her father, was a zealous Roman Catholic, and, as may be supposed, a warm adherent of James the Second. He followed that prince in his exile, held the post of lord chamberlain in his melancholy Court, and received from him further the patent of duke, which was never acknowledged in England. He died in 1697, but his wife and daughter continued to reside at St. Germains under the protection of the queen, Mary of Modena.

William fifth Earl of Nithsdale had been left a minor by his father's untimely death, but was brought up by his surviving parent in the same principles of devoted attachment to the House of Stuart and to the Church of Rome. On attaining his majority he repaired to St. Germains, and did homage to the prince, whom he continued to regard as his rightful king. A more tender motive arose to detain him. He fell in love with Lady Winifred Herbert, who proved no inexorable beauty. They were married in the spring of 1699, and he bore away his bride to his house and fair gardens of Terregles. Since her noble exploit in the Tower these gardens have been examined with interest for any trace of the departed heroine. But, as Mr. Fraser informs us, they have been greatly changed since her time. Only " some old beech hedges and a broad green terrace still remain much the same as then."

We may take occasion to observe of the new-married pair that there was some diversity in the spelling of their name. English writers have most commonly inserted an *i*, and made it Nithisdale ; but the earl and countess themselves signed Nithsdaill.

The countess bore her lord five children, three of whom, however, died in early childhood. At the insurrection of 1715 they had but two surviving—a son, William Lord Maxwell, and an infant daughter, Lady

Anne. And here in ordinary course might close the record of her life, but for the shining events of 1715, which called forth her energies both to act and to endure.

It need scarcely be related even to the least literary of our readers, how, in 1715, the standard of the Chevalier—" James the Third," as his adherents called him —was raised, by Lord Mar in the Highlands and by Mr. Forster and Lord Derwentwater in Northumberland. Lord Kenmure gave the like example to the Scottish peers of the southern counties, setting out to join Forster with a small band of retainers. Considering the principles of Lord Nithsdale in Church and State, his course could not be doubtful. He, too, at the head of a few horsemen, appeared in Forster's camp, and shared the subsequent fortunes of that little army. To Lord Kenmure, who was a Protestant, was assigned the chief command of the Scottish levies. But, as Mr. Fraser tells us, "the Earl of Nithsdale, from his position, and from the devotion of his family to the House of Stuart, would have been placed at the head of the insurrection in the north of Scotland had he not been a Roman Catholic." But though Mr. Fraser has printed "north," he, beyond all doubt, means "south." There was never any question as to either Kenmure's or Nithsdale's command beyond the Forth.

We need not relate in any detail the well-known fate of these hasty levies. They found themselves encompassed at Preston by a regular force under General Wills, and were compelled to surrender without obtaining any better terms than the promise to await the orders of the Government and protect them from any immediate slaughter by the soldiery. It was only a short respite that most of the chiefs then obtained. They were at once sent off as prisoners to London. The painful circumstances of their entry are described as follows in the journal of Lady Cowper, the wife of the Lord Chancellor :—

"*December* 5, 1715.—This week the prisoners were brought to town from Preston. They came in with their arms tied, and their horses, whose bridles were taken off, led each by a soldier. The mob insulted them terribly, carrying a warming-pan before them, and saying a thousand barbarous things, which some of the prisoners returned with spirit. The chief of my father's family was amongst them. He is above seventy years old. A desperate fortune had drove him from home, in hopes to have repaired it. I did not see them come into town, nor let any of my children do so. I thought it would be an insulting of the relatives I had here, though almost everybody went to see them."

The captive peers being thus brought to London were sent for safe custody to the Tower, while preparations for their trial by the House of Lords were making in Westminster Hall. Here again we may borrow from Lady Cowper's journal :—

"*February* 9, 1716.—The day of the trials. My lord was named High Steward by the king, to his vexation and mine; but it could not be helped, and so we must submit, though we both heartily wished it had been Lord Nottingham. . . . . I was told it was customary to make fine liveries upon this occasion, but I had them all plain. I think it very wrong to make a parade upon so dismal an occasion as that of putting to death one's fellow-creatures, nor could I go to the trial to see them receive their sentences, having a relation among them—Lord Widdrington. The prince was there, and came home much touched with compassion. What a pity it is that such cruelties should be necessary!"

But were they necessary? Certainly not, according to the temper of present times; while in 1716, on the contrary, far from exceeding, they seem rather to have fallen short of the popular expectation and demands.

The trials were quickly despatched. None of the prisoners could deny that they had risen in arms against the king. It only remained for them to plead "Guilty," and throw themselves on the royal mercy. They were condemned to death as traitors; and the execution of Lord Nithsdale, with that of others, was appointed to take place upon Tower Hill on Wednesday, the 24th of the month.

While Forster's insurrection lasted Lady Nithsdale remained with her children at Terregles. But on learning her lord's surrender and his imprisonment in London, she resolved at once to join him. Leaving her infant daughter in the charge of her sister-in-law, the Countess of Traquair, and burying the family papers in a nook of the gardens, she set out, attended only by her faithful maid, who had been with her ever since her marriage, a Welshwoman, Cecilia Evans by name. A journey from Scotland in mid-winter was then no such easy task. She made her way on horseback across the Border, and then from Newcastle to York. There she found a place in the coach for herself alone, and was forced to hire a horse for Evans. Nor did her troubles end there, as she writes from Stamford, on Christmas Day, to Lady Traquair—

"The ill weather, ways, and other accidents, has made the coach not get further than Grentum (Grantham); and the snow is so deep it is impossible it should stir without some change of weather; upon which I have again hired horses, and shall go the rest of the journey on horseback to London, though the snow is so deep that our horses yesterday were in several places almost buried in it. . . . . To-morrow I shall set forward again. I must confess such a journey, I believe, was scarce ever made, considering the weather, by a woman. But an earnest desire compasses a great deal with God's help. If I met my dear lord well, and am so happy as to be able to serve him, I shall think all my trouble well repaid."

The writer adds: "I think myself most fortunate in having complied with your kind desire of leaving my little girl with you. Had I her with me, she would have been in her grave by this time, with the excessive cold." It was indeed a season of most unusual rigour. The Thames was fast bound in ice, and many wayfarers throughout England were, it is said, found frozen to death.

The countess reached London in safety, but, on her arrival, was thrown by the hardships of the journey into "a violent sickness," which confined her for some days to her bed. All this time she was anxiously pleading for admittance to her lord in the Tower, which at last, though with some difficulty and under some restrictions, she obtained. As she writes: "Now and then by favour I get a sight of him." There are some hurried notes from her at this period to Lady Traquair. But her proceedings are far more fully to be traced in a letter which some years afterwards she addressed to her sister, Lady Lucy Herbert, the abbess of an English convent at Bruges. It thus commences: "Dear sister, my lord's escape is such an old story now, that I have almost forgot it; but since you desire the account, to whom I have too many obligations to refuse it, I will endeavour to call it to mind, and be as exact in the relation as I can possible." And so the narrative proceeds.

This most interesting letter had remained unknown for many years. It was not till 1792 that it was published by the Society of Antiquaries of Scotland, in the first volume of their "Translations." But it came from a faulty, or, rather we may call it, a *touched-up* copy, putting "the king," for example, where Lady Nithsdale had written "the elector," and often interspersing the phrase "his Majesty," which she would never have applied to George the First. In the same spirit a few trifling inaccuracies of grammar and language are corrected.

Sometimes, also, it might be desired to soften some roughness of tone. Thus, for example, the published letter makes the countess say, in reference to the joint petition which it was intended to lay before the House of Lords, "We were, however, disappointed, for the Duke of St. Albans, who had promised my Lady Derwentwater to present it, failed in his word." But what Lady Nithsdale really wrote was this: "Being disappointed because the Duke of ——, I forget which of the bastard dukes."

In all these cases the motive of the finishing touches seems perfectly clear. But there are some other changes that really seem made only for the love of change. Is the phrase, as Lady Nithsdale wrote, "I took the resolution to endeavour his escape," improved by making it, "I formed the resolution to attempt his escape?" Or, again, when the countess describes how, when at St. James's Palace, she presented the separate petition to George the First, he turned from her while she clung to the skirts of his coat, and in that manner was dragged along the passage on her knees until she fell back fainting, and the petition dropped to the ground in the "struggle"—Lady Nithsdale calls it—then why alter it to "scuffle"?

The original, meanwhile, in Lady Nithsdale's own handwriting, was still preserved at Bruges. It was brought from thence so recently as 1828, as a present from the English nuns, and is now among Lord Herries's papers. As Mr. Fraser informs us, it consists of eleven closely written pages of paper quarto size. At the foot of the last leaf a small piece has been cut out, which is thought to have contained the signature of the writer, and to have been abstracted by some one of the autograph collectors—an evil-minded race, alas! to whom, in many cases, the eighth commandment appears to be quite unknown.

This letter is not dated. The omission might seem to be sufficiently supplied by a copy in the library at

Terregles, which, as Mr. Fraser assures us, is "finely bound in morocco," and which bears the date "Royal Palais de Rome, April 16, 1718." This date is accordingly accepted by Mr. Fraser. We must confess, however, that we see very strong objections to it, which, though derived from Mr. Fraser's volumes, have not, it appears, occurred to Mr. Fraser himself.

In the first place, although Lord Nithsdale was at Rome in April, 1718, Lady Nithsdale certainly was not. This may be shown beyond dispute from the correspondence now before us. In 1717 Lady Nithsdale had gone to a place she calls "Flesh," that is, La Flèche, in Anjou. There she received a visit from her nephew, Lord Linton, eldest son of the Earl of Traquair. We find her writing to her sister-in-law on the 1st of September, 1717: "I hope you have heard something from my nephew L., who came to take his leave of me on Friday last, to begin his journey into Italie, and was to leave Angiers yesterday in order to it." On the 1st of January, 1718, we find her writing again: "My husband was very well the last letter I had from him. . . . . I hope very soon to hear of your son's being happily arrived at his journey's end." And on the 1st of May following: "In one of the 10th of March from my husband, he expected his nephew the next day." On the 22nd of June Lord Linton writes himself from Rome as follows: "I am glad to hear that the good lady I saw at La Flèche is well, though I have not as yet received any letter from her; yet I did not fail to deliver the commission she gave me for her husband." It is quite clear from these extracts that Lady Nithsdale was not in the Eternal City during any part of the period mentioned; and that the date of "Rome, April 16, 1718," assigned to her letter is entirely erroneous.

There is another circumstance which leads us to think that the real date was several years later. Lady Nithsdale mentions in this letter—as we shall presently see—a servant of the name of Mitchell, who followed Lord Nithsdale abroad, and who, she adds, "is now very well placed with our young master." The allusion is, of course, to the exiled royal family. But "the Chevalier de St. George," or, as we used to call him, "the Old Pretender," was in 1718 about thirty years of age. He had no especial claim to this distinguishing epithet as "our young master;" and is constantly mentioned in this correspondence as "our master," without any epithet at all. It is probable, therefore, that the allusion is rather to his son Charles Edward, who was born in December, 1720, and who from his early boyhood appears, according to the custom of princes, to have had a small household assigned him. It may also perhaps be thought that a longer interval would better accord with that failure of recollection on some points, which in her opening sentence Lady Nithsdale mentions.

Passing from this point of chronology, in which we cannot help thinking that the editor might have shown a little more critical care, we have further to complain of a slight injustice that he does to, we admit, not a very great historian. In one of his notes to the first volume, he remarks: "It is certainly necessary here to notice that Smollett was so ignorant of this fact, that, in his 'History of England,' he says that the Earl of Nithsdale made his escape in woman's apparel, furnished or conveyed to him by his own mother." No doubt that Smollett did commit the error here described. But if Mr. Fraser had been more widely conversant with the other writers of that or the next ensuing period, he would have known that such was then the common impression or belief. As the agent in Lord Nithsdale's escape, his wife is not mentioned, but his mother instead, by Boyer, John Wesley, and, above all, Tindall in his valuable "History of England." So far as we can see, it was not till the publication of Lady Nithsdale's own narrative that the true facts of the transaction were established. It seems a little hard, therefore, to single out Smollett for especial blame, when he did no more than repeat the current and accepted story of his time.

Full of interest as is Lady Nithsdale's letter, we do not propose to give any further extracts from it in this place, since it has several times already, though with verbal variations, appeared in print. It may be found, for instance, in the appendix to the second volume of Lord Mahon's "History of England." Moreover, it is a little confused in its arrangement. Thus the delivery of her petition to the king, which should stand first of the events in order of time, stands by retrospect the last in her relation. But we will endeavour, with Mr. Fraser's aid, to deduce from it a narrative of her lord's escape, which shall be more concise and equally clear.

Lord Nithsdale was confined in the house of Colonel D'Oyly, lieutenant deputy of the Tower, in a small room which looked out on Water Lane, the ramparts, and the wharf, and was 60 feet from the ground. The way from the room was through the Council Chamber and the passages and stairs of Colonel D'Oyly's house. The door of his room was guarded by one sentinel, that floor by two, the passages and stairs by several, and the outer gate by two. Escape under such circumstances seemed to be impossible, and, as Lady Nithsdale notes, it was one of her main difficulties, when the moment came, to persuade her lord to acquiesce in an attempt which, as he believed, would end in nothing but ignominious failure.

The countess still placed some reliance on the proceedings that impended in the House of Lords. There, on the 22nd of February, only two days before that fixed for the execution, a petition was presented, praying the House to intercede with the king in favour of the peers under sentence of death. Lady Nithsdale herself stood in the lobby, with many other ladies of rank, imploring the compassion of each peer as he passed. A motion to the same effect as the petition was made in the House, and, notwithstanding the resistance of the Government, it was carried through the unexpected aid of Lord Nottingham, and by a majority of five. But there was added to it a proviso limiting the intercession with the king to such of the condemned lords as should deserve his mercy. The meaning was that those only should be recommended for pardon who would give information against others who had engaged, although less openly, in the same unprosperous cause. This extinguished all Lady Nithsdale's hopes. She well knew, as she says, that her lord would never purchase life on such terms. "Nor," adds the high-minded woman, "would I have desired it."

The axe, as we have seen, was appointed to do its bloody work on the next day but one, and there was no time to lose if Lady Nithsdale sought to carry out the project she had secretly formed of effecting her lord's escape in woman's clothes. No sooner was the debate concluded than she hastened from the House of Peers to the Tower, where, putting on a face of joy, she went up to the guards at each station and told them that she brought good news. "No more fear for the prisoners," she cried, "since now their petition has passed." Nor, in saying this, was she without an object. She rightly judged that the soldiers, believing that the prisoners were on the point of being pardoned, would become, of course, less vigilant. Moreover, at each station she drew some money from her pocket, and gave it to the guards, bidding them drink "the king's health and the peers'." But she was careful, as she says, to be sparing in what she gave; enough to put the guard in good humour, and not enough to raise their suspicions as though their connivance was desired.

All this time she had never acquainted the earl with her design. This plainly appears from a letter which Lord Herries has published, dated on this very day, the 22nd. It is addressed by Lord Nithsdale to his brother-in-law, the Earl of Traquair, and bids an affectionate farewell to him and his sister, speaking of himself as fully expecting and calmly resigned to death.

The next morning, the last before the intended execution, was spent by Lady Nithsdale in the needful preparations, and, above all, in securing the assistance of one Mrs. Morgan, a friend of her faithful Evans. When she was ready to go, she sent for Mrs. Mills, at whose house she was lodging, and said, "Finding now there is no further room for hope of my lord's pardon, nor longer time than this night, I am resolved to endeavour his escape. I have provided all that is requisite for it; and I hope you will not refuse to come along with me to the end that he may pass for you. Nay, more, I must beg you will come immediately, because we are full late." Lady Nithsdale had, with excellent judgment, delayed this appeal to the last possible moment; so that her landlady might be put to an immediate decision on the spur of pity, and have no leisure to think of the danger she was herself incurring by any share in the escape of a man convicted of treason. Mrs. Mills having in this surprise assented, Lady Nithsdale bade Mrs. Morgan, who was tall and slender—her height not unlike Lord Nithsdale's—to put under her own riding-hood another which Lady Nithsdale had provided, and after this all three stepped into the coach, which was ready at the door. As they drove to the Tower, Lady Nithsdale has noted that she never ceased to talk with her two companions, so as to leave them no time to reflect.

On arriving at their destination the countess found that, as usual, she was allowed to take in but one person at a time. She first took Mrs. Morgan, and while they went upstairs spoke, so as to be overheard, of the necessity that, besides the Lords' vote, she should present a separate petition of her own. Within the prisoner's chamber she bade Mrs. Morgan take out and leave the riding-hood that she had brought beneath her clothes, and then conducted her out again, saying as she went, "Pray do me the kindness to send my maid to me that I may be dressed, else I shall be too late with my petition."

Having thus dismissed Mrs. Morgan, the countess next brought in Mrs. Mills. As they passed she bade Mrs. Mills hold her handkerchief to her face, as though in tears, designing that the earl should go forth in the same manner, and thus conceal, in part at least, his face from the guards. When alone with him in his chamber, they proceeded as they best could to disguise him. He had a long beard, which there was not time to shave, but the countess daubed it over with some white paint that she had provided. In like manner she put some red paint on his cheeks and some yellow on his eyebrows, which were black and thick, while Mrs. Mills's were *blonde* and slight; and she had also ready some ringlets of the same coloured hair. Next she made Mrs. Mills take off the riding-hood in which she came and put on instead that which Mrs. Morgan had brought. Finally they proceeded to equip Lord Nithsdale in female attire by the aid of the riding-hood which the guards had just before seen on Mrs.

Mills—by the aid also of all Lady Nithsdale's petticoats but one.

Matters being so far matured, Lady Nithsdale opened the door and led out the real Mrs. Mills, saying aloud, in a tone of great concern, " Dear Mrs. Catherine, I must beg you to go in all haste and look for my woman, for she certainly does not know what o'clock it is, and has forgot the petition I am to give, which should I miss is irreparable, having but this one night; let her make all the haste she can possible, for I shall be upon thorns till she comes."

In the anteroom there were then eight or nine persons, the wives and daughters of the guards; they all seemed to feel for the countess, and quickly made way for her companion. The sentry at the outer door in like manner opened it with alacrity, and thus Mrs. Mills went out. Lady Nithsdale then returning to her lord, put a finishing touch to his disguise, and waited patiently until it was nearly dark, and she was afraid that candles would be brought. This she determined was the best time to go; so she led forth by the hand the pretended Mrs. Mills, who, as though weeping, held up a handkerchief to her eyes, while Lady Nithsdale, with every expression of grief, loudly lamented herself that her maid Evans had been so neglectful, and had ruined her by her long delay. " So, dear Mrs. Betty," she added, " run and bring her with you, for God's sake; you know my lodgings, and if ever you made haste in your life, do it now, for I am almost distracted with this disappointment." The guards, not a little mollified by Lady Nithsdale's gifts the day before, and fully persuaded that a reprieve was at hand, had not taken much heed of the ladies whom they saw pass to and fro, nor exactly reckoned their number. They opened the door, without the least suspicion, to Lady Nithsdale and the false Mrs. Mills, and both accordingly went out. But no sooner past the door than Lady Nithsdale slipped behind her lord on the way downstairs, and made him precede her, lest the guards, on looking back, should observe his gait, as far different from a lady's. All the time that they walked down she continued to call to him aloud in a tone of great distress, entreating him to make all possible haste, for the sake of her petition; and at the foot of the last stairs she found, as agreed, her trusty Evans, into whose hands she put him.

It had further been settled by Lady Nithsdale that Mr. Mills should wait for them in the open space before the Tower. Mr. Mills had come accordingly, but was so thoroughly convinced of the hopeless nature of the enterprise, that, on seeing Mrs. Evans and the false Mrs. Mills approach him, he grew quite dazed, and, in his confusion, instead of helping them, ran home. Evans, however, retained her presence of mind. She took her precious charge, in the first place, to some friends on whom she could rely, and thence proceeding alone to Mr. Mills's house, learnt from him which was the hiding-place he had provided. To this they now conducted the earl. It was a house just before the Court of Guards, and belonged to a poor woman who had but one tiny room, up a small pair of stairs, and containing one poor little bed.

Meanwhile Lady Nithsdale, after seeing her husband pass the gates in his disguise, had returned to the chamber, lately his, upstairs. There, so as to be heard outside, she affected to speak to him, and to answer as if he had spoken to her, imitating his voice as nearly as she could, and walking up and down, as though they had walked and talked together. This she continued to do until she thought he had time to get out of his enemies' reach. "I then began to think," she adds, "it was fit for me to get out of it also." Then opening the door to depart, she went half out, and holding it in her hand so that those without might hear, she took what seemed to be a solemn leave of her lord for that night, complaining again of Evans's delay, and saying there was no remedy but to go herself in search of her. She promised that if the Tower were still open after she had done, she would see him again that night; but that otherwise, as soon as ever it was opened in the morning, she would certainly be with him, and hoped to bring him good news. Before shutting the door she drew to the inside a little string that lifted up a wooden latch, so that it could only be opened by those within, and she then shut the door with a flap, so that it might be securely closed. This being done, she took her departure. As she passed by she told the earl's *valet de chambre*, who knew nothing of the plan of escape, that my lord would not have candles till he called for them, for that he would finish some prayers first.

On leaving the Tower Lady Nithsdale observed several hackney-coaches waiting in the open space, and taking one, she drove first to her own lodgings. There she dismissed the coach for fear of being traced, and went on in a sedan-chair to the house of Anne Duchess of Buccleuch, widow of the ill-fated Monmouth. The duchess had promised to be ready to go with her to present, even almost at the last moment, her single petition; and Lady Nithsdale now left a message at her door, with her "most humble service," to say that her Grace need not give herself any further trouble, it being now thought fit to give a general petition in the name of all.

From the Duchess of Buccleuch's Lady Nithsdale, again changing her conveyance, and calling a second sedan-chair, went on to the Duchess of Montrose's. The duke was on the Government side, but the duchess was her personal friend. Lady Nithsdale, being shown into a room upstairs, the duchess hastened to join her. Then, as Lady Nithsdale writes, "as my heart was very light, I smiled when she came into the chamber and ran to her in great joy. She really started when she saw me, and since owned that she thought my head was turned with trouble, till I told her my good fortune."

The duchess, on hearing what had passed, cordially took part in the joy of her friend, and declared that she would go at once to Court and see how the news of the escape was received. She went accordingly, and next time she saw Lady Nithsdale told her that "the elector"—for so she termed him—had, in her own phrase, "stormed terribly," and said he was betrayed, for he was sure it could not have been done without some connivance; and he sent immediately two of his suite to the Tower to see that the other prisoners were well guarded. On the opposite side it was related that his Majesty—perhaps at a later and calmer moment—made a far more good-natured remark. He is rumoured to have said on Lord Nithsdale's escape, "It was the best thing that a man in his situation could do." Indeed, according to one account, Lord Nithsdale's name was included in a list to be sent out that very evening of the peers to be reprieved. In fact, only two—Lords Derwentwater and Kenmure—were executed the next day.

Lady Nithsdale paid no more visits that evening. From the duchess's house she went straight to her husband's hiding-place. There, in that single narrow room upstairs, they remained closely shut up, making as little stir as possible, and relying for their sustenance on some bread and wine which Mrs. Mills brought them in her pocket. Thus they continued for some days, until there arose a favourable opportunity for Lord Nithsdale to leave the kingdom. A servant of the Venetian ambassador, Mitchell by name, was ordered to go down to Dover in his Excellency's coach-and-six, and bring back his Excellency's brother. By the contrivance of Mitchell, and without the ambassador's knowledge, the earl slipped on a livery coat and travelled as one in the ambassador's train to Dover, where, hiring a small vessel, he crossed without suspicion, and, taking Mitchell with him, landed safe at Calais. Lady Nithsdale, for whom no search was made, remained for the time in London.

In concluding the narrative of this remarkable escape, we think that even the most cursory reader cannot fail to notice its close resemblance to that other escape of Count Lavalette from the *Conciergerie* prison at Paris on the evening of the 20th December, 1815. The countess having changed dresses with her husband in his prison chamber, he passed out in woman's attire, leaning on his daughter's arm and holding a handkerchief to his face, as though in an agony of tears. Yet, great as is the likeness between the two cases, it arose from coincidence, and not at all from imitation. The detailed account of the whole affair, as given by Count Lavalette in the second volume of his "Memoirs," clearly shows that they had never heard of Lady Nithsdale, and knew nothing of any similar attempt in England.

The heroine of this later deliverance was a niece of the Empress Josephine; her maiden name Emilie de Beauharnais. Her letters since her marriage, several of which we have seen, are signed Beauharnais-Lavalette. She had been in childbirth only a few weeks before the 20th of December, her nerves were still unstrung, and her strength was not yet restored. There was also a great difficulty in the way of the disguise which she had planned; she was tall and slender in person, while Count Lavalette was short and stout. But muffled up as he was, the difference passed unperceived by the officers on duty, and his escape from the prison was successfully accomplished.

It is well known, and we need not repeat, how the generous spirit of Sir Robert Wilson, with two others

P

of our countrymen, effected a few days afterwards his further escape from France to Belgium. The husband was safe, but hard—hard indeed—was the fate of the wife. She had to remain behind in the prison chamber, there to sustain, on the discovery of the escape, the first fury of the exasperated jailers, all trembling for their places. During six weeks she was kept in close captivity, all access of friends or domestics, or even of her daughter, denied her. Weak in health as she had been from the first, it is no wonder that her mind would not bear the strain that was put upon it. Her reason became obscured, and soon after she was set free from prison she had to be removed to a *Maison de Santé*. When, after six years of exile, her husband obtained his pardon and was able to return to France, she did not know him again.

The mental malady of Madame Lavalette hung upon her for full twelve years. At the end of that time her reason was, partially at least, restored, and she could go back to her husband's house. But she continued subject to a settled melancholy, and could only lead a life of strict retirement. Her husband died in 1830, while she survived till June, 1855.

Reverting to Lady Nithsdale, we may observe that while the publication of her narrative in 1792 made clear all the circumstances of her lord's escape, nothing further was known of his or her further fortunes beyond the dates of their respective deaths in Italy. It is therefore with pleasure that, in the correspondence now before us, we find numerous letters from the countess subsequent to the great act and exploit of her life on the 23rd of February, 1716. To these letters, as well as to some others by which they are illustrated, we shall now apply ourselves, hoping that our readers may feel some part at least of the interest that we do in the life of this high-minded lady.

Lord Nithsdale, on landing at Calais, had gone straight to Paris. There, in the course of the spring, he received a pressing invitation from the prince, whom he constantly regarded as his rightful king. One phrase of that letter is cited by his nephew, Lord Linton: "As long as I have a crust of bread in the world, assure yourself you shall always have a share of it." The earl accordingly set out for Italy, there to do homage, and remain for at least a few weeks' visit. The countess, on her part, finding no pursuit made for her in London, ventured, a little later, to ride back to Scotland with her faithful Evans, desiring to arrange her family affairs. For several weeks she lived without molestation, and took a fond—it proved to be a final—farewell of her own Terregles. When again in London she was advised that she was in great risk of arrest, and would do wisely to leave England. Embarking accordingly, she landed on the coast of Flanders, where she was detained some time by a miscarriage and dangerous illness. Only half-recovered, she set out again to join, first her sister at Bruges, and next, in October, her husband at Lille. Alas! that reunion did not bring her all the happiness that she had fondly hoped. Her letter from Lille to Lady Traquair has not been preserved, but a later one from

Paris gives a full account of her proceedings and plans: it is dated February 29, 1717.

"I could not resolve to leave this place, dearest sister, without giving you an account of the situation of your brother's affairs and mine. I suppose you have received mine from Lille, so you are acquainted with the reasons of our quitting that place, and consequently have only to tell you that I immediately went to my old mistress [Mary of Modena, Queen Dowager of England], who, though she received me very kindly, yet there was great complaints of poverty, and no likelihood of my getting into her service again. My first attempt was to endeavour to get a recommendation from her to her son to take my husband into his service; but all in vain, it being alleged that as matters now stand with him, he could not augment his family. . . . . My next business was to see what I could get to live on, that we might take our resolutions where to go accordingly. But all that I could get was 100 livres a month to maintain me in everything—meat, drink, fire, candle, washing, clothes, lodging, servants' wages; in fine, all manner of necessaries. My husband has 200 livres a month, but considering his way of managing, it was impossible to live upon it. . . . . For, let me do what I will, he cannot be brought to submit to live according to what he has; and when I endeavoured to persuade him to keep in compass, he attributed my advice to my grudging him everything, which stopped my mouth, since I am very sure that I would not [grudge] my heart's blood if it could do him any service. . . . . It was neither in gaming, company, nor much drinking, that it was spent, but in having the nicest of meat and wine; and all the service I could do was to see he was not cheated in the buying it. I had a little, after our meeting at Lille, endeavoured to persuade him to go back to his master, upon the notice he received that 50 livres a month was taken off of his pension; but that I did not dare persist in, for he seemed to imagine that I had a mind to be rid of him, which one would have thought could scarce come into his mind.

"And now, he finding, what I had often warned him, that we could get no more, some of his friends has persuaded him to follow his master, he having sent him notice where he was going, and that he might come after him if he pleased; and I, having no hopes of getting anything out of England, am forced to go to the place where my son is, to endeavour to live, the child and me, upon what I told you. All my satisfaction is, that at least my husband has twice as much to maintain himself and man as I have; so I hope when he sees there is no resource, as, indeed, now there is not, having sold all, even to the necessary little plate I took so much pains to bring over, he will live accordingly, which will be some comfort to me, though I have the mortification to be from him, which, after we met again, I hoped never to have separated; but God's will be done, and I submit to this cross, as well as many others I have had in the world, though I must confess living from a husband I love so well is a very great one. . . . . He was to be at Lions last Tuesday, and I cannot hear from him till I am arrived at La Flesh, for I go from hence to-morrow morning at seven o'clock. . . . Pray burn this as soon as you have read it, and keep the contents to yourself."

Lady Nithsdale, it will be noticed, speaks of having no hopes of anything from England. Her meaning here is best elucidated by the following passage from her long letter to Lady Lucy Herbert, which refers to the scene at Court, when she was dragged along the passage by the skirts of George the First:—

"My being so rudely treated had made a noise, and

gave no good reputation to the Duke of Hanover; for several said, what had they brought themselves to? For the kings of England was never used to refuse a petition from the poorest woman's hand; and to use a person of my quality in such a manner as he had done was a piece of unheard-of brutality. These talks made the elector have a particular dislike to me, which he showed afterwards; for when all the ladies whose lords had been concerned in this business put in claims for their jointures, mine was given in amongst the rest; but he said I was not, nor did deserve, the same privilege, so I was excepted, and he would never hear speak in my favour."

We give the passage as Lady Nithsdale wrote it, not desiring to emulate, even at a humble distance, the very great politeness of the Scottish Society of Antiquaries. But we may observe that these words of the countess, like many others from her pen, are most strongly coloured by political resentment. Ungenerous as was, beyond all doubt, the exception made of Lady Nithsdale in the matter of the peeresses' jointures, there is no ground to regard it otherwise than as a ministerial measure—not a tittle of evidence to derive it personally from the king. We may add that, judging from the records of this reign, we do not believe that George the First, whatever may have been his other failings, was capable of the petty spite which is here imputed to him.

In her letter from Paris Lady Nithsdale mentions that she was going to La Flèche, on purpose to be with her son, who, we may conclude, was receiving his education at the great Jesuit College there established. From La Flèche she continued her correspondence with Lady Traquair; and, for fear of its being intercepted, commonly signed herself "W. Joanes," or sometimes "W. Johnstone," while she addressed her sister countess as "Mrs. Young."

Writing on the 10th of June, 1717, after reverting to the recovery from an illness of her nephew Lord Linton, then in France, she gives the last news of her husband :—

"Now that I have given you an account of what is nearest to you, I must let you know that your friend and mine is well, at least was so the last time I was so happy as to hear from him. He has had another great preservation, being six days in so great a danger at sea that all the seamen left off working, and left themselves to the mercy of the waves; and was at last cast into Antibes, from whence they coasted it to Lighorn. However, he is now safe with his master, and both of them in good health. I hope these two narrow escapes in so short a time is not for nothing, and that God reserves him for some great good."

Lord Nithsdale, however, was not well pleased with Italy. He did not receive from the Chevalier the cordial welcome to which, with good reason, he deemed himself entitled; and was exposed to divers mortifications at that melancholy little court, then established at Urbino. Nor was he at all edified by his nearer view of the Pope's government in ecclesiastical or in civil affairs. Here are his own words to Lady Nithsdale as she transcribes them: "Be assured there is nothing in this damnable country that can tend to the good either of one's soul or body."

We must say that we give Lord Herries great credit for his candour in allowing the passage to be printed without change or comment, since we dare say that no very zealous Roman Catholic could read it without something of an *Abi Satanas!* feeling.

Lady Nithsdale herself may have disliked still more what follows, as she reports it to Lady Traquair:—

"The remainder of his letter did not much please me, it running all upon the inconveniences of living where he was, and a full and fixed resolution of leaving his master. . . . . However, as I sent him word, I hope God Almighty reserved his reward for a better place, and that after the favour he had received in his two late preservations, he ought also to accept the trials from the same hand, with some other little motives for the doing it, whose reflections I hoped might render it more easy as well as meritorious. But he answered it in so great a banter upon my virtue and resignation, that I believe that it will be the last time that I shall venture to inspire him with any such thoughts, not doubting that he makes better use of them than I do. But it proceeded from my good will alone. However, in what regards his temporal good, I shall not be so far wanting in my duty as not to tell him my thoughts, with a reference to his better judgment; after which I have performed my part, and shall submit, as I ever have done, to what he thinks fit."

Lady Nithsdale therefore, in her next ensuing letter, takes her stand on temporal grounds:—

"You may be sure, my dear lord, that having you with me, or near me, would be the greatest natural satisfaction I could have in this world; but I should be a very ill wife if, to procure it myself, I would let you run into those inconveniences you would do if you followed the method you propose of leaving your master. . . . . So, if you have any regard for your honour and family, leave off any such thoughts; for from that time your master will have a pretence to do nothing for you, whereas if ever he comes to be in a condition [and with you near him] he cannot avoid it. . . . . But what would go nearer my heart, if it were possible, chameleon-like, to live on air, is that it would ruin your reputation; and that all your enemies, or rather enviers, who think others pretentions a diminution of theirs, might make it their business to say that it was not desire of serving your master that made you do what you did, but because you could not live at home on what you had."

Writing from Scotland, Lady Traquair argued strongly in the same sense as Lady Nithsdale, and the earl yielded in some degree to their joint representations. It induced him at least to pause and think again before the final step was taken. Besides, there was now a stronger rumour of the Chevalier's intended marriage, which would afford an opening for good places in the new and larger household to be formed.

Meanwhile Lady Nithsdale was enduring some of the sharpest privations of poverty. But for a little timely aid from the kind-hearted Lady Traquair she would have wanted all through the winter both warmth and light. Thus she writes in reply :—

"May God Almighty reward you in this and the next world for your goodness to us and ours! . . . . My nephew paid me the sum you ordered, and never thing came more providentially, for I had tugged on in summer with much ado; but did not know in the world what to do for the addition of wood and candle, which it will enable me to get. But I fear I must soon think of repaying it again, since I took it up from a gentleman, who took my bill for it on the goldsmith you bid me take it from. . . . . Had I not had so pressing a need of it, I would not have taken it, your son having lent your brother 200 livres."

Another calamity was now close impending on this ill-fated lady. On the 7th of May, 1718, died at St. Germains her former mistress and her constant friend, the Queen Dowager of England. It was a grievous blow to the whole melancholy train of exiles. Father James Carnegy, a Roman Catholic priest, writes thus from Paris:—

"The desolation amongst the followers of her son, her servants, and other poor dependants, amongst whom she used to divide all her pension, is inexpressible. It is said the regent will assist the most indigent of them; but nothing is yet certain. It is feared, whatever he do to others, he dare not help the king's followers."

Lady Nithsdale herself writes as follows from Paris on the 28th of June, and still to Lady Traquair:—

"My husband is now fully resolved not to leave his master; for when he went to take his leave of him, his master was pleased to tell him that he had so few about him, that he would not part with him; that he should probably be married before winter, and then he desired to have me in his family, and so desired him to leave off the thoughts of a journey for two or three months, which you may be sure he agreed to."

Full of these hopes, Lord Nithsdale desired that the countess should join him in Italy as soon as possible, since as he observes in these matters it is "first come, first served." He could send her no funds for the journey, but bade her apply to Lord and Lady Traquair, which Lady Nithsdale, mindful of their many obligations, was most unwilling to do. However, in the same letter of the 28th of June, she proceeds to say:—

"Though he bid me lose no time in writing to you about borrowing money, I would not do it, because, though he did not know it, my dear mistress, who was, underhand, the occasion of furthering my promotion, and who, though it must never be known, was resolved I should be about her daughter-in-law, had promised me to give me notice when it was fit for me to go, and would have given me what was requisite to carry me; and writ to me four days before her illness what she would have me write to her son in order to it, which I did the first post, and sent it inclosed in a letter to her. But, alas, it arrived the day she died, some hours after her death. Imagine you, whether her loss is not a great one to me. I may truly say I have lost a kind mother, for she was truly that to me whilst I had her. I would not write to you, being sensible that you have already done a great deal; so that nothing but unavoidable necessity could make me mention any such thing. But, alas, I am so far from being able to comply with my husband's desire now, that I know not how scarce to keep myself from starving, with the small credit I have here, being reduced to the greatest of straits."

The kindness of Lord and Lady Traquair, as shown on many former occasions, was not denied her on this. A small sum in addition was paid her by order of the Chevalier. There was also as it chanced one of her sisters then at Paris—Lady Anne Herbert by birth, and married to Francis Smith, Lord Carrington—"a person," writes Lady Nithsdale, "that no one would have thought should have helped me in this juncture. But so far from it that I have not got a sixpence, but a promise to keep my little girl who stays with her. But I oblige myself to pay what masters she has, without which she would have lost all the learning I have done my endeavours to give her, notwithstanding all my strait."

By the aid of the Traquair subsidy and that from her so-called royal "master," Lady Nithsdale was enabled to join her husband at Urbino, and, after a brief interval, proceed with him in the Chevalier's train to Rome. From Rome there soon went forth another melancholy letter to Lady Traquair:—

"*January* 3, 1719.—Dearest sister, I have still deferred writing to you since I came to this place, hoping to have some agreeable news to make a letter welcome that had so far to go; but we still are in the same situation, and live upon hopes; and, indeed, without hope, hearts would break; but I can say no more. . . . . I found him [my lord] still the same man as to spending, not being able to conform himself to what he has, which really troubles me. And to the end that he might not make me the pretence, which he ever did, I do not touch a penny of what he has, but leave it to him to maintain him and his man, which is all he has, and live upon what is allowed me. . . . . Now as to other things: the great expectations I had some reason to have conceived from my husband's letters when he sent for me hither, are far from answered. I am kept at as great a distance from my master as can well be, and as much industry used to let me have none of his ear as they can; and though he is going to a house that his family can scarce fill, I could not obtain to be admitted under his roof. But that and many other things must be looked over; at least we shall have bread by being near him, and I have the happiness once again to be with my dear husband that I love above my life."

The real fact, as explaining the cold reception of Lord and Lady Nithsdale, appears to be that the Chevalier was at this time greatly under the dominion of two unworthy favourites—Colonel the Hon. John Hay, a son of Lord Kinnoul, and his wife Marjory, a daughter of Lord Stormont. Some years later James named John Hay his Secretary of State, with high rank in his titular peerage as Earl of Inverness. Both the wife and husband are described as follows in Lockhart of Carnwath's "Memoirs": "The lady was a mere coquette, tolerably handsome, but withal prodigiously vain and arrogant. Her lord was a cunning, false, avaricious creature of very ordinary parts, cultivated by no sort of literature, and altogether void of experience in business." It was now the object of this well-matched pair to confirm and maintain their influence by keeping away as much as possible all persons who would not declare themselves their followers and their dependants.

Within a few weeks, however, of Lord and Lady Nithsdale's arrival at Rome, James himself was suddenly called away from it. He was summoned to Spain, there to sanction and direct the expedition against Great Britain, which the Prime Minister Cardinal Alberoni had been preparing. It is well known how soon and how signally that project was baffled by the winds and tempests, and with how much of disappointment the Chevalier had to return to Italy.

In this journey to Spain James appears to have been attended by Lord Nithsdale, while the countess remained at Rome. There she witnessed the arrival of James's bride, the Princess Clementina Sobieski, whom she describes (May 17, 1719) as follows:—

"This, dearest sister, is barely to acquaint you that yesterday night arrived here our young mistress. I and my companion went out a post to meet her, and, indeed, she is one of the charmingest, obliging, and well-bred young ladies that ever was seen. Our master cannot but be extremely happy in her, and all those who has the good fortune to have any dependence on her. To add to it, she is very pretty; has good eyes, a fine skin, well-shaped for her height; but is not tall, but may be so as yet, for she is but seventeen, and looks even younger. She has chosen a retired place in the town in our master's absence."

It had been hoped by Lord and Lady Nithsdale that on the return of James to Italy there would be expressed to them some disapproval of the mortifications to which they had almost daily been exposed. But it did not prove so. Lady Nithsdale writes, October 10, 1719:—

"The first of August our young mistress went to meet her husband, who could not come hither by reason of the great heats, in which time it is thought dangerous to come into this town; so she went to a small place six or seven posts from hence, a very good air, but so small a place that she took but one person with her, which was Mrs. Hay. The straitness of the place was the reason given for my companion's and my stay behind; but there is some reason to believe that our master did not care for to have more about him than what he has there. He has not permitted anybody to go to him but those he sends for, which has been but few persons, and such only as those who addressed themselves to Mrs. Hay's brother or husband. . . . As before mentioned, our master and mistress comes hither, and are, probably speaking, to stay this winter, though the master of this town [the Pope] does not much approve of it. Where we shall go after God knows. His company he used to have about him is much diminished; many are gone, and more is a-going daily. My companion is a-going to her husband, and I fear neither he nor she intend to return; so that I am the only one now left of my station, and shall in all appearance be yet more trampled on than were both in our master's absence. At his return we hoped for some redress, but now we have reason to believe we are to expect none, for everything is approved that was done in his absence, which has made many one withdraw; and I wish that may be the greatest ill that follows from the retirement of some. My husband would fain have been of the number, and have had me, but I told him my pleasure did not draw me hither, nor the slights and troubles I daily meet should make me go, but be overlooked by me for the same end that brought me, which was the good of my children and family; so I intend to act as if I saw nothing but what pleased me, and expect God Almighty's time for an alteration."

In this same letter Lady Nithsdale laments to her sister-in-law her husband's want of forethought and consideration in borrowing, or, as she calls it, "taking up" money where he finds it practicable, and, above all, in drawing bills on Lord or Lady Traquair without their consent and approval first obtained. She grieves at this money being "all taken up and spent already, which," she adds, "is but too true; so that if his master does not pay it, as I very much fear he will not, his reputation is quite lost. . . . . All my comfort is that I have no share in this misfortune, for he has never been the man that has offered me one farthing of all the money he has taken up, and as yet all is spent, but how, is a riddle to me, for what he spends at home is but 30 pence a day in his eating. He has had but one suit of clothes since, and now he must have one for winter. For my part I continue in mourning as yet for want of wherewithal to buy clothes, and I brought my mourning with me that has served ever since I came, and was neither with my master's or husband's money bought. But now I have nobody to address myself to but my master for wherewithal to buy any.

"I know, between you and I, but that I need not tell my master, that he [my lord] blames me and his daughter for what he is obliged to take up; whereas I have not had one single penny, and as for our daughter, whose masters I must pay, or she forget all the little I have been at the expense of before, and have done it hitherto, I have neither paid out of his nor my own pension, which is too small to do it, but that I had 30 pistoles from the Pope for her, which had done it. But now they are at an end, and I know not what to do. For as to my sister I suppose she will not see her starve or go naked, but for more I cannot rely on."

Thus wearily and heavily the months dragged along at Rome. In March, 1720, however, there came a gleam of joy when Lady Nithsdale found herself able to announce that the princess gave hopes of an heir. Even this brief gleam was clouded over by signal mortifications. James would allow at this juncture no intimate access of any lady to his consort, except only Mrs. Hay—

"who is one as you know," Lady Nithsdale writes, " that has never had any children; . . . and though I have had occasion to be better versed in these things, having been so long married and had so many children, yet they prefer one who has had no experience of that kind, and my mistress has not so much as ever let me know how she was in any kind. And when she was indisposed, which she has been frequently since her being with child was spoken of, and that I was there constantly three times a day to see how she did, I never was thought fit to be admitted into the secret, but it was told me by herself and others that it was nothing but a cold, though I knew in what condition she was."

In spite of these unpromising signs, Lady Nithsdale ventured at this juncture, " humbly begging," to know whether she " might have any hopes of having care of the young lord or lady when it pleased God to send it." She was not precisely refused—that is, there was no other person preferred. But the chevalier answered that, " having taken a resolution to take no servants while I am abroad, I will make neither governess nor under-governess. My wife has but little to do, and will look to it herself."

Great was the delight of the whole mournful company of exiles when, on the last day of the year, the princess gave birth to a son, Charles Edward, the hero of " The Forty-five." Henceforth the letters of Lady Nithsdale teem with accounts of his teething and weaning, and other incidents of childhood. Scarcely less were they rejoiced when, four years afterwards, there came a second son, Henry, afterwards Cardinal York.

But during this time the circumstances of the Nithsdales by no means improved. They were constantly reduced to dismal straits. Thus, on the occasion of Prince Charles's birth, when some gala dresses were required, Lady Nithsdale writes:—

"I have had the happiness to have one handsome suit procured me by means of a Cardinal, who got it from the Pope, but that is between you and I, for I was forbid to let it be known. I have bought two others, the one as good as that, the other more for bad weather, being obliged to walk on foot to my master's several times in the day, so that I am much out of pocket, but shall in time get free, I hope, without taking a farthing from my husband for it. The reason why I thought myself obliged to provide myself so well, was that my master might not think that because I was disappointed of what I had some reason to expect I did not care how I went; and also that if I had not he might have taken the pretence that he was ashamed I should be seen with his wife because I had not decent clothes."

Still more grievous was it, for Lady Nithsdale at least, when dire necessity compelled them to draw bills on Lord Traquair, and trust to his generosity for their acceptance. In 1722 there went out a bill of a larger amount than usual, namely 150*l.*, and for this Lord Nithsdale desired that his sister should sell a little household furniture which his wife had left in her care, and apply the proceeds in its discharge.

"But," as Lady Nithsdale writes, "it will not answer our end if the money be not paid twenty days after the receipt of the bill; so I beg you by all that is dear to you to have compassion of us; for if this fails, if we were starving nobody would let us have a sixpence. We have pawned all our credit to hinder our being molested till this can be answered, and have had no small difficulty in getting it done, and are quite out of the power of doing it longer."

Lord Nithsdale, on his part, adds, in another letter, 'this, if not answered, will infallibly ruin me."

Neither in this instance, nor in any other, so far as we are made aware of it, did Lord Traquair fail in the expected aid. But it must be owned that Lord Nithsdale made him a strange return. This was in 1723. Either to enhance his own importance, or for some other object, he intimated to the Chevalier that some property, belonging of right to himself, was unfairly detained by his brother-in-law. Hereupon James, desiring to do an act of justice at the same time with an act of kindness, wrote as follows to one of his agents in Scotland :—

"The Earl of Nidsdale tells me he has private means of his own in the Earl of Traquair's hands, from whom he has never yet got any account of them; and as you know the just regard I have, particularly for the first, I would have you get Mr. Carnegy to take a proper method of letting Traquair know that I should take it kindly if he would settle these affairs with his kinsman here to his satisfaction, which I am persuaded he will do when he knows it will be agreeable to me."

Even the most placable of men must here have been roused to resentment. Here, in complete reversal of the real facts, was Lord Traquair, a steady adherent of the exiled prince, held up to that prince, whose good opinion he was of course anxious to secure, as the spoiler of that kinsman whom he had so constantly befriended. No wonder if we find Lady Traquair writing to her brother as follows (January, 1724):—

"It is but within these few days that my husband was in a condition that he could know the contents of your letter, or what Sir John [the king] writ of your affairs. I do not pretend to write to you what his sentiments were upon knowing this most unexpected and unaccountable piece of news. He was not a little grieved that matters had been so misrepresented as if he had effects of yours in his hands, and were so unjust to so near a relation as not to transmit your own to you, though you be straitened and suffer in such a cause. This is indeed, dear brother, a very strange office from you to my husband, after so many services done by him to you and your family. I must say it is very unkind and a sad return for all the favours my husband has done you before and since you went last abroad; for he having no effects of yours save a little household furniture of no use to us and what I could not get disposed of, has honoured your bills, supplied your wants without scrape of pen from you; besides the considerable sum you owed him formerly, he even under God has preserved your family which without his money credit, and his son's assiduous attendance and application, must, humanly speaking, have sunk. He might reasonably have expected other returns from you than complaints to one we value so infinitely as we do Sir John, as if my husband had wronged you and detained your own when your sufferings justly call for the greatest consideration."

This affair, however little to the credit of Lord Nithsdale, produced no breach between the sisters:

'I having been always kept ignorant of his affairs," writes Lady Nithsdale, in a previous letter (March 22, 1723). And subsequently (March 7, 1725), adverting to this very incident, she says to Lady Traquair:—

"As to what you imagined to be the reason of my not writing you wronged me very much in the matter, for what happens between your brother and you yourselves are best able to judge. I am only sorry that he should do anything that gives you reason to take ill, and if it lay in my power I am sure he would not. As for my part I am so sensible of all your kindnesses and favours to my son and family, that I never think I can sufficiently acknowledge them, or return you my grateful thanks."

But although there might be no absolute breach of friendship, there was certainly a decline of correspondence. From this period the letters, as we find them, of Lady Nithsdale to her sister-in-law are few and far between. The latest of all, after six years' interval, bears date January 29, 1739, and in this she excuses herself that "my great troubles, and illnesses occasioned by them, has hindered me from writing hitherto."

In this period of years, however, there had been several events to cheer her. Lord Maxwell, her sole surviving son, after much litigation in the Court of Session and the House of Lords, was admitted by the latter tribunal to the benefit of an early entail which Lord Nithsdale had made, so that at his father's death he would, notwithstanding his father's forfeiture, succeed to Terregles and the family estates. Practically he succeeded to them—in part, at least—even sooner, since the life-interest of his father was purchased from the Government in his behalf.

Pass we to the daughter, Lady Anne, who had come to join her parents in Italy. There she chanced to meet Lord Bellew, an Irish nobleman upon his travels. He conceived for her a strong attachment, apparently on but slight acquaintance. As he writes himself to Lord Nithsdale (April 27, 1731):—

"I propose to be entirely happy in the possession of the lady, who has so fine a character with all those that know her. But it is not only hearsay on which I ground my happiness, having had the honour and pleasure to see Lady Anne, though, perchance, not the good fortune to be remembered by her."

The offer of his hand, which this letter conveyed, was by the young lady accepted, and the marriage took place at Lucca in the course of the same year.

Another marriage, at nearly the same period, must have been still more interesting to Lord and Lady Nithsdale. Lord Maxwell, now a resident in Scotland, had become attached to his cousin Lady Catherine Stuart, daughter of Lord and Lady Traquair. Considering the old connection, and the constant friendship between the two families, and their agreement both in religion and in politics, to say nothing of the benefits conferred by the one earl upon the other, it might have been supposed that the prospect of this alliance would have given Lord Nithsdale especial pleasure. But such was by no means the case. We may perceive the contrary from the following sentence of Lady Nithsdale, writing to Lady Traquair (October 2, 1731): "Dear sister, I have this considerable while been expecting every post the good news of the conclusion of my son's happy marriage with Lady Catherine; a happiness he has long coveted, and I as long been endeavouring to procure him his father's consent to." The marriage, however, did take place in the course of the same year. It appears to have been a happy one, as Lady Nithsdale, by anticipation, called it. No sons were born from it, and only one daughter, through whom the line of Maxwell was continued.

Lord Nithsdale did not live to witness the last enterprise on behalf of the exiled Stuarts. He died at Rome in March, 1744. After his decease his widow was induced, though not without difficulty, to accept an annuity of 200*l.* from her son, who then came into full possession of the family estates. Of this annuity she resolved to apply one-half to the discharge of her husband's debts, which would in that manner be paid off at the end of three years.

Lady Nithsdale herself survived till the spring of 1749. Nothing further is known of her declining years. We conjecture, however, that she had grown very infirm, since her signature, of which some specimens are given at this period, is tremulous and indistinct to a most uncommon degree.

Both Lord and Lady Nithsdale died at Rome, and, in all probability, were buried there. When the late Mr. Marmaduke Maxwell, of Terregles, came to that city in the year 1870—so the editor of these volumes informs us—he made inquiries for any monument or grave of these two ancestors; but, after much research, was unable to find the least trace of any such.

Here then ends our narrative of the life of Winifred Herbert, as she was by birth, the worthy descendant of that first Earl of Pembroke of the last creation, the chief of the English forces at the battle of St. Quentin and the Lord President of Wales. In her was nobly sustained the spirit of that ancient race. Nor in our own century has that spirit declined. When we look to what they have done, or may probably yet do, in the present age—to the past of Sidney Herbert—to the future of Lord Carnarvon—to the future also perhaps of that son of Sidney Herbert, who, young as he is, has already wielded his pen with considerable power, though not always quite discreetly, and who has been so recently named Under-Secretary of State in that very War Department where his father gained and deserved such high distinction—we cannot but feel how much of sap and growth is left in the ancestral stem, and how aptly it might take for its motto REVIRESCIT.

VII.
THE STATUE OF MEMNON.

THE STATUE OF MEMNON.*

THEBES in Egypt—who has not heard of its wonders? Who has not longed to behold them? That city of the hundred gates, as Homer calls it, has indeed long since passed away; but even now some of its massy monuments and vast sepulchral chambers bear witness to its ancient grandeur. Above all, those twin statues of colossal size—"the Pair," for so our countrymen have named them—continue to look down on the valley of the Nile, and more than any other monuments arrest the stranger's eye. "There they sat"—so writes Miss Harriet Martineau, describing her first sight of them—"together yet apart, in the midst of the plain, serene and vigilant, still keeping their untired watch over the lapse of ages and the eclipse of Egypt. I can never believe that anything else so majestic as this Pair has been conceived of by the imagination of Art.

---

* 1. *L'Empire Romain en Orient.* Par Gaston Boissier. Publié dans la *Revue des Deux Mondes,* Juillet, 1874.
2. *La Statue Vocale de Memnon, considérée dans ses rapports avec l'Egypte et la Grèce.* Par Jean Antoine Letronne. Paris, 1833.

Nothing even in nature certainly ever affected me so unspeakably; no thunderstorm in my childhood, nor any aspect of Niagara, or the great lakes of America, or the Alps or the Desert, in my later years."

Such were Miss Martineau's words of wonder derived only from a transient glance in her up-stream voyage. But on her return, when she passed many days at Thebes, she found her first admiration very far from enfeebled, and she has expressed it with her wonted vividness of style: "The Pair sitting alone amidst the expanse of verdure, with islands of ruin behind them, grew more striking to us every day. To-day, for the first time, we looked up at them from their base. The impression of sublime tranquillity which they convey, when seen from distant points, is confirmed by a nearer approach. There they sit, keeping watch—hands on knees, gazing straight forward, seeming, though so much of the faces is gone, to be looking over to the monumental piles on the other side of the river, which became gorgeous temples after these throne-seats were placed here—the most immovable thrones that have ever been established on this earth!"

These gigantic statues, as Sir Gardner Wilkinson has measured or computed, are forty-seven feet in height; that is, above the present soil, for they extend to seven feet more below it. They appear like islands during the yearly inundations of the Nile which cover the plain around them. Each was at first of a single block, although the one to which we shall presently and more in detail advert has been repaired in five blocks, from the middle upwards. Those five blocks came from a neighbouring quarry; but each original monolith was of a stone not known within several days' journey of the place, so that the means adopted for their transport are not easy to imagine or explain. What countless multitudes must have been required to move these stupendous masses!

Our readers, we are sure, need not be reminded how since the commencement of the present century the patient industry of some eminent men has poured a flood of light upon Ancient Egypt. Not only have its pyramids and sepulchral chambers been explored, but its hieroglyphics deciphered and its inscriptions read. By these means—that is, by the tablets at the back of the Colossi—we learn that both represent King Amunoph the Third, who began his reign about 1400 years before the Christian Era. They were designed as the entrance to an avenue leading to the temple-palace of Amunoph, about 1100 feet farther inland. This palace-temple, once so richly adorned with its sculpture, sphinxes, and columns, is now a mere heap of sandstone—"a little roughness in the plain," says Miss Martineau, "when seen from the heights behind."

Many centuries later, when Greeks began to settle in Egypt, they found that the easternmost statue of the Pair had been shattered down to the waist. According to one report, this mutilation was due to the capricious fury of Cambyses, as conqueror of Egypt. We regard it, however, as highly improbable that if Cambyses had been swayed by such an impulse, he would have been satisfied with the demolition, and that only partial, of only one of the statues. It is far more likely that, as Strabo, the geographer, was assured, an earthquake was the cause of the disaster. To the half-statue, which then remained, the Greeks gave the name of Memnon. They believed it—notwithstanding the strong asseverations of the natives, who rightly alleged Amunoph—to represent the fabled son of Tithonus and Aurora, the valiant prince extolled by Homer, who brought a host of Ethiopians to the aid of Priam.

But ere long a rumour rose that this was no ordinary statue. As ear-witnesses affirmed, it would sometimes, in the first hour after sunrise, send forth a musical voice. The sound, they said, was like that when a harp-string breaks. "What more natural," exclaimed the Greeks, "than that the son of Aurora should hail in tuneful tones the advent of his mother!" Even those philosophers who might not admit the argument could not deny the fact. Men and women of rank came from distant lands "to hear Memnon," as was then the phrase; and we find the Vocal Statue celebrated all through the classic times. Thus when Juvenal, in his fifteenth Satire, is describing Egypt, he speaks of it as the country—

"Dimidio magicæ resonant ubi Memnone chordæ."

Not all, nor nearly all, who came "to hear Memnon" succeeded in their object. On many mornings the Statue remained obstinately dumb. When, on the contrary, the expected Voice came forth at daybreak, the foreign visitors frequently desired to engrave on the Statue itself a record of their gratification. Thus at the present day we find the whole lower part of the

Statue covered with inscriptions from the classic times, in Greek or in Latin, in prose or in verse.

It is very strange that this huge mass, so conspicuous an object from the river, should have been unknown a century or more ago, and been subsequently, as it were, re-discovered. We have now before us a quarto volume, published at Paris in 1733, and at present become very rare, a "Description de l'Egypte," by M. de Maillet, formerly French Consul at Cairo. In this book an account of the Statue, with its name of Memnon, is given from the ancient writers, and M. de Maillet adds: " Quoiqu'il en soit, il ne reste plus de traces aujourd'hui de ce colosse."

In our own time the writers who have treated of this subject have mostly been disposed to connect the "magical chords of Memnon," as Juvenal calls them, with some artifice of the priests. They "no doubt contrived the sound of the Statue"—so says, for example, Sir Gardner Wilkinson, in his "Handbook of Egypt." For our part we are not at all concerned about the character of the hierophants at Thebes, or bound in any manner to defend them:—

"Oh, worthy thou of Egypt's blest abodes,
A decent priest where monkeys were the gods!"

But our regard for historical truth obliges us to say that, as we believe, there was no priestcraft whatever in this case. The priests heard the Voice, as did the visitors, but were as ignorant of its real cause. They did no more than share the common error, although no doubt they benefited by it.

We are glad to find that the opinion which we have now expressed entirely accords with that of a most competent judge on any subject connected with classic times, M. Gaston Boissier. He has touched upon this question incidentally, while discussing the inscriptions on the Statue, in an Essay on the Roman Monuments in the East, which appeared in the *Revue des Deux Mondes* of July last year. But for full details we would refer to the earlier and more special treatise of M. Letronne; a rare book, however, of which there were only two hundred copies printed; and even of these no more than one hundred were on sale. It is mainly by the aid, then, of these two able archæologists—Boissier and Letronne—that we hope to render the whole case clear and convincing to our readers.

And first, as to the shattering of the Statue. Admitting an earthquake to have been the cause, there still remains the question by which, or at what period, these huge fragments were hurled down. M. Letronne has produced a passage from the "Chronicle of Eusebius," as translated by St. Jerome. It refers to the year 27 before Christ, when, as it states, the edifices of Thebes were levelled to the ground. "Thebæ Egypti usque ad solum dirutæ." Judging even from what now remains, it is clear that this is a great exaggeration. Yet still the fact remains beyond dispute, that in the year alleged there was a violent convulsion of nature, which wrought great havoc at Thebes. Now, earthquakes are, or were, extremely rare in the valley of the Nile. This has been noticed by Pliny, who, in one sentence, has rather strangely lumped together

Gaul and Egypt. "Gallia et Ægyptus minime quatiuntur." If then any person be inclined to doubt that the partial destruction of the Statue took place in the year 27 before Christ, he will find it very difficult to name any other earthquake to which within the necessary limits of time that partial destruction can be ascribed.

But farther, this date accurately tallies with the other circumstances of the case. The visit of Strabo to Egypt was made between the years 18 and 7 of the Christian Era, that is ten or twenty years after the earthquake which Eusebius has recorded. At Thebes he found the natives full of traditional resentment at the long past Persian conquest. They appear to have pointed out, or enumerated to him, various of their monuments as mutilated by Cambyses. But they always excepted the colossal Statue, which, as was said among them, had been rent asunder by a convulsion of the earth. That convulsion was then too recent for them to entertain or express any doubt upon the subject. But in the reign of the Emperor Hadrian, a hundred and fifty years later, the memory of the earthquake appears to have faded away, and the Colossus was then included in the list of monuments which Cambyses had attempted to destroy. Several of the inscriptions dating from that reign, and still to be traced along the base of the Statue, allude to this as to a certain fact.

It is to be borne in mind, that until the Statue was shattered to its waist there was no thought or question of its musical sound at sunrise. It was only since then

R

that the "Voice of Memnon" was heard, or that by degrees the rumour of it spread abroad. Miss Martineau is therefore quite in error when, after mentioning how the easternmost statue was shattered by Cambyses, she adds, "after which, however, it still gave out its gentle music to the morning sun." It was not in spite of, but in consequence of, the mutilation that the musical sound was heard.

On the rumours, as they gradually went forth of this wonderful Voice, travellers, some of princely rank, were attracted to the spot, and bore witness to the miracle. Thus, when in the year 19 of the Christian Era Germanicus appeared in Egypt, and sailed up the Nile, we are informed by Tacitus that he visited the Vocal Statue. But, as we have already noted, Memnon was by no means constant or discriminating in his favours. On some mornings the pilgrims were gratified with the expected Voice, on others they went disappointed away.

From this variation there ensued, ere long, the common idea that to hear Memnon was a high privilege—a special favour of the Gods. The inscriptions at the base of the Statue, beginning, so far as their dates can be traced, in the reign of Nero, are forward to commemorate the fact.

Here follow some of these inscriptions as translated, the originals being partly in Latin and partly in very indifferent Greek.

"I, Funisulana Vetulla, wife of Caius Lælius Africanus, Præfect of Egypt, heard Memnon an hour and a half before sunrise on the Ides of February, in the first year of the august Emperor Domitian."

This date corresponds to the year 82 of the Christian Era.

———

"In the seventeenth year of the Emperor Domitian, Cæsàr Augustus, Germanicus, I, Titus Petronius Secundus, Præfect, heard Memnon at the first hour in the Ides of March, and gave him honour in the Greek verses inscribed below."

Here then follow the verses, which seem of but moderate merit; although M. Letronne, considering the authorship, is disposed to view them with indulgence: "*Fort passables,*" he says, "*pour être l'ouvrage d'un Préfet.*"

"After the first hour, and when in the course of the second the genial day (*alma dies*) irradiates the ocean, the Memnonian Voice was happily heard by me three times.

"Viaticus Theramenes made (this inscription) when he heard Memnon in the Calends of June, Servianus being for the third time Consul. With him was his wife Asidonia Calpe."

The third Consulship of Servianus answers to the year of our Lord 134.

———

(*Greek Verses*) *by Cæcilia Trebulla.*

"Hearing the sacred voice of Memnon, I longed for thee, O my mother, and desired that thou also mightest hear it."

———

(*In Greek Verse.*)

"Thy mother, O renowned Memnon, the Goddess, the rosy-fingered Aurora, has rendered thee vocal for me who desired to hear thee. In the twelfth year of the illustrious Antoninus, and in the month of Pachon, counting thirteen days, twice, O Divine Being, did I hear thy Voice as the sun was leaving the majestic waves of Ocean.

"Once the son of Saturn, great Jove, had made thee monarch of the East; now thou art but a stone; and it is from a stone that thy Voice proceeds."

"Gemellus wrote these verses in his turn, having come hither with his dear wife Rufilla and his children."

The 12th year of the reign of Antoninus answers to 150 of our Era.

But by far the most interesting visit ever paid to Memnon was from the Emperor Hadrian, in the year of Christ 140. That Emperor, whose intelligent curiosity led him to view in their turn almost every place of note in his dominions, appears to have passed many days, perhaps even a whole month, at Thebes. With him came his Empress Sabina; and in their train was a blue-stocking matron, Julia Balbilla by name. This lady desiring to do honour to her patron, inscribed at the base of the statue several pieces of pedantic verse composed by herself. In one of them she triumphantly relates that the Emperor heard Memnon no less than three times—"a clear proof," adds Balbilla, "that the Gods love Hadrian."

Sabina was not quite so fortunate. She was greatly displeased that when she first appeared before him Memnon remained mute. Her displeasure is still attested by an inscription in Greek verse, composed, it would seem, by one of her attendants, perhaps by the same blue-stocking matron who wrote the rest.

"Having failed to hear Memnon yesterday, we prayed to him not to be again unfavourable to us, nor withhold his Divine Sound; for the venerable features of the Empress were inflamed with anger. The Emperor himself might be irritated, and a lasting sadness might invade his venerable consort. Memnon accordingly, dreading the wrath of these immortal princes, has of a sudden sent forth his melodious voice, thus showing that he takes pleasure in the companionship of Gods."

The accounts of the Memnon Statue and of its Voice at sunrise, as transmitted to us by divers Pagan writers since the beginning of the Christian Era, are clear, distinct, and consistent with each other. There is, however, a remarkable exception in that historical romance, "The Life of Apollonius of Tyana," by Philostratus. Dr. Jowett, in the article on Apollonius which he contributed to one of Dr. Smith's Classical Dictionaries, describes that book as a "mass of incongruities and fables;" nor shall we find any reason to modify that general judgment by the particular instance which is now before us.

Philostratus then, writing in the reign of Alexander Severus, that is between the years 222 and 235 of our Era, describes the wanderings and the miracles of Apollonius in the first century since the birth of Christ. He makes his hero visit the Memnon, which he represents as not mutilated but entire. The head, he says, is of a beardless young man; his arms rest upon his throne, his figure leans forward as though in act to rise, his mouth and eyes betoken a man in the act to speak, and when the Voice does issue his eyes shine forth with especial brilliancy, like those of a man on whom the sunlight falls.

But what a fancy fabric is here! All the other effigies of Amunoph the Third represent him as bearded: it seems therefore all but certain that this Colossus when entire was bearded also. As to the figure bending forward as though ready to rise, M. Letronne assures us that no such attitude is to be found in any other Egyptian statue. The eyes that betoken an intention of speaking, and that beam with preternatural light whenever the Voice is heard, are plainly the work of the imagination, and of the imagination only.

But further still, it is expressly stated by Philostratus, though M. Letronne was the first to notice it, as bearing on this question, that Philostratus does not profess to give this description on his own authority, but quotes the words of Damis, who was a writer in Assyria a century and a half before. The account which Philostratus, still following Damis, proceeds to give of the first cataract, may vie for its inaccuracy with his account of the Memnon. Here he says the Nile is flowing along mountains, like to those of Tmolus, in Lydia, from which its waters dash down with so prodigious a noise, that many persons who approached them nearly, have lost in consequence all power of hearing. May we not, then, upon the whole adopt the judgment of M. Chassang, the last translator of the "Life of Apollonius?" "Tout porte à croire que cette description de la Statue de Memnon n'est qu'une amplification de rhétorique."

If, as the Ancients did, we were to regard the Voice of Memnon as a miracle—as the manifestation of a Godhead to man—we must own that not many miracles could be better attested. We should have in its support an unbroken chain of testimonies, derived from the most various sources, and extending over scores of years. But in this case the light of modern science has supplied a natural and simple explanation. " On sait que cette découverte est due à notre illustre Letronne,"—such are the words of M. Gaston Boissier. But in spite of this positive *on sait*, we will venture to assert that no such thing is known, for no such thing is true. Even for ourselves, the writers in this Review, we may claim precedence in the explanation over M. Letronne. And this the following dates will clearly show.

The volume of M. Letronne on this subject appeared in 1833. We of the *Quarterly*, on the other hand, in our 88th number, published in February, 1831, were reviewing Herschel's " Treatise on Sound." Nor will it be any breach of confidence, after so long an interval, to state that this article was contributed by one of the foremost men of science in his day—by Mr., since Sir David, Brewster.

In his article, then, upon Herschel, Sir David took occasion to advert, though not at length, to the case of the Statue of Memnon. Here are the words he used: " We have no hesitation in avowing our belief that the sound or sounds which it [the Statue of Memnon] discharged were the offspring of a natural cause." In common with some travellers, whom we alleged, we "ascribed these sounds to the transmission of rarefied air through the crevices of a sonorous stone." And he adds: "The phenomenon proceeded without doubt from the sudden change of temperature which takes place at the rising of the sun."

It is plain, we may now subjoin, that in such a case the phenomenon could not be uniform or constant, but would depend on the varying conditions of temperature or season.

In the same article we proceeded to point out that this is no solitary instance. There are several other well-attested cases of musical sounds which issue at sunrise from the like crevices, and which are explained by the same cause. Above all, we quoted the observations of the celebrated traveller, Baron Humboldt, when wandering on the banks of the Oronooko: "The granite rock," he says, "on which we lay is one of those where travellers on the Oronooko have heard from time to time towards sunrise subterranean sounds resembling those of the organ. The missionaries call these stones *loxas de musica*. 'It is witchcraft,' said our young Indian pilot. . . . But the existence of a phenomenon that seems to depend on a certain state of the atmosphere cannot be denied. The shelves of rock are full of very narrow and deep crevices. They are heated during the day to about 50°. I often found their temperature at the surface during the night at 39°. It may easily be conceived that the difference of temperature between the subterraneous and the external air would attain its *maximum* about sunrise, or at that moment which is at the same time farthest from the period of the *maximum* of the heat of the preceding day."

Nor did the acute mind of Humboldt fail to notice, even though very vaguely, the close connection between this case and that of the Theban Colossus. For he goes on to ask: "May we not admit that the ancient inhabitants of Egypt, in passing incessantly up and down the Nile, had made the same observation on some rock of the Thebaid, and that the music of the rocks there led to the jugglery of the priests in the Statue of Memnon?"

In the same article we also called attention to the analogous phenomena among the sandstone rocks of El Nakous, in Arabia Petræa. But without quitting the soil of Egypt, or even the neighbourhood of Thebes, a striking parallel can be adduced. We called as witnesses three French artists, Messrs. Jomard, Jollois, and Devilliers, who state that, being in a monument of granite placed in the centre of the spot on which the palace of Karnak stood, they heard a noise which resembled that of a chord breaking—the very comparison employed by Pausanias—issue from the blocks at sunrise. And they were of opinion that these sounds "might," in their own words, "have suggested to the Egyptian priests to invent the juggleries of the Memnonium." The fact indeed may be taken as now accepted and admitted by men of science. It is no longer, we think, doubted in any quarter that the action of the morning sun on the chilled air in the crevices of rock may and does produce the same effect as was observed in the Statue of Memnon.

We would observe that, although in this explanation we claim priority of M. Letronne, we most cheerfully accord it to Baron Humboldt and to the other explorers, whose remarks we have transcribed. Still earlier precedence is due to M. Dussaulx, the French translator of Juvenal, who was the first, we rather think, to suggest the true theory of the *magicæ chordæ* in his author.

It is also to be noted that M. Letronne himself never made that claim of priority which his countryman has thought fit to make in his behalf. On the contrary, he expressly quoted in his margin our article of February, 1831, and derived from it the remarkable account by Baron Humboldt of the Oronooko sound. His industry has also collected some further parallel cases—one, for instance, near the Maladetta mountain in the Pyrenees—and devoting a whole volume, instead of a mere digression in a quarterly article, to this subject, he has treated it in a most complete and convincing manner, with which our own cursory remarks could never pretend to vie.

Admitting then, as no one seems at present to deny, that the phenomenon of the Theban Colossus was produced by the vibration of the air, the question would still remain whether, as some persons persistently assert, "the jugglery of the priests," as they term it, was at all concerned. As we have already stated, we are convinced that it was not. Let it, in the first place, be considered that there is no hiding-place or secret chamber in or near the Statue; and that without the aid of these, it seems impossible that the Voice of

THE STATUE OF MEMNON. 251

Memnon could be either promoted or restrained. Secondly, had the priests really possessed any such power of promoting the miraculous Voice, they would certainly have used it in behalf of the great and powerful—of those whose favour they desired to gain. How then could we explain the fact that the wife of a Præfect of Egypt was allowed to make two visits without hearing the desired sound; that in like manner the consort of an Emperor came for the first time in vain, to her great displeasure and at the risk of her resentment; while a common soldier has put on record that he enjoyed the privilege no less than thirteen times?

The latest inscription that bears a date upon the Statue is by Marcus Ulpius Primianus, Præfect of Egypt, in the second Consulship of Septimius Severus, and in the year of our Lord 194; and the restoration of the Statue was, in all probability, made a few years afterwards. In its mutilated state, the lower half from which the Voice proceeded was part of the original monolith; when restored, or rather rebuilt, that lower half bore, as it still bears upon it, five ranges of enormous blocks of stone. The magnitude and cost of this construction must be held to indicate an Emperor's work, and the result of an Emperor's visit. Now, since the time of Hadrian, no Emperor, except Septimius Severus, ever came to Upper Egypt. His biographer, Spartianus, records of him that "he carefully examined Memphis, the Pyramids, the Labyrinth, and Memnon."

Such being the fact, it cannot but be thought surprising that while there are so many inscriptions on the base of the Colossus to commemorate the visit of Hadrian, not a single one appears to commemorate the visit of Severus. As is argued by M. Letronne, there is only one explanation that can be assigned as satisfactory or sufficient to account for the omission —namely, to presume that when Severus came to the Statue it remained obstinately dumb. These inscriptions, it should be remembered, were never put up when there was a failure in the sound, unless in the case when the first failures were followed by success.

It may also be inferred, with considerable probability, that the silence of the Statue in the august presence was the cause of its reconstruction. Severus was a sincere and zealous Pagan; and he lived in an age when the adherents of the old Mythology, alarmed at the progress of the Christians, strove hard to regain the public confidence and favour. It was during his reign that the main attempt was made to hold forth Apollonius of Tyana as a worker of wonders and religious teacher, in opposition to our Lord. In like manner the Voice of Memnon, as a Pagan prodigy, was esteemed a counterpoise to the Christian miracles. The priests and devotees, as M. Boissier puts it, would assure Severus that since Memnon even in his mutilated state gave his greeting often, though not quite so often as he ought, his Voice would certainly become both more distinct and more unfailing if once his Statue were restored. This is no mere vague conjecture of the popular belief. Several of the inscriptions on the base express or imply the idea that Memnon, when entire, could speak in language, but since his mutilation, was reduced to inarticulate sounds.

But there is yet another point of view from which the Emperor might be urged. The silence of the Statue denoted the displeasure of the Gods. Did it not, then, become a devout worshipper, such as was Severus, to take some step for removing that displeasure? Should he not appease the offended deity by a splendid reconstruction of his Statue?

Yielding, perhaps—for there is no positive statement on the subject—to some such representations, the Emperor gave orders for the costly work required. But alas for the result! In his new construction he, of course, filled up the ancient crevices, and in consequence silenced Memnon for ever. Aurora continued to rise as usual, but received no further greetings from her son.

We have thus endeavoured to trace the varied fortunes, the rise and the fall, of this celebrated prodigy. Well pleased shall we be if any future traveller, as in his Nile boat he nears that majestic monument, shall feel that he owes to our pages a more accurate knowledge of its history, and a warmer interest in its survey.

50A, Albemarle Street, London,
January, 1876.

MR. MURRAY'S

GENERAL LIST OF WORKS.

ALBERT (THE) MEMORIAL. A Descriptive and Illustrated Account of the National Monument erected to the PRINCE CONSORT at Kensington. Illustrated by Engravings of its Architecture, Decorations, Sculptured Groups, Statues, Mosaics, Metalwork, &c. With Descriptive Text. By DOYNE C. BELL. With 24 Plates. Folio. 12*l*. 12*s*.
——— (PRINCE) SPEECHES AND ADDRESSES with an Introduction, giving some outline of his Character. With Portrait. 8vo. 10*s*. 6*d*.; or *Popular Edition*, fcap. 8vo. 1*s*.
ALBERT DURER; his Life and Works. By DR. THAUSING, Keeper of Archduke Albert's Art Collection at Vienna. Translated from the German. With Portrait Illustrations. Medium 8vo.
[*In the Press.*
ABBOTT'S (REV. J.) Memoirs of a Church of England Missionary in the North American Colonies. Post 8vo. 2*s*.
ABERCROMBIE'S (JOHN) Enquiries concerning the Intellectual Powers and the Investigation of Truth. Fcap. 8vo. 3*s*. 6*d*.
——— Philosophy of the Moral Feelings. Fcap. 8vo. 2*s*. 6*d*.
ACLAND'S (REV. CHARLES) Popular Account of the Manners and Customs of India. Post 8vo. 2*s*.
ÆSOP'S FABLES. A New Version. With Historical Preface. By Rev. THOMAS JAMES. With 100 Woodcuts, by TENNIEL and WOLF. Post 8vo. 2*s*. 6*d*.
AGRICULTURAL (ROYAL) JOURNAL. (*Published half yearly.*)
AIDS TO FAITH: a Series of Theological Essays. 8vo. 9*s*.
CONTENTS.

Miracles	DEAN MANSEL.
Evidences of Christianity	BISHOP FITZGERALD.
Prophecy & Mosaic Record of Creation	DR. MCCAUL.
Ideology and Subscription	Canon COOK.
The Pentateuch	Canon RAWLINSON.
Inspiration	BISHOP HAROLD BROWNE.
Death of Christ	ARCHBISHOP THOMSON.
Scripture and its Interpretation	BISHOP ELLICOTT.

AMBER-WITCH (THE). A most interesting Trial for Witchcraft. Translated by LADY DUFF GORDON. Post 8vo. 2*s*.
ARMY LIST (THE). *Published Monthly by Authority.*
ARTHUR'S (LITTLE) History of England. By LADY CALLCOTT. *New Edition, continued to* 1872. With 36 Woodcuts. Fcap. 8vo. 1*s*. 6*d*.
AUSTIN'S (JOHN) LECTURES ON GENERAL JURISPRUDENCE; or, the Philosophy of Positive Law. Edited by ROBERT CAMPBELL. 2 Vols. 8vo. 32*s*.
——— STUDENT'S EDITION, compiled from the above work. Post 8vo. 12*s*.
ARNOLD'S (THOS.) Ecclesiastical and Secular Architecture of Scotland: The Abbeys, Churches, Castles, and Mansions. With Illustrations. Medium 8vo. [*In Preparation.*

B

ADMIRALTY PUBLICATIONS; Issued by direction of the Lords Commissioners of the Admiralty:—

A MANUAL OF SCIENTIFIC ENQUIRY, for the Use of Travellers. *Fourth Edition.* Edited by ROBERT MAIN, M.A. Woodcuts. Post 8vo. 3s. 6d.

GREENWICH ASTRONOMICAL OBSERVATIONS 1841 to 1846, and 1847 to 1871. Royal 4to. 20s. each.

MAGNETICAL AND METEOROLOGICAL OBSERVATIONS. 1840 to 1847. Royal 4to. 20s. each.

APPENDICES TO OBSERVATIONS.
  1837. Logarithms of Sines and Cosines in Time. 3s.
  1842. Catalogue of 1439 Stars, from Observations made in 1836 to 1841. 4s.
  1845. Longitude of Valentia (Chronometrical). 3s.
  1847. Description of Altazimuth. 3s.
       Twelve Years' Catalogue of Stars, from Observations made in 1836 to 1847. 4s.
       Description of Photographic Apparatus. 2s.
  1851. Maskelyne's Ledger of Stars. 3s.
  1852. I. Description of the Transit Circle. 3s.
  1853. Refraction Tables. 3s.
  1854. Description of the Zenith Tube. 3s.
       Six Years' Catalogue of Stars, from Observations. 1848 to 1853. 4s.
  1862. Seven Years' Catalogue of Stars, from Observations. 1854 to 1860. 10s.
       Plan of Ground Buildings. 3s.
       Longitude of Valentia (Galvanic). 2s.
  1864. Moon's Semid. from Occultations. 2s.
       Planetary Observations, 1831 to 1835. 2s.
  1868. Corrections of Elements of Jupiter and Saturn. 2s.
       Second Seven Years' Catalogue of 2760 Stars for 1861 to 1867. 4s.
       Description of the Great Equatorial. 3s.
  1856. Descriptive Chronograph. 3s.
  1860. Reduction of Deep Thermometer Observations. 2s.
  1871. History and Description of Water Telescope. 3s.
  Cape of Good Hope Observations (Star Ledgers). 1856 to 1863. 2s.
  ——————— 1856. 5s.
  ——————— Astronomical Results. 1857 to 1858. 5s.
  Report on Teneriffe Astronomical Experiment. 1856. 5s.
  Paramatta Catalogue of 7385 Stars. 1822 to 1826. 4s.

ASTRONOMICAL RESULTS. 1847 to 1871. 4to. 3s. each.

MAGNETICAL AND METEOROLOGICAL RESULTS. 1847 to 1871. 4to. 3s. each.

REDUCTION OF THE OBSERVATIONS OF PLANETS. 1750 to 1830. Royal 4to. 20s. each.

——————————————— LUNAR OBSERVATIONS. 1750 to 1830. 2 Vols. Royal 4to. 20s. each.

——————— 1831 to 1851. 4to. 10s. each.

BERNOULLI'S SEXCENTENARY TABLE. 1779. 4to. 5s.

BESSEL'S AUXILIARY TABLES FOR HIS METHOD OF CLEARING LUNAR DISTANCES. 8vo. 2s.

ENCKE'S BERLINER JAHRBUCH, for 1830. *Berlin*, 1828. 8vo. 9s.

HANSEN'S TABLES DE LA LUNE. 4to. 20s.

LAX'S TABLES FOR FINDING THE LATITUDE AND LONGITUDE. 1821. 8vo. 10s.

ADMIRALTY PUBLICATIONS—*continued.*

 LUNAR OBSERVATIONS at GREENWICH. 1783 to 1819. Compared with the Tables, 1821. 4to. 7s. 6d.
 MACLEAR ON LACAILLE'S ARC OF MERIDIAN. 2 Vols. 20s. each.
 MAYER'S DISTANCES of the MOON'S CENTRE from the PLANETS. 1822, 3s.; 1823, 4s. 6d. 1824 to 1835. 8vo. 4s. each.
 —— TABULÆ MOTUUM SOLIS ET LUNÆ. 1770. 5s.
 —— ASTRONOMICAL OBSERVATIONS MADE AT GOTTINGEN, from 1756 to 1761. 1826. Folio. 7s. 6d.
 NAUTICAL ALMANACS, from 1767 to 1877. 2s. 6d. each.
 —— SELECTIONS FROM, up to 1812. 8vo. 5s. 1834-54. 5s.
 —— SUPPLEMENTS, 1828 to 1833, 1837 and 1838. 2s. each.
 —— TABLE requisite to be used with the N.A. 1781. 8vo. 5s.
 SABINE'S PENDULUM EXPERIMENTS to DETERMINE THE FIGURE OF THE EARTH. 1825. 4to. 40s.
 SHEPHERD'S TABLES for CORRECTING LUNAR DISTANCES. 1772. Royal 4to. 21s.
 —— TABLES, GENERAL, of the MOON'S DISTANCE from the SUN, and 10 STARS. 1787. Folio. 5s. 6d.
 TAYLOR'S SEXAGESIMAL TABLE. 1780. 4to. 15s.
 —— TABLES OF LOGARITHMS. 4to. 60s.
 TIARK'S ASTRONOMICAL OBSERVATIONS for the LONGITUDE of MADEIRA. 1822. 4to. 5s.
 —— CHRONOMETRICAL OBSERVATIONS for DIFFERENCES of LONGITUDE between DOVER, PORTSMOUTH, and FALMOUTH. 1823. 4to. 5s.
 VENUS and JUPITER: OBSERVATIONS of, compared with the TABLES. *London,* 1822. 4to. 2s.
 WALES' AND BAYLY'S ASTRONOMICAL OBSERVATIONS. 1777. 4to. 21s.
 —— REDUCTION OF ASTRONOMICAL OBSERVATIONS MADE IN THE SOUTHERN HEMISPHERE. 1764—1771. 1788. 4to. 10s. 6d.

BARBAULD'S (MRS.) Hymns in Prose for Children. With Illustrations. Crown 8vo. 5s.

BARROW'S (SIR JOHN) Autobiographical Memoir, from Early Life to Advanced Age. Portrait. 8vo. 16s.

—— (JOHN) Life, Exploits, and Voyages of Sir Francis Drake. Post 8vo. 2s.

BARRY'S (SIR CHARLES) Life and Works. By CANON BARRY. With Portrait and Illustrations. Medium 8vo. 15s.

BATES' (H. W.) Records of a Naturalist on the River Amazon during eleven years of Adventure and Travel. Illustrations. Post 8vo. 7s. 6d.

BAX'S (CAPTAIN) Russian Tartary, Eastern Siberia, China, Japan, and Formosa. A Narrative of a Cruise in the Eastern Seas. With Map and Illustrations. Crown 8vo. 12s.

BEAUCLERK'S (LADY DIANA) Summer and Winter in Norway. With Illustrations. Small 8vo. 6s.

BELCHER'S (LADY) Account of the Mutineers of the 'Bounty,' and their Descendants; with their Settlements in Pitcairn and Norfolk Islands. With Illustrations. Post 8vo. 12s.

BELL'S (SIR CHAS.) Familiar Letters. Portrait. Post 8vo. 12s.

BELT'S (THOS.) Naturalist in Nicaragua, including a Residence at the Gold Mines of Chontales; with Journeys in the Savannahs and Forests; and Observations on Animals and Plants. Illustrations. Post 8vo. 12s.

BERTRAM'S (JAS. G.) Harvest of the Sea: an Account of British Food Fishes, including sketches of Fisheries and Fisher Folk. With 50 Illustrations. 8vo. 9s.

BIBLE COMMENTARY. EXPLANATORY and CRITICAL. With a REVISION of the TRANSLATION. By BISHOPS and CLERGY of the ANGLICAN CHURCH. Edited by F. C. COOK, M.A., Canon of Exeter. Medium 8vo. VOL. I., 30s. VOLS. II. and III., 36s. VOL IV., 24s. Vol. V., 20s. Vol. VI., 20s.

Vol. I.	GENESIS. EXODUS. LEVITICUS. NUMBERS. DEUTERONOMY.	VOL. IV.	JOB. PSALMS. PROVERBS. ECCLESIASTES. SONG OF SOLOMON.
Vols. II. and III.	JOSHUA. JUDGES, RUTH, SAMUEL. KINGS, CHRONICLES, EZRA, NEHEMIAH, ESTHER.	Vol. V. Vol. VI.	ISAIAH. JEREMIAH. EZEKIEL. DANIEL. MINOR PROPHETS.

BIRCH'S (SAMUEL) History of Ancient Pottery and Porcelain: Egyptian, Assyrian, Greek, Roman, and Etruscan. With Coloured Plates and 200 Illustrations. Medium 8vo. 42s.

BIRD'S (ISABELLA) Hawaiian Archipelago; or Six Months Among the Palm Groves, Coral Reefs, and Volcances of the Sandwich Islands. With Illustrations. Crown 8vo. 12s.

BISSET'S (ANDREW) History of the Commonwealth of England, from the Death of Charles I. to the Expulsion of the Long Parliament by Cromwell. Chiefly from the MSS. in the State Paper Office. 2 vols. 8vo. 30s.

—————— (GENERAL) Sport and War in South Africa from 1834 to 1867, with a Narrative of the Duke of Edinburgh's Visit. With Map and Illustrations. Crown 8vo. 14s.

BLACKSTONE'S COMMENTARIES; adapted to the Present State of the Law. By R. MALCOLM KERR. LL.D. *Revised Edition*, incorporating all the Recent Changes in the Law. 4 vols. 8vo.

BLUNT'S (REV. J. J.) Undesigned Coincidences in the Writings of the Old and New Testaments, an Argument of their Veracity: containing the Books of Moses, Historical and Prophetical Scriptures, and the Gospels and Acts. Post 8vo. 6s.

—————— History of the Church in the First Three Centuries. Post 8vo. 6s.

—————— Parish Priest; His Duties, Acquirements and Obligations. Post 8vo. 6s.

—————— Lectures on the Right Use of the Early Fathers. 8vo. 9s.

—————— University Sermons. Post 8vo. 6s.

—————— Plain Sermons. 2 vols. Post 8vo. 12s.

BLOMFIELD'S (BISHOP) Memoir, with Selections from his Correspondence. By his Son. Portrait, post 8vo. 12s.

BOSWELL'S (JAMES) Life of Samuel Johnson, LL.D. Including the Tour to the Hebrides. By Mr. CROKER. *New Edition.* Portraits. 4 vols. 8vo.   [*In Preparation.*

BRACE'S (C. L.) Manual of Ethnology; or the Races of the Old World. Post 8vo. 6s.

BOOK OF COMMON PRAYER. Illustrated with Coloured Borders, Initial Letters, and Woodcuts. 8vo. 18s.

BORROW'S (GEORGE) Bible in Spain; or the Journeys, Adventures, and Imprisonments of an Englishman in an Attempt to circulate the Scriptures in the Peninsula. Post 8vo. 5s.
—————— Gypsies of Spain; their Manners, Customs, Religion, and Language. With Portrait. Post 8vo. 5s.
—————— Lavengro; The Scholar—The Gypsy—and the Priest. Post 8vo. 5s.
—————— Romany Rye—a Sequel to "Lavengro." Post 8vo. 5s.
—————— Wild Wales: its People, Language, and Scenery. Post 8vo. 5s.
—————— Romano Lavo-Lil; Word-Book of the Romany, or English Gypsy Language; with Specimens of their Poetry, and an account of certain Gypsyries. Post 8vo. 10s. 6d.

BRAY'S (MRS.) Life of Thomas Stothard, R.A. With Portrait and 60 Woodcuts. 4to. 21s.
—————— Revolt of the Protestants in the Cevennes. With some Account of the Huguenots in the Seventeenth Century. Post 8vo. 10s. 6d.

BRITISH ASSOCIATION REPORTS. 8vo.

York and Oxford, 1831-32, 13s. 6d.
Cambridge, 1833, 12s.
Edinburgh, 1834, 15s.
Dublin, 1835, 13s. 6d.
Bristol, 1836, 12s.
Liverpool, 1837, 16s. 6d.
Newcastle, 1838, 15s.
Birmingham, 1839, 13s. 6d.
Glasgow, 1840, 15s.
Plymouth, 1841, 13s. 6d.
Manchester, 1842, 10s. 6d.
Cork, 1843, 12s.
York, 1844, 20s.
Cambridge, 1845, 12s.
Southampton, 1846, 15s.
Oxford, 1847, 18s.
Swansea, 1848, 9s.
Birmingham, 1849, 10s.
Edinburgh, 1850, 15s.
Ipswich, 1851, 16s. 6d.
Belfast, 1852, 15s.
Hull, 1853, 10s. 6d.

Liverpool, 1854, 18s.
Glasgow, 1855, 15s.
Cheltenham, 1856, 18s.
Dublin, 1857, 15s.
Leeds, 1858, 20s.
Aberdeen, 1859, 15s.
Oxford, 1860, 25s.
Manchester, 1861, 15s.
Cambridge, 1862, 20s.
Newcastle, 1863, 25s.
Bath, 1864, 18s.
Birmingham, 1865, 25s.
Nottingham, 1866, 24s.
Dundee, 1867, 26s.
Norwich, 1868, 25s.
Exeter, 1869, 22s.
Liverpool, 1870, 18s.
Edinburgh, 1871, 16s.
Brighton, 1872, 24s.
Bradford, 1973, 25s.
Belfast, 1874.

BROUGHTON'S (LORD) Journey through Albania, Turkey in Europe and Asia, to Constantinople. Illustrations. 2 Vols. 8vo. 30s.
—————— Visits to Italy. 2 Vols. Post 8vo. 18s.

BROWNLOW'S (LADY) Reminiscences of a Septuagenarian. From the year 1802 to 1815. Post 8vo. 7s. 6d.

BRUGSCH'S (PROFESSOR) History of Ancient Egypt. Derived from Monuments and Inscriptions. New Edition. Translated by H. DANBY SEYMOUR. 8vo. [In Preparation.

BUCKLEY'S (ARABELLA B.) Short History of Natural Science, and the Progress of Discovery from the time of the Greeks to the present day, for Schools and young Persons. Illustrations. Post 8vo. 9s.

BURGON'S (REV. J. W.) Christian Gentleman; or, Memoir of Patrick Fraser Tytler. Post 8vo. 9s.
—————— Letters from Rome. Post 8vo. 12s.

BURN'S (COL.) Dictionary of Naval and Military Technical Terms, English and French—French and English. Crown 8vo. 15s.

BURROW'S (MONTAGU) Constitutional Progress. A Series of Lectures delivered before the University of Oxford. Post 8vo. 5s.

BUXTON'S (CHARLES) Memoirs of Sir Thomas Fowell Buxton, Bart. With Selections from his Correspondence. Portrait. 8vo. 16s. *Popular Edition*. Fcap. 8vo. 5s.

―――― Notes of Thought. With Biographical Sketch. By Rev. LLEWELLYN DAVIES. With Portrait. Crown 8vo. 10s. 6d.

BURCKHARDT'S (DR. JACOB) Cicerone ; or Art Guide to Painting in Italy. Edited by REV. DR. A. VON ZAHN, and Translated from the German by MRS. A. CLOUGH. Post 8vo. 6s.

BYLES' (SIR JOHN) Foundations of Religion in the Mind and Heart of Man. Post 8vo. 6s.

BYRON'S (LORD) Life, Letters, and Journals. By THOMAS MOORE. *Cabinet Edition*. Plates. 6 Vols. Fcap. 8vo. 18s.; or One Volume, Portraits. Royal 8vo., 7s. 6d.

―――――― and Poetical Works. *Popular Edition.* Portraits. 2 vols. Royal 8vo. 15s.

―― Poetical Works. *Library Edition.* Portrait. 6 Vols. 8vo. 45s.
―――― *Cabinet Edition.* Plates. 10 Vols. 12mo. 30s.
―――― *Pocket Edition.* 8 Vols. 24mo. 21s. *In a case.*
―――― *Popular Edition.* Plates. Royal 8vo. 7s. 6d.
―――― *Pearl Edition.* Crown 8vo. 2s. 6d.
―――― Childe Harold. With 80 Engravings. Crown 8vo. 12s.
―――――― 16mo. 2s. 6d.
―――――― Vignettes. 16mo. 1s.
―――――― Portrait. 16mo. 6d.
―――― Tales and Poems. 24mo. 2s. 6d.
―――― Miscellaneous. 2 Vols. 24mo. 5s.
―――― Dramas and Plays. 2 Vols. 24mo. 5s.
―――― Don Juan and Beppo. 2 Vols. 24mo. 5s.
―――― Beauties. Poetry and Prose. Portrait. Fcap. 8vo. 3s. 6d.

BUTTMAN'S Lexilogus ; a Critical Examination of the Meaning of numerous Greek Words, chiefly in Homer and Hesiod. By Rev. J. R. FISHLAKE. 8vo. 12s.

―――― Irregular Greek Verbs. With all the Tenses extant—their Formation, Meaning, and Usage, with Notes, by Rev. J. R. FISHLAKE. Post 8vo. 6s.

CALLCOTT'S (LADY) Little Arthur's History of England. *New Edition, brought down to* 1872. With Woodcuts. Fcap. 8vo. 1s. 6d.

CARNARVON'S (LORD) Portugal, Gallicia, and the Basque Provinces. Post 8vo. 3s. 6d.

―――――― Reminiscences of Athens and the Morea. With Map. Crown 8vo. 7s. 6d.

―――――― Recollections of the Druses of Lebanon. With Notes on their Religion. Post 8vo. 5s. 6d.

CASTLEREAGH (THE) DESPATCHES, from the commencement of the official career of Viscount Castlereagh to the close of his life. 12 Vols. 8vo. 14s. each.

PUBLISHED BY MR. MURRAY.

CAMPBELL'S (LORD) Lord Chancellors and Keepers of the Great Seal of England. From the Earliest Times to the Death of Lord Eldon in 1838. 10 Vols. Crown 8vo. 6s. each.

―――― Chief Justices of England. From the Norman Conquest to the Death of Lord Tenterden. 4 Vols. Crown 8vo. 6s. each.

―――― Lords Lyndhurst and Brougham. 8vo. 16s.

―――― Shakspeare's Legal Acquirements. 8vo. 5s. 6d.

―――― Lord Bacon. Fcap. 8vo. 2s. 6d.

―――― (SIR NEIL) Account of Napoleon at Fontainebleau and Elba. Being a Journal of Occurrences and Notes of his Conversations, &c. Portrait. 8vo. 15s.

―――― (SIR GEORGE) India as it may be: an Outline of a proposed Government and Policy. 8vo.

―――― (THOS.) Essay on English Poetry. With Short Lives of the British Poets. Post 8vo. 3s. 6d.

CATHCART'S (SIR GEORGE) Commentaries on the War in Russia and Germany, 1812-13. Plans. 8vo. 14s.

CAVALCASELLE AND CROWE'S History of Painting in NORTH ITALY, from the 14th to the 16th Century. With Illustrations. 2 Vols. 8vo. 42s.

―――― Early Flemish Painters, their Lives and Works. Illustrations. Post 8vo. 10s. 6d.; or Large Paper, 8vo. 15s.

CHILD'S (G. CHAPLIN, M.D.) Benedicite; or, Song of the Three Children; being Illustrations of the Power, Beneficence, and Design manifested by the Creator in his works. Post 8vo. 6s.

CHISHOLM'S (Mrs.) Perils of the Polar Seas; True Stories of Arctic Discovery and Adventure. Illustrations. Post 8vo. 6s.

CHURTON'S (ARCHDEACON) Gongora. An Historical Essay on the Age of Philip III. and IV. of Spain. With Translations. Portrait. 2 Vols. Small 8vo. 12s.

―――― Poetical Remains, Translations and Imitations. Portrait. Post 8vo. 7s. 6d.

―――― New Testament. Edited with a Plain Practical Commentary for Families and General Readers. With 100 Panoramic and other Views, from Sketches made on the Spot. 2 vols. 8vo. 2s.

CICERO'S LIFE AND TIMES. His Character as a Statesman, Orator, and Friend, with a Selection from his Correspondence and Orations. By WILLIAM FORSYTH, M.P. With Illustrations. 8vo. 10s. 6d.

CLARK'S (SIR JAMES) Memoir of Dr. John Conolly. Comprising a Sketch of the Treatment of the Insane in Europe and America. With Portrait. Post 8vo. 10s. 6d.

CLIVE'S (LORD) Life. By REV. G. R. GLEIG. Post 8vo. 3s. 6d.

CLODE'S (C. M.) Military Forces of the Crown; their Administration and Government. 2 Vols. 8vo. 21s. each.

―――― Administration of Justice under Military and Martial Law, as applicable to the Army, Navy, Marine, and Auxiliary Forces. 8vo. 12s.

COLCHESTER (THE) Papers. The Diary and Correspondence of Charles Abbott, Lord Colchester, Speaker of the House of Commons, 1802-1817. Portrait. 3 Vols. 8vo. 42s.

CHURCH (THE) & THE AGE. Essays on the Principles and Present Position of the Anglican Church. 2 vols. 8vo. 26s. Contents:—

VOL. I.
Anglican Principles.—Dean Hook.
Modern Religious Thought.—Bishop Ellicott.
State, Church, and Synods.—Rev. Dr. Irons.
Religious Use of Taste.—Rev. R. St. John Tyrwhitt.
Place of the Laity.—Professor Burrows.
Parish Priest.—Rev. Walsham How.
Divines of 16th and 17th Centuries. —Rev. A. W. Haddan.
Liturgies and Ritual, Rev. M. F. Sadler.
Church & Education.—Canon Barry.
Indian Missions.— Sir Bartle Frere.
Church and the People.—Rev. W. D. Maclagan.
Conciliation and Comprehension.— Rev. Dr. Weir.

VOL. II.
Church and Pauperism.—Earl Nelson.
American Church.—Bishop of Western New York.
Church and Science. — Prebendary Clark.
Ecclesiastical Law.—Isambard Brunel.
Church & National Education.— Canon Norris.
Church and Universities.—John G. Talbot.
Toleration.—Dean Cowie.
Eastern Church and Anglican Communion.—Rev. Geo. Williams.
A Disestablished Church.—Dean of Cashel.
Christian Tradition.—Rev. Dr. Irons.
Dogma.—Rev. Dr. Weir.
Parochial Councils. — Archdeacon Chapman.

COLERIDGE'S (SAMUEL TAYLOR) Table-Talk. Portrait. 12mo. 3s. 6d.

COLLINGWOOD'S (CUTHBERT) Rambles of a Naturalist on the Shores and Waters of the China Sea. With Illustrations. 8vo. 16s.

COLONIAL LIBRARY. [See Home and Colonial Library.]

COOK'S (Canon) Sermons Preached at Lincoln's Inn. 8vo. 9s.

COOKE'S (E. W.) Artist's Portfolio. Being Sketches made during Tours in Holland, Germany, Italy, Egypt, &c. 50 Plates. Royal 4to. [In Preparation.

COOKERY (MODERN DOMESTIC). Founded on Principles of Economy and Practical Knowledge, By a Lady. Woodcuts. Fcap. 8vo. 5s.

COOPER'S (T. T.) Travels of a Pioneer of Commerce on an Overland Journey from China towards India. Illustrations. 8vo. 16s.

CORNWALLIS (THE) Papers and Correspondence during the American War,—Administrations in India,—Union with Ireland, and Peace of Amiens. 3 Vols. 8vo. 63s.

COWPER'S (COUNTESS) Diary while Lady of the Bedchamber to Caroline, Princess of Wales, 1714—20. Portrait. 8vo. 10s. 6d.

CRABBE'S (REV. GEORGE) Life and Poetical Works. With Illustrations. Royal 8vo. 7s.

CRAWFORD & BALCARRE'S (Earl of) Etruscan Inscriptions. Analyzed, Translated, and Commented upon. 8vo. 12s.

——————— Argo ; or the Quest of the Golden Fleece. In Ten Books. 8vo.

CROKER'S (J. W.) Progressive Geography for Children. 18mo. 1s. 6d.

——————— Stories for Children, Selected from the History of England. Woodcuts. 16mo. 2s. 6d.

——————— Boswell's Life of Johnson. Including the Tour to the Hebrides. *New Edition.* Portraits. 4 vols. 8vo. [In Preparation.

——————— Early Period of the French Revolution. 8vo. 15s.

——————— Historical Essay on the Guillotine. Fcap. 8vo. 1s.

CUMMING'S (R. GORDON) Five Years of a Hunter's Life in the Far Interior of South Africa. Woodcuts. Post 8vo. 6s.

CROWE'S AND CAVALCASELLE'S Lives of the Early Flemish Painters. Woodcuts. Post 8vo, 10s. 6d.; or Large Paper, 8vo, 15s.

———— History of Painting in North Italy, from 14th to 16th Century. Derived from Researches into the Works of Art in that Country. With Illustrations. 2 Vols. 8vo. 42s.

CUNYNGHAME'S (SIR ARTHUR) Travels in the Eastern Caucasus, on the Caspian, and Black Seas, in Daghestan and the Frontiers of Persia and Turkey. With Map and Illustrations. 8vo. 18s.

CURTIUS' (PROFESSOR) Student's Greek Grammar, for the Upper Forms. Edited by DR. WM. SMITH. Post 8vo. 6s.

———— Elucidations of the above Grammar. Translated by EVELYN ABBOT. Post 8vo. 7s. 6d.

———— Smaller Greek Grammar for the Middle and Lower Forms. Abridged from the larger work. 12mo. 3s. 6d.

———— Accidence of the Greek Language. Extracted from the above work. 12mo. 2s. 6d.

———— Principles of Greek Etymology. Translated by A. S. WILKINS, M.A., and E. B. ENGLAND, B.A. Vol. I. 8vo. 15s.

CURZON'S (HON. ROBERT) ARMENIA AND ERZEROUM. A Year on the Frontiers of Russia, Turkey, and Persia. Woodcuts. Post 8vo. 7s. 6d.

———— Visits to the Monasteries of the Levant. Illustrations. Post 8vo. 7s. 6d.

CUST'S (GENERAL) Warriors of the 17th Century—The Thirty Years' War. 2 Vols. 16s. Civil Wars of France and England. 2 Vols. 16s. Commanders of Fleets and Armies. 2 Vols. 18s.

———— Annals of the Wars—18th & 19th Century, 1700—1815. With Maps. 9 Vols. Post 8vo. 5s. each.

DAVIS'S (NATHAN) Ruined Cities of Numidia and Carthaginia. Illustrations. 8vo. 16s.

DAVY'S (SIR HUMPHRY) Consolations in Travel; or, Last Days of a Philosopher. Woodcuts. Fcap. 8vo. 3s. 6d.

———— Salmonia; or, Days of Fly Fishing. Woodcuts. Fcap. 8vo. 3s. 6d.

DARWIN'S (CHARLES) Journal of a Naturalist during a Voyage round the World. Crown 8vo. 9s.

———— Origin of Species by Means of Natural Selection; or, the Preservation of Favoured Races in the Struggle for Life. Crown 8vo. 7s. 6d.

———— Variation of Animals and Plants under Domestication. With Illustrations. 2 Vols. Crown 8vo. 18s.

———— Descent of Man, and Selection in Relation to Sex. With Illustrations. Crown 8vo. 9s.

———— Expressions of the Emotions in Man and Animals. With Illustrations. Crown 8vo. 12s.

———— Fertilization of Orchids through Insect Agency, and as to the good of Intercrossing. Woodcuts. Post 8vo. 9s.

———— Movements and Habits of Climbing Plants. Woodcuts. Crown 8vo. 6s.

———— Insectivorous Plants. Woodcuts. Crown 8vo. 14s.

———— Fact and Argument for Darwin. By FRITZ MÜLLER. Translated by W. S. DALLAS. Woodcuts. Post 8vo. 6s.

DELEPIERRE'S (OCTAVE) History of Flemish Literature. 8vo. 9s.
——————— Historic Difficulties & Contested Events.' Post 8vo. 6s.

DENISON'S (E. B.) Life of Bishop Lonsdale. With Selections from his Writings. With Portrait. Crown 8vo. 10s. 6d.

DERBY'S (EARL OF) Iliad of Homer rendered into English Blank Verse. 2 Vols. Post 8vo. 10s.

DE ROS'S (LORD) Young Officer's Companion; or, Essays on Military Duties and Qualities: with Examples and Illustrations from History. Post 8vo. 9s.

DEUTSCH'S (EMANUEL) Talmud, Islam, The Targums and other Literary Remains. 8vo. 12s.

DILKE'S (SIR C. W.) Papers of a Critic. Selected from the Writings of the late CHAS. WENTWORTH DILKE. With a Biographical Sketch. 2 Vols. 8vo. 24s.

DOG-BREAKING; the Most Expeditious, Certain, and Easy Method, whether great excellence or only mediocrity be required. With a Few Hints for those who Love the Dog and the Gun. By LIEUT.-GEN. HUTCHINSON. With 40 Woodcuts. Crown 8vo. 9s.

DOMESTIC MODERN COOKERY. Founded on Principles of Economy and Practical Knowledge, and adapted for Private Families. Woodcuts. Fcap. 8vo. 5s.

DOUGLAS'S (SIR HOWARD) Life and Adventures. Portrait. 8vo. 15s.
——————— Theory and Practice of Gunnery. Plates. 8vo. 21s.
——————— Construction of Bridges and the Passage of Rivers, in Military Operations. Plates. 8vo. 21s.
——————— (WM.) Horse-Shoeing; As it Is, and As it Should be. Illustrations. Post 8vo. 7s. 6d.

DRAKE'S (SIR FRANCIS) Life, Voyages, and Exploits, by Sea and Land. By JOHN BARROW. Post 8vo. 2s.

DRINKWATER'S (JOHN) History of the Siege of Gibraltar, 1779-1783. With a Description and Account of that Garrison from the Earliest Periods. Post 8vo. 2s.

DUCANGE'S MEDIÆVAL LATIN-ENGLISH DICTIONARY. Translated by Rev. E. A. DAYMAN, M.A. Small 4to. [In preparation.

DU CHAILLU'S (PAUL B.) EQUATORIAL AFRICA, with Accounts of the Gorilla, the Nest-building Ape, Chimpanzee, Crocodile, &c. Illustrations. 8vo. 21s.
——————— Journey to Ashango Land; and Further Penetration into Equatorial Africa. Illustrations. 8vo. 21s.

DUFFERIN'S (LORD) Letters from High 'Latitudes; a Yacht Voyage to Iceland, Jan Mayen, and Spitzbergen. Woodcuts. Post 8vo. 7s. 6d.

DUNCAN'S (MAJOR) History of the Royal Artillery. Compiled from the Original Records. With Portraits. 2 Vols. 8vo. 30s.

DYER'S (THOS. H.) History of Modern Europe, from the taking of Constantinople by the Turks to the close of the War in the Crimea. With Index. 4 Vols. 8vo. 42s.

EASTLAKE'S (SIR CHARLES) Contributions to the Literature of the Fine Arts. With Memoir of the Author, and Selections from his Correspondence. By LADY EASTLAKE. 2 Vols. 8vo. 24s.

EDWARDS' (W. H.) Voyage up the River Amazons, including a Visit to Para. Post 8vo. 2s.

EIGHT MONTHS AT ROME, during the Vatican Council, with a Daily Account of the Proceedings. By POMPONIO LETO. Translated from the Original. 8vo. [*Nearly ready.*

ELDON'S (LORD) Public and Private Life, with Selections from his Correspondence and Diaries. By HORACE TWISS. Portrait. 2 Vols. Post 8vo. 21s.

ELGIN'S (LORD) Letters and Journals. Edited by THEODORE WALROND. With Preface by Dean Stanley. 8vo. 14s.

ELLESMERE'S (LORD) Two Sieges of Vienna by the Turks. Translated from the German. Post 8vo. 2s.

ELLIS'S (W.) Madagascar, including a Journey to the Capital, with notices of Natural History and the People. Woodcuts. 8vo. 16s.

———————— Madagascar Revisited. Setting forth the Persecutions and Heroic Sufferings of the Native Christians. Illustrations. 8vo. 16s.

———————— Memoir. By HIS SON. With his Character and Work. By REV. HENRY ALLON, D.D. Portrait. 8vo. 10s. 6d.

———————— (ROBINSON) Poems and Fragments of Catullus. 16mo. 5s.

ELPHINSTONE'S (HON. MOUNTSTUART) History of India—the Hindoo and Mahomedan Periods. Edited by PROFESSOR COWELL. Map. 8vo. 18s.

———————— (H. W.) Patterns for Turning; Comprising Elliptical and other Figures cut on the Lathe without the use of any Ornamental Chuck. With 70 Illustrations. Small 4to. 15s.

ENGLAND. See CALLCOTT, CROKER, HUME, MARKHAM, SMITH, and STANHOPE.

ESSAYS ON CATHEDRALS. With an Introduction. By DEAN HOWSON. 8vo. 12s.

CONTENTS.

Recollections of a Dean.—Bishop of Carlisle.
Cathedral Canons and their Work.—Canon Norris.
Cathedrals in Ireland, Past and Future.—Dean of Cashel.
Cathedrals in their Missionary Aspect.—A. J. B. Beresford Hope.
Cathedral Foundations in Relation to Religious Thought.—Canon Westcott.
Cathedral Churches of the Old Foundation.—Edward A. Freeman.
Welsh Cathedrals.—Canon Perowne.
Education of Choristers.—Sir F. Gore Ouseley.
Cathedral Schools.—Canon Durham.
Cathedral Reform.—Chancellor Massingberd.
Relation of the Chapter to the Bishop. Chancellor Benson.
Architecture of the Cathedral Churches.—Canon Venables.

ELZE'S (KARL) Life of Lord Byron. With a Critical Essay on his Place in Literature. Translated from the German. With Portrait. 8vo. 16s.

FARRAR'S (A. S.) Critical History of Free Thought in reference to the Christian Religion. 8vo. 16s.

FERGUSSON'S (JAMES) History of Architecture in all Countries from the Earliest Times. With 1,600 Illustrations. 4 Vols. Medium 8vo. 31s. 6d. each.

Vol. I. & II. Ancient and Mediæval.
Vol. III. Indian and Eastern. Vol. IV. Modern.

———————— Rude Stone Monuments in all Countries; their Age and Uses. With 230 Illustrations. Medium 8vo. 24s.

———————— Holy Sepulchre and the Temple at Jerusalem. Woodcuts. 8vo. 7s. 6d.

FLEMING'S (Professor) Student's Manual of Moral Philosophy.
With Quotations and References. Post 8vo. 7s. 6d.

FLOWER GARDEN. By Rev. Thos. James. Fcap. 8vo. 1s.

FORD'S (Richard) Gatherings from Spain. Post 8vo. 3s. 6d.

FORSYTH'S (William) Life and Times of Cicero. With Selections from his Correspondence and Orations. Illustrations. 8vo. 10s. 6d.

―――――― Hortensius; an Historical Essay on the Office and Duties of an Advocate. Illustrations. 8vo. 12s.

―――――― History of Ancient Manuscripts. Post 8vo. 2s. 6d.

―――――― Novels and Novelists of the 18th Century, in Illustration of the Manners and Morals of the Age. Post 8vo. 10s. 6d.

FORTUNE'S (Robert) Narrative of Two Visits to the Tea Countries of China, 1843-52. Woodcuts. 2 Vols. Post 8vo. 18s.

FORSTER'S (John) Life of Jonathan Swift. Vol. I. 1667-1711. With Portrait. 8vo. 15s.

FOSS' (Edward) Biographia Juridica, or Biographical Dictionary of the Judges of England, from the Conquest to the Present Time, 1066-1870. Medium 8vo. 21s.

―――――― Tabulæ Curiales; or, Tables of the Superior Courts of Westminster Hall. Showing the Judges who sat in them from 1066 to 1864. 8vo. 10s. 6d.

FRANCE. *⁎* See Markham—Smith—Student's.

FRENCH (The) in Algiers; The Soldier of the Foreign Legion— and the Prisoners of Abd-el-Kadir. Translated by Lady Duff Gordon. Post 8vo. 2s.

FRERE'S (Sir Bartle) Indian Missions. Small 8vo. 2s. 6d.

―――――― Eastern Africa as a field for Missionary Labour. With Map. Crown 8vo. 5s.

―――――― Bengal Famine. How it will be Met and How to Prevent Future Famines in India. With Maps. Crown 8vo. 5s.

GALTON'S (Francis) Art of Travel; or, Hints on the Shifts and Contrivances available in Wild Countries. Woodcuts. Post 8vo. 7s. 6d.

GEOGRAPHICAL SOCIETY'S JOURNAL. (Published Yearly.)

GEORGE'S (Ernest) Mosel; a Series of Twenty Etchings, with Descriptive Letterpress. Imperial 4to. 42s.

―――――― Loire and South of France; a Series of Twenty Etchings, with Descriptive Text. Folio. 42s.

GERMANY (History of). See Markham.

GIBBON'S (Edward) History of the Decline and Fall of the Roman Empire. Edited by Milman and Guizot. Edited, with Notes, by Dr. Wm. Smith. Maps. 8 Vols. 8vo. 60s.

―――――― (The Student's Gibbon); Being an Epitome of the above work, incorporating the Researches of Recent Commentators. By Dr. Wm. Smith. Woodcuts. Post 8vo. 7s. 6d.

GIFFARD'S (EDWARD) Deeds of Naval Daring; or, Anecdotes of the British Navy. Fcap. 8vo. 3s. 6d.

GLADSTONE'S (W. E.) Financial Statements of 1853, 1860, 63–65. 8vo. 12s.

—————— Rome and the Newest Fashions in Religion. Three Tracts. *Collected Edition.* With a new Preface. 8vo. 7s. 6d.

GLEIG'S (G. R.) Campaigns of the British Army at Washington and New Orleans. Post 8vo. 2s.

—————— Story of the Battle of Waterloo. Post 8vo. 3s. 6d.

—————— Narrative of Sale's Brigade in Affghanistan. Post 8vo. 2s.

—————— Life of Lord Clive. Post 8vo. 3s. 6d.

—————— Sir Thomas Munro. Post 8vo. 3s. 6d.

GOLDSMITH'S (OLIVER) Works. Edited with Notes by PETER CUNNINGHAM. Vignettes. 4 Vols. 8vo. 30s.

GORDON'S (SIR ALEX.) Sketches of German Life, and Scenes from the War of Liberation. Post 8vo. 3s. 6d.

—————— (LADY DUFF) Amber-Witch: A Trial for Witchcraft. Post 8vo. 2s.

—————— French in Algiers. 1. The Soldier of the Foreign Legion. 2. The Prisoners of Abd-el-Kadir. Post 8vo. 2s.

GRAMMARS. See CURTIUS; HALL; HUTTON; KING EDWARD; MATTHIÆ; MAETZNER; SMITH.

GREECE. *See* GROTE—SMITH—Student.

GREY'S (EARL) Correspondence with King William IVth and Sir Herbert Taylor, from 1830 to 1832. 2 Vols. 8vo. 30s.

—————— Parliamentary Government and Reform; with Suggestions for the Improvement of our Representative System. *Second Edition.* 8vo.

GUIZOT'S (M.) Meditations on Christianity, and on the Religious Questions of the Day. 3 Vols. Post 8vo.

GROTE'S (GEORGE) History of Greece. From the Earliest Times to the close of the generation contemporary with the death of Alexander the Great. *Library Edition.* Portrait, Maps, and Plans. 10 Vols. 8vo. 120s. *Cabinet Edition.* Portrait and Plans. 12 Vols. Post 8vo. 6s. each.

—————— PLATO, and other Companions of Socrates. 3 Vols. 8vo. 45s.

—————— ARISTOTLE. 2 Vols. 8vo. 32s.

—————— Minor Works. With Critical Remarks on his Intellectual Character, Writings, and Speeches. By ALEX. BAIN, LL.D. Portrait. 8vo. 14s.

—————— Fragments on Ethical Subjects. Being a Selection from his Posthumous Papers. With an Introduction. By ALEXANDER BAIN, M.A. 8vo.

—————— Personal Life. Compiled from Family Documents, Private Memoranda, and Original Letters to and from Various Friends. By Mrs. Grote. Portrait. 8vo. 12s.

—————— (MRS.) Memoir of Ary Scheffer. Portrait. 8vo. 8s. 6d.

HALL'S (T. D.) School Manual of English Grammar. With Copious Exercises. 12mo. 3s. 6d.

—————— Primary English Grammar for Elementary Schools. 16mo. 1s.

—————— Child's First Latin Book, including a Systematic Treatment of the New Pronunciation, and a full Praxis of Nouns, Adjectives, and Pronouns. 16mo. 1s. 6d.

HALLAM'S (HENRY) Constitutional History of England, from the Accession of Henry the Seventh to the Death of George the Second. *Library Edition.* 3 Vols. 8vo. 30s. *Cabinet Edition*, 3 Vols. Post 8vo. 12s.

———— Student's Edition of the above work. Edited by WM. SMITH, D.C.L. Post 8vo. 7s. 6d.

———— History of Europe during the Middle Ages. *Library Edition.* 3 Vols. 8vo. 30s. *Cabinet Edition*, 3 Vols. Post 8vo. 12s.

———— Student's Edition of the above work. Edited by WM. SMITH, D.C.L. Post 8vo. 7s. 6d.

———— Literary History of Europe, during the 15th, 16th and 17th Centuries. *Library Edition.* 3 Vols. 8vo. 36s. *Cabinet Edition.* 4 Vols. Post 8vo. 16s.

———— (ARTHUR) Literary Remains; in Verse and Prose. Portrait. Fcap. 8vo. 3s. 6d.

HAMILTON'S (GEN. SIR F. W.) 'History of the Grenadier Guards. From Original Documents in the Rolls' Records, War Office, Regimental Records, &c. With Illustrations. 3 Vols. 8vo. 63s.

HART'S ARMY LIST. (*Published Quarterly and Annually.*)

HAY'S (SIR J. H. DRUMMOND) Western Barbary, its Wild Tribes and Savage Animals. Post 8vo. 2s.

HEAD'S (SIR FRANCIS) Royal Engineer. Illustrations. 8vo. 12s.

———— Life of Sir John Burgoyne. Post 8vo. 1s.

———— Rapid Journeys across the Pampas. Post 8vo. 2s.

———— Bubbles from the Brunnen of Nassau. Illustrations. Post 8vo. 7s. 6d.

———— Emigrant. Fcap. 8vo. 2s. 6d.

———— Stokers and Pokers; or, the London and North Western Railway. Post 8vo. 2s.

———— (SIR EDMUND) Shall and Will; or, Future Auxiliary Verbs. Fcap. 8vo. 4s.

HEBER'S (BISHOP) Journals in India. 2 Vols. Post 8vo. 7s.

———— Poetical Works. Portrait. Fcap. 8vo. 3s. 6d.

———— Hymns adapted to the Church Service. 16mo. 1s. 6d.

HERODOTUS. A New English Version. Edited, with Notes and Essays, historical, ethnographical, and geographical, by CANON RAWLINSON, assisted by SIR HENRY RAWLINSON and SIR J. G. WILKINSON. Maps and Woodcuts. 4 Vols. 8vo. 48s.

HERSCHEL'S (CAROLINE) Memoir and Correspondence. By MRS. JOHN HERSCHEL. With Portraits. Crown 8vo.

HATHERLEY'S (LORD) Continuity of Scripture, as Declared by the Testimony of our Lord and of the Evangelists and Apostles. 8vo. 6s. *Popular Edition.* Post 8vo. 2s. 6d.

HOLLWAY'S (J. G.) Month in Norway. Fcap. 8vo. 2s.

HONEY BEE. By REV. THOMAS JAMES. Fcap. 8vo. 1s.

HOOK'S (DEAN) Church Dictionary. 8vo. 16s.

———— (THEODORE) Life. By J. G. LOCKHART. Fcap. 8vo. 1s.

HOPE'S (T. C.) ARCHITECTURE OF AHMEDABAD, with Historical Sketch and Architectural Notes. With Maps, Photographs, and Woodcuts. 4to. 5l. 5s.

———— (A. J. BERESFORD) Worship in the Church of England. 8vo. 9s., or, *Popular Selections from.* 8vo. 2s. 6d.

FOREIGN HANDBOOKS.

HAND-BOOK—TRAVEL-TALK. English, French, German, and Italian. 18mo. 3s. 6d.

——— ——— HOLLAND,—BELGIUM, RHENISH PRUSSIA, and the Rhine from Holland to Mayence. Map and Plans. Post 8vo. 6s.

——— NORTH GERMANY,—From the Baltic to the Black Forest, the Hartz, Thüringerwald, Saxon Switzerland, Rügen, the Giant Mountains, Taunus, Odenwald, and the Rhine Countries, from Frankfort to Basle. Map and Plans. Post 8vo. 6s.

——— SOUTH GERMANY,—Wurtemburg, Bavaria, Austria, Styria, Salzburg, the Austrian and Bavarian Alps, Tyrol, Hungary, and the Danube, from Ulm to the Black Sea. Map. Post 8vo. 10s.

——— PAINTING. German, Flemish, and Dutch Schools. Illustrations. 2 Vols. Post 8vo. 24s.

——— LIVES OF EARLY FLEMISH PAINTERS. By CROWE and CAVALCASELLE. Illustrations. Post 8vo. 10s. 6d.

——— SWITZERLAND, Alps of Savoy, and Piedmont. Maps. Post 8vo. 9s.

——— FRANCE, Part I. Normandy, Brittany, the French Alps, the Loire, the Seine, the Garonne, and the Pyrenees. Post 8vo. 7s. 6d.

——— Part II. Central France, Auvergne, the Cevennes, Burgundy, the Rhone and Saone, Provence, Nimes, Arles, Marseilles, the French Alps, Alsace, Lorraine, Champagne, &c. Maps. Post 8vo. 7s. 6d.

——— MEDITERRANEAN ISLANDS—Malta, Corsica, Sardinia, and Sicily. Maps. Post 8vo. [*In the Press.*]

——— ALGERIA. Algiers, Constantine, Oran, the Atlas Range. Map. Post 8vo. 9s.

——— PARIS, and its Environs. Map. 16mo. 3s. 6d.
⁎ MURRAY'S PLAN OF PARIS, mounted on canvas. 3s. 6d.

——— SPAIN, Madrid, The Castiles, The Basque Provinces, Leon, The Asturias, Galicia, Estremadura, Andalusia, Ronda, Granada, Murcia, Valencia, Catalonia, Aragon, Navarre, The Balearic Islands, &c. &c. Maps. 2 Vols. Post 8vo. 24s.

——— PORTUGAL, LISBON, Porto, Cintra, Mafra, &c. Map. Post 8vo. 9s.

——— NORTH ITALY, Turin, Milan, Cremona, the Italian Lakes, Bergamo, Brescia, Verona, Mantua, Vicenza, Padua, Ferrara, Bologna, Ravenna, Rimini, Piacenza, Genoa, the Riviera, Venice, Parma, Modena, and Romagna. Map. Post 8vo. 10s.

——— CENTRAL ITALY, Florence, Lucca, Tuscany, The Marches, Umbria, and the late Patrimony of St. Peter's. Map. Post 8vo. 10s.

——— ROME AND ITS ENVIRONS. Map. Post 8vo. 10s.

——— SOUTH ITALY, Two Sicilies, Naples, Pompeii, Herculaneum, and Vesuvius. Map. Post 8vo. 10s.

——— KNAPSACK GUIDE TO ITALY. 16mo.

——— PAINTING. The Italian Schools. Illustrations. 2 Vols. Post 8vo. 30s.

——— LIVES OF ITALIAN PAINTERS, FROM CIMABUE to BASSANO. By Mrs. JAMESON. Portraits. Post 8vo. 12s.

——— NORWAY, Christiania, Bergen, Trondhjem. The Fjelds and Fjords. Map. Post 8vo. 9s.

——— SWEDEN, Stockholm, Upsala, Gothenburg, the Shores of the Baltic, &c. Post 8vo. 6s.

——— DENMARK, Sleswig, Holstein, Copenhagen, Jutland, Iceland. Map. Post 8vo. 6s.

LIST OF WORKS

HAND-BOOK—RUSSIA, St. Petersburg, Moscow, Poland, and Finland. Maps. Post 8vo. 15s.
—————— GREECE, the Ionian Islands, Continental Greece, Athens, the Peloponnesus, the Islands of the Ægean Sea, Albania, Thessaly, and Macedonia. Maps. Post 8vo. 15s.
—————— TURKEY IN ASIA—Constantinople, the Bosphorus, Dardanelles, Brousa, Plain of Troy, Crete, Cyprus, Smyrna, Ephesus, the Seven Churches, Coasts of the Black Sea, Armenia, Mesopotamia, &c. Maps. Post 8vo. 15s.
—————— EGYPT, including Descriptions of the Course of the Nile through Egypt and Nubia, Alexandria, Cairo, and Thebes, the Suez Canal, the Pyramids, the Peninsula of Sinai, the Oases, the Fyoom, &c. Map. Post 8vo. 15s
—————— HOLY LAND—Syria, Palestine, Peninsula of Sinai, Edom, Syrian Deserts, Petra, Damascus, and Palmyra. Maps. Post 8vo.
⁎ Travelling Map of Palestine. In a case. 12s.
—————— INDIA — Bombay and Madras. Map. 2 Vols. Post 8vo. 12s. each.

ENGLISH HANDBOOKS.

HAND-BOOK—MODERN LONDON. Map. 16mo. 3s. 6d.
—————— EASTERN COUNTIES, Chelmsford, Harwich, Colchester, Maldon, Cambridge, Ely, Newmarket, Bury St. Edmunds, Ipswich, Woodbridge, Felixstowe, Lowestoft, Norwich, Yarmouth, Cromer, &c. Map and Plans. Post 8vo. 12s.
—————— CATHEDRALS of Oxford, Peterborough, Norwich, Ely, and Lincoln. With 90 Illustrations. Crown 8vo. 18s.
—————— KENT AND SUSSEX, Canterbury, Dover, Ramsgate, Sheerness, Rochester, Chatham, Woolwich, Brighton, Chichester, Worthing, Hastings, Lewes, Arundel, &c. Map. Post 8vo. 10s.
—————— SURREY AND HANTS, Kingston, Croydon, Reigate, Guildford, Dorking, Boxhill, Winchester, Southampton, New Forest, Portsmouth, and Isle of Wight. Maps. Post 8vo. 10s.
—————— BERKS, BUCKS, AND OXON, Windsor, Eton, Reading, Aylesbury, Uxbridge, Wycombe, Henley, the City and University of Oxford, Blenheim, and the Descent of the Thames. Map. Post 8vo. 7s. 6d.
—————— WILTS, DORSET, AND SOMERSET, Salisbury, Chippenham, Weymouth, Sherborne, Wells, Bath, Bristol, Taunton, &c. Map. Post 8vo. 10s.
—————— DEVON AND CORNWALL, Exeter, Ilfracombe, Linton, Sidmouth, Dawlish, Teignmouth, Plymouth, Devonport, Torquay, Launceston, Truro, Penzance, Falmouth, the Lizard, Land's End, &c. Maps. Post 8vo. 12s.
—————— CATHEDRALS of Winchester, Salisbury, Exeter, Wells, Chichester, Rochester, Canterbury. With 110 Illustrations. 2 Vols. Crown 8vo. 24s.
—————— GLOUCESTER, HEREFORD, and WORCESTER, Cirencester, Cheltenham, Stroud, Tewkesbury, Leominster, Ross, Malvern, Kidderminster, Dudley, Bromsgrove, Evesham. Map. Post 8vo. 9s.
—————— CATHEDRALS of Bristol, Gloucester, Hereford, Worcester, and Lichfield. With 50 Illustrations. Crown 8vo. 16s.
—————— NORTH WALES, Bangor, Carnarvon, Beaumaris, Snowdon, Llanberis, Dolgelly, Cader Idris, Conway, &c. Map. Post 8vo. 7s.
—————— SOUTH WALES, Monmouth, Llandaff, Merthyr, Vale of Neath, Pembroke, Carmarthen, Tenby, Swansea, and The Wye, &c. Map. Post 8vo. 7s.

HAND-BOOK—CATHEDRALS OF BANGOR, ST. ASAPH, Llandaff, and St. David's. With Illustrations. Post 8vo. 15s.

————— DERBY, NOTTS, LEICESTER, STAFFORD, Matlock, Bakewell, Chatsworth, The Peak, Buxton, Hardwick, Dove Dale, Ashborne, Southwell, Mansfield, Retford, Burton, Belvoir, Melton Mowbray, Wolverhampton, Lichfield, Walsall, Tamworth. Map. Post 8vo. 9s

————— SHROPSHIRE, CHESHIRE AND LANCASHIRE —Shrewsbury, Ludlow, Bridgnorth, Oswestry, Chester, Crewe, Alderley, Stockport, Birkenhead, Warrington, Bury, Manchester, Liverpool, Burnley, Clitheroe, Bolton, Blackburn, Wigan, Preston, Rochdale, Lancaster, Southport, Blackpool, &c. Map. Post 8vo. 10s.

————— YORKSHIRE, Doncaster, Hull, Selby, Beverley, Scarborough, Whitby, Harrogate, Ripon, Leeds, Wakefield, Bradford, Halifax, Huddersfield, Sheffield. Map and Plans. Post 8vo. 12s.

————— CATHEDRALS of York, Ripon, Durham, Carlisle, Chester, and Manchester. With 60 Illustrations. 2 Vols. Crown 8vo. 21s.

————— DURHAM AND NORTHUMBERLAND, Newcastle, Darlington, Gateshead, Bishop Auckland, Stockton, Hartlepool, Sunderland, Shields, Berwick-on-Tweed, Morpeth, Tynemouth, Coldstream, Alnwick, &c. Map. Post 8vo. 9s.

————— WESTMORLAND AND CUMBERLAND—Lancaster, Furness Abbey, Ambleside, Kendal, Windermere, Coniston, Keswick, Grasmere, Ulswater, Carlisle, Cockermouth, Penrith, Appleby. Map. Post 8vo. 6s.

*** MURRAY'S MAP OF THE LAKE DISTRICT, on canvas. 3s. 6d.

————— SCOTLAND, Edinburgh, Melrose, Kelso, Glasgow, Dumfries, Ayr, Stirling, Arran, The Clyde, Oban, Inverary, Loch Lomond, Loch Katrine and Trossachs, Caledonian Canal, Inverness, Perth, Dundee, Aberdeen, Braemar, Skye, Caithness, Ross, Sutherland, &c. Maps and Plans. Post 8vo. 9s.

————— IRELAND, Dublin, Belfast, Donegal, Galway, Wexford, Cork, Limerick, Waterford, Killarney, Munster, &c. Maps. Post 8vo. 12s.

HORACE; a New Edition of the Text. Edited by DEAN MILMAN. With 100 Woodcuts. Crown 8vo. 7s. 6d.

————— Life of. By DEAN MILMAN. Illustrations. 8vo. 9s.

HOUGHTON'S (LORD) Monographs, Vol. I., Personal and Social. With Portraits. Crown 8vo. 10s. 6d.

————— POETICAL WORKS. *Collected Edition.* With Portrait. 2 Vols Fcap. 8vo. 12s.

HUME'S (The Student's) History of England, from the Invasion of Julius Cæsar to the Revolution of 1688. Corrected and continued to 1868. Woodcuts. Post 8vo. 7s. 6d.

HUTCHINSON (GEN.), on the most expeditious, certain, and easy Method of Dog-Breaking. With 40 Illustrations. Crown 8vo. 9s.

HUTTON'S (H. E.) Principia Græca; an Introduction to the Study of Greek. Comprehending Grammar, Delectus, and Exercise-book, with Vocabularies. *Sixth Edition.* 12mo. 3s. 6d.

IRBY AND MANGLES' Travels in Egypt, Nubia, Syria, and the Holy Land. Post 8vo. 2s.

JACOBSON'S (BISHOP) Fragmentary Illustrations of the History of the Book of Common Prayer; from Manuscript Sources (Bishop SANDERSON and Bishop WREN). 8vo. 5s.

JAMES' (REV. THOMAS) Fables of Æsop. A New Translation, with Historical Preface. With 100 Woodcuts by TENNIEL and WOLF. Post 8vo. 2s. 6d.

C

18   LIST OF WORKS

HOME AND COLONIAL LIBRARY. A Series of Works adapted for all circles and classes of Readers, having been selected for their acknowledged interest, and ability of the Authors. Post 8vo. Published at 2s. and 3s. 6d. each, and arranged under two distinctive heads as follows:—

CLASS A.
HISTORY, BIOGRAPHY, AND HISTORIC TALES.

1. SIEGE OF GIBRALTAR. By JOHN DRINKWATER. 2s.
2. THE AMBER-WITCH. By LADY DUFF GORDON. 2s.
3. CROMWELL AND BUNYAN. By ROBERT SOUTHEY. 2s.
4. LIFE OF SIR FRANCIS DRAKE. By JOHN BARROW. 2s.
5. CAMPAIGNS AT WASHINGTON. By REV. G. R. GLEIG. 2s.
6. THE FRENCH IN ALGIERS. By LADY DUFF GORDON. 2s.
7. THE FALL OF THE JESUITS. 2s.
8. LIVONIAN TALES. 2s.
9. LIFE OF CONDÉ. By LORD MAHON. 3s. 6d.
10. SALE'S BRIGADE. By REV. G. R. GLEIG. 2s.
11. THE SIEGES OF VIENNA. By LORD ELLESMERE. 2s.
12. THE WAYSIDE CROSS. By CAPT. MILMAN. 2s.
13. SKETCHES OF GERMAN LIFE. By SIR A. GORDON. 3s. 6d.
14. THE BATTLE OF WATERLOO. By REV. G. R. GLEIG. 3s. 6d.
15. AUTOBIOGRAPHY OF STEFFENS. 2s.
16. THE BRITISH POETS. By THOMAS CAMPBELL. 3s. 6d.
17. HISTORICAL ESSAYS. By LORD MAHON. 3s. 6d.
18. LIFE OF LORD CLIVE. By REV. G. R. GLEIG. 3s. 6d.
19. NORTH-WESTERN RAILWAY. By SIR F. B. HEAD. 2s.
20. LIFE OF MUNRO. By REV. G. R. GLEIG. 3s. 6d.

CLASS B.
VOYAGES, TRAVELS, AND ADVENTURES.

1. BIBLE IN SPAIN. By GEORGE BORROW. 3s. 6d.
2. GYPSIES OF SPAIN. By GEORGE BORROW. 3s. 6d.
3 & 4. JOURNALS IN INDIA. By BISHOP HEBER. 2 Vols. 7s.
5. TRAVELS IN THE HOLY LAND. By IRBY and MANGLES. 2s.
6. MOROCCO AND THE MOORS. By J. DRUMMOND HAY. 2s.
7. LETTERS FROM THE BALTIC. By a LADY. 2s.
8. NEW SOUTH WALES. By MRS. MEREDITH. 2s.
9. THE WEST INDIES. By M. G. LEWIS. 2s.
10. SKETCHES OF PERSIA. By SIR JOHN MALCOLM. 3s. 6d.
11. MEMOIRS OF FATHER RIPA. 2s.
12 & 13. TYPEE AND OMOO. By HERMANN MELVILLE. 2 Vols. 7s.
14. MISSIONARY LIFE IN CANADA. By REV. J. ABBOTT. 2s.
15. LETTERS FROM MADRAS. By a LADY. 2s.
16. HIGHLAND SPORTS. By CHARLES ST. JOHN. 3s. 6d.
17. PAMPAS JOURNEYS. By SIR F. B. HEAD. 2s.
18. GATHERINGS FROM SPAIN. By RICHARD FORD. 3s. 6d.
19. THE RIVER AMAZON. By W. H. EDWARDS. 2s.
20. MANNERS & CUSTOMS OF INDIA. By REV. C. ACLAND. 2s.
21. ADVENTURES IN MEXICO. By G. F. RUXTON. 3s. 6d.
22. PORTUGAL AND GALLICIA. By LORD CARNARVON. 3s. 6d.
23. BUSH LIFE IN AUSTRALIA. By REV. H. W. HAYGARTH. 2s.
24. THE LIBYAN DESERT. By BAYLE ST. JOHN. 2s.
25. SIERRA LEONE. By A LADY. 3s. 6d.

*** Each work may be had separately.

JAMESON'S (MRS.) Lives of the Early Italian Painters—
and the Progress of Painting in Italy—Cimabue to Bassano. With
50 Portraits. Post 8vo. 12s.

JENNINGS' (L. J.) Eighty Years of Republican Government in
the United States. Post 8vo. 10s. 6d.

JERVIS'S (REV. W. H.) Gallican Church, from the Con-
cordat of Bologna, 1516, to the Revolution. With an Introduction.
Portraits. 2 Vols. 8vo. 28s.

JESSE'S (EDWARD) Gleanings in Natural History. Fcp. 8vo. 3s. 6d.

JEX-BLAKE'S (REV. T. W.) Life in Faith: Sermons Preached
at Cheltenham and Rugby. Fcap. 8vo.

JOHNS' (REV. B. G.) Blind People; their Works and Ways. With
Sketches of the Lives of some famous Blind Men. With Illustrations.
Post 8vo. 7s. 6d.

JOHNSON'S (DR. SAMUEL) Life. By James Boswell. Including
the Tour to the Hebrides. Edited by MR. CROKER. *New Edition.*
Portraits. 4 Vols. 8vo. [*In Preparation.*

——— Lives of the most eminent English Poets, with
Critical Observations on their Works. Edited with Notes, Corrective
and Explanatory, by PETER CUNNINGHAM. 3 vols. 8vo. 22s. 6d.

JUNIUS' HANDWRITING Professionally investigated. By Mr. CHABOT,
Expert. With Preface and Collateral Evidence, by the Hon. EDWARD
TWISLETON. With Facsimiles, Woodcuts, &c. 4to. £3 3s.

KEN'S (BISHOP) Life. By a LAYMAN. Portrait. 2 Vols. 8vo. 18s.

——— Exposition of the Apostles' Creed. 16mo. 1s. 6d.

KERR'S (ROBERT) GENTLEMAN'S HOUSE; OR, HOW TO PLAN ENG-
LISH RESIDENCES FROM THE PARSONAGE TO THE PALACE. With
Views and Plans. 8vo. 24s.

——— Small Country House. A Brief Practical Discourse on
the Planning of a Residence from 2000l. to 5000l. With Supplementary Estimates to 7000l. Post 8vo. 3s.

——— Ancient Lights; a Book for Architects, Surveyors,
Lawyers, and Landlords. 8vo. 5s. 6d.

——— (R. MALCOLM) Student's Blackstone. A Systematic
Abridgment of the entire Commentaries, adapted to the present state
of the law. Post 8vo. 7s. 6d.

KING EDWARD VITH's Latin Grammar. 12mo. 3s. 6d.

——— First Latin Book. 12mo. 2s 6d.

KING GEORGE IIIRD's Correspondence with Lord North,
1769-82. Edited, with Notes and Introduction, by W. BODHAM DONNE.
2 vols. 8vo. 32s.

KING'S (R. J.) Archæology, Travel and Art; being Sketches and
Studies, Historical and Descriptive. 8vo. 12s.

KIRK'S (J. FOSTER) History of Charles the Bold, Duke of Burgundy. Portrait. 3 Vols. 8vo. 45s.

KIRKES' Handbook of Physiology. Edited by W. MORRANT
BAKER, F.R.C.S. With 240 Illustrations. Post 8vo. 12s. 6d.

KUGLER'S Handbook of Painting.—The Italian Schools. Revised and Remodelled from the most recent Researches. By LADY
EASTLAKE. With 140 Illustrations. 2 Vols. Crown 8vo. 30s.

——— Handbook of Painting.—The German, Flemish, and
Dutch Schools. Revised and in part re-written. By J. A. CROWE.
With 60 Illustrations. 2 Vols. Crown 8vo. 24s.

LANE'S (E. W.) Account of the Manners and Customs of Modern
Egyptians. With Illustrations. 2 Vols. Post 8vo. 12s

LAWRENCE'S (Sir Geo.) Reminiscences of Forty-three Years' Service in India; including Captivities in Cabul among the Affghans and among the Sikhs, and a Narrative of the Mutiny in Rajputana. Crown 8vo. 10s. 6d.

LAYARD'S (A. H.) Nineveh and its Remains. Being a Narrative of Researches and Discoveries amidst the Ruins of Assyria. With an Account of the Chaldean Christians of Kurdistan; the Yezedis, or Devil-worshippers; and an Enquiry into the Manners and Arts of the Ancient Assyrians. Plates and Woodcuts. 2 Vols. 8vo. 36s.
*** A Popular Edition of the above work. With Illustrations. Post 8vo. 7s. 6d.

——— Nineveh and Babylon; being the Narrative of Discoveries in the Ruins, with Travels in Armenia, Kurdistan and the Desert, during a Second Expedition to Assyria. With Map and Plates. 8vo. 21s.
*** A Popular Edition of the above work. With Illustrations. Post 8vo. 7s. 6d.

LEATHES' (Stanley) Practical Hebrew Grammar. With the Hebrew Text of Genesis i.—vi., and Psalms i.—vi. Grammatical Analysis and Vocabulary. Post 8vo. 7s. 6d.

LENNEP'S (Rev. H. J. Van) Missionary Travels in Asia Minor. With Illustrations of Biblical History and Archæology. With Map and Woodcuts. 2 Vols. Post 8vo. 24s.

——— Modern Customs and Manners of Bible Lands in Illustration of Scripture. With Coloured Maps and 300 Illustrations. 2 Vols. 8vo. 21s.

LESLIE'S (C. R.) Handbook for Young Painters. With Illustrations. Post 8vo. 7s. 6d.

——— Life and Works of Sir Joshua Reynolds. Portraits and Illustrations. 2 Vols. 8vo. 42s.

LETTERS From the Baltic. By a Lady. Post 8vo. 2s.

——— Madras. By a Lady. Post 8vo. 2s.

——— Sierra Leone. By a Lady. Post 8vo. 3s. 6d.

LEVI'S (Leone) History of British Commerce; and of the Economic Progress of the Nation, from 1763 to 1870. 8vo. 16s.

LIDDELL'S (Dean) Student's History of Rome, from the earliest Times to the establishment of the Empire. With Woodcuts. Post 8vo. 7s. 6d.

LLOYD'S (W. Watkiss) History of Sicily to the Athenian War; with Elucidations of the Sicilian Odes of Pindar. With Map 8vo. 14s.

LISPINGS from LOW LATITUDES; or, the Journal of the Hon. Impulsia Gushington. Edited by Lord Dufferin. With 24 Plates. 4to. 21s.

LITTLE ARTHUR'S History of England. By Lady Callcott. New Edition, continued to 1872. With Woodcuts. Fcap. 8vo. 1s. 6d.

LIVINGSTONE'S (Dr.) Popular Account of his First Expedition to Africa, 1840-56. Illustrations. Post 8vo. 7s 6d.

——— Popular Account of his Second Expedition to to Africa, 1858-64. Map and Illustrations. Post 8vo. 7s. 6d.

——— Last Journals in Central Africa, from 1865 to his Death. Continued by a Narrative of his last moments and sufferings. By Rev Horace Waller. Maps and Illustrations. 2 Vols 8vo. 28s.

LIVONIAN TALES. By the Author of "Letters from the Baltic." Post 8vo. 2s.

LOCH'S (H. B.) Personal Narrative of Events during Lord Elgin's Second Embassy to China. With Illustrations. Post 8vo. 9s.

LOCKHART'S (J. G.) Ancient Spanish Ballads. Historical and Romantic. Translated, with Notes. With Portrait and Illustrations. Crown 8vo. 5s.

—————— Life of Theodore Hook. Fcap. 8vo. 1s.

LONSDALE'S (Bishop) Life. With Selections from his Writings. By E. B. Denison. With Portrait. Crown 8vo. 10s. 6d.

LOUDON'S (Mrs.) Gardening for Ladies. With Directions and Calendar of Operations for Every Month. Woodcuts. Fcap. 8vo. 3s 6d.

LUCKNOW: A Lady's Diary of the Siege. Fcap. 8vo. 4s. 6d.

LYELL'S (Sir Charles) Principles of Geology; or, the Modern Changes of the Earth and its Inhabitants considered as illustrative of Geology. With Illustrations. 2 Vols. 8vo. 32s.

—————— Student's Elements of Geology. With Table of British Fossils and 600 Illustrations. Post 8vo. 9s.

—————— Geological Evidences of the Antiquity of Man, including an Outline of Glacial Post-Tertiary Geology, and Remarks on the Origin of Species. Illustrations. 8vo. 14s.

—————— (K. M.) Geographical Handbook of Ferns. With Tables to show their Distribution. Post 8vo. 7s. 6d.

LYTTELTON'S (Lord) Ephemera. 2 Vols. Post 8vo. 19s. 6d.

LYTTON'S (Lord) Memoir of Julian Fane. With Portrait. Post 8vo. 5s.

McCLINTOCK'S (Sir L.) Narrative of the Discovery of the Fate of Sir John Franklin and his Companions in the Arctic Seas. With Illustrations. Post 8vo. 7s. 6d.

MACDOUGALL'S (Col.) Modern Warfare as Influenced by Modern Artillery. With Plans. Post 8vo. 12s.

MACGREGOR'S (J.) Rob Roy on the Jordan, Nile, Red Sea, Gennesareth, &c. A Canoe Cruise in Palestine and Egypt and the Waters of Damascus. With Map and 70 Illustrations. Crown 8vo. 7s. 6d

MACPHERSON'S (Major) Services in India, while Political Agent at Gwalior during the Mutiny. Illustrations. 8vo. 12s.

MAETZNER'S English Grammar. A Methodical, Analytical, and Historical Treatise on the Orthography, Prosody, Inflections, and Syntax of the English Tongue. Translated from the German. By Clair J. Grece, LL.D. 3 Vols. 8vo. 36s.

MAHON (Lord), see Stanhope.

MAINE'S (Sir H. Sumner) Ancient Law: its Connection with the Early History of Society, and its Relation to Modern Ideas. 8vo. 12s.

—————— Village Communities in the East and West. 8vo. 9s.

—————— Early History of Institutions. 8vo. 12s.

MALCOLM'S (Sir John) Sketches of Persia. Post 8vo. 3s. 6d.

MANSEL'S (Dean) Limits of Religious Thought Examined. Post 8vo. 8s. 6d.

—————— Letters, Lectures, and Papers, including the Phrontisterion, or Oxford in the XIXth Century. Edited by H. W. Chandler, M.A. 8vo. 12s.

—————— Gnostic Heresies of the First and Second Centuries. With a sketch of his life and character By Lord Carnarvon. Edited by Canon Lightfoot. 8vo 10s. 6d.

MANUAL OF SCIENTIFIC ENQUIRY. For the Use of Travellers. Edited by Rev. R. Main. Post 8vo. 3s. 6d. (*Published by order of the Lords of the Admiralty*.)

MARCO POLO. The Book of Ser Marco Polo, the Venetian. Concerning the Kingdoms and Marvels of the East. A new English Version. Illustrated by the light of Oriental Writers and Modern Travels. By Col. Henry Yule. Maps and Illustrations. 2 Vols. Medium 8vo. 63s.

MARKHAM'S (MRS.) History of England. From the First Invasion by the Romans to 1867. Woodcuts. 12mo. 3s. 6d.
—————— History of France. From the Conquest by the Gauls to 1861. Woodcuts. 12mo. 3s. 6d.
—————— History of Germany. From the Invasion by Marius to 1867. Woodcuts. 12mo. 3s. 6d.
MARLBOROUGH'S (SARAH, DUCHESS OF) Letters. Now first published from the Original MSS. at Madresfield Court. With an Introduction. 8vo. 10s. 6d.
MARRYAT'S (JOSEPH) History of Modern and Mediæval Pottery and Porcelain. With a Description of the Manufacture. Plates and Woodcuts. 8vo. 42s.
MARSH'S (G. P.) Student's Manual of the English Language. Post 8vo. 7s. 6d.
MATTHIÆ'S GREEK GRAMMAR. Abridged by BLOMFIELD, Revised by E. S. CROOKE. 12mo. 4s.
MAUREL'S Character, Actions, and Writings of Wellington. Fcap. 8vo. 1s. 6d.
MAYNE'S (CAPT.) Four Years in British Columbia and Vancouver Island. Illustrations. 8vo. 16s.
MEADE'S (HON. HERBERT) Ride through the Disturbed Districts of New Zealand, with a Cruise among the South Sea Islands. With Illustrations. Medium 8vo. 12s.
MELVILLE'S (HERMANN) Marquesas and South Sea Islands. 2 Vols. Post 8vo. 7s.
MEREDITH'S (MRS. CHARLES) Notes and Sketches of New South Wales. Post 8vo. 2s.
MESSIAH (THE): The Life, Travels, Death, Resurrection, and Ascension of our Blessed Lord. By A Layman. Map. 8vo. 18s.
MILLINGTON'S (REV. T. S.) Signs and Wonders in the Land of Ham, or the Ten Plagues of Egypt, with Ancient and Modern Illustrations. Woodcuts. Post 8vo. 7s. 6d.
MILMAN'S (DEAN) History of the Jews, from the earliest Period down to Modern Times. 3 Vols. Post 8vo. 18s.
—————— Early Christianity, from the Birth of Christ to the Abolition of Paganism in the Roman Empire. 3 Vols. Post 8vo. 18s.
—————— Latin Christianity, including that of the Popes to the Pontificate of Nicholas V. 9 Vols. Post 8vo. 54s.
—————— Annals of St. Paul's Cathedral, from the Romans to the funeral of Wellington. Portrait and Illustrations. 8vo. 18s.
—————— Character and Conduct of the Apostles considered as an Evidence of Christianity. 8vo. 10s. 6d.
—————— Quinti Horatii Flacci Opera. With 100 Woodcuts. Small 8vo. 7s. 6d.
—————— Life of Quintus Horatius Flaccus. With Illustrations. 8vo. 9s.
—————— Poetical Works. The Fall of Jerusalem—Martyr of Antioch—Balshazzar—Tamor—Anne Boleyn—Fazio, &c. With Portrait and Illustrations. 3 Vols. Fcap. 8vo. 18s.
—————— Fall of Jerusalem. Fcap. 8vo. 1s.
—————— (CAPT. E. A.) Wayside Cross. Post 8vo. 2s.
MIVART'S (ST. GEORGE) Lessons from Nature; as manifested in Mind and Matter. 8vo.
MODERN DOMESTIC COOKERY. Founded on Principles of Economy and Practical Knowledge. New Edition. Woodcuts. Fcap. 8vo. 5s.

MONGREDIEN'S (AUGUSTUS) Trees and Shrubs for English Plantation. A Selection and Description of the most Ornamental which will flourish in the open air in our climate. With Classified Lists. With 30 Illustrations. 8vo. 16s.

MOORE & JACKMAN on the Clematis as a Garden Flower. Descriptions of the Hardy Species and Varieties, with Directions for their Cultivation. 8vo. 10s. 6d

MOORE'S (THOMAS) Life and Letters of Lord Byron. *Cabinet Edition.* With Plates. 6 Vols. Fcap. 8vo. 18s.; *Popular Edition*, with Portraits. Royal 8vo. 7s. 6d.

MOSSMAN'S (SAMUEL) New Japan; the Land of the Rising Sun; its Annals and Progress during the past Twenty Years, recording the remarkable Progress of the Japanese in Western Civilisation. With Map. 8vo. 15s.

MOTLEY'S (J. L.) History of the United Netherlands: from the Death of William the Silent to the Twelve Years' Truce, 1609. *Library Edition.* Portraits. 4 Vols. 8vo. 60s. *Cabinet Edition.* 4 Vols. Post 8vo. 6s. each.

—————— Life and Death of John of Barneveld, Advocate of Holland. With a View of the Primary Causes and Movements of the Thirty Years' War. *Library Edition.* Illustrations. 2 Vols. 8vo. 28s. *Cabinet Edition.* 2 vols. Post 8vo. 12s.

MOUHOT'S (HENRI) Siam, Cambojia, and Lao; a Narrative of Travels and Discoveries. Illustrations. 2 Vols. 8vo.

MOZLEY'S (CANON) Treatise on Predestination. 8vo. 14s.

—————— Primitive Doctrine of Baptismal Regeneration. 8vo. 7s. 6d.

MUIRHEAD'S (JAS.) Vaux-de-Vire of Maistre Jean Le Houx, Advocate of Vire. Translated and Edited. With Portrait and Illustrations. 8vo.

MUNRO'S (GENERAL) Life and Letters. By REV. G. R. GLEIG. Post 8vo. 3s. 6d.

MURCHISON'S (SIR RODERICK) Siluria; or, a History of the Oldest rocks containing Organic Remains. Map and Plates. 8vo. 18s.

—————— Memoirs. With Notices of his Contemporaries, and Rise and Progress of Palæozoic Geology. By ARCHIBALD GEIKIE. Portraits. 2 Vols. 8vo. 30s.

MURRAY'S RAILWAY READING. Containing:—

WELLINGTON. By LORD ELLESMERE. 6d.
NIMROD ON THE CHASE. 1s.
MUSIC AND DRESS. 1s.
MILMAN'S FALL OF JERUSALEM. 1s.
MAHON'S "FORTY-FIVE." 3s.
LIFE OF THEODORE HOOK. 1s.
DEEDS OF NAVAL DARING. 3s. 6d.
THE HONEY BEE. 1s.
ÆSOP'S FABLES. 2s. 6d.
NIMROD ON THE TURF. 1s. 6d.
ART OF DINING. 1s. 6d.
MAHON'S JOAN OF ARC. 1s.
HEAD'S EMIGRANT. 2s. 6d.
NIMROD ON THE ROAD. 1s.
CROKER ON THE GUILLOTINE. 1s.
HOLLWAY'S NORWAY. 2s.
MAUREL'S WELLINGTON. 1s. 6d.
CAMPBELL'S LIFE OF BACON. 2s. 6d.
THE FLOWER GARDEN. 1s.
TAYLOR'S NOTES FROM LIFE. 2s.
REJECTED ADDRESSES. 1s.
PENN'S HINTS ON ANGLING. 1s.

MUSTERS' (CAPT.) Patagonians; a Year's Wanderings over Untrodden Ground from the Straits of Magellan to the Rio Negro. Illustrations. Post 8vo. 7s. 6d.

NAPIER'S (SIR CHAS.) Life, Journals, and Letters. Portraits. 4 Vols. Crown 8vo. 48s.

—————— (SIR WM.) Life and Letters. Portraits. 2 Vols. Crown 8vo. 28s.

—————— English Battles and Sieges of the Peninsular War. Portrait. Post 8vo. 9s.

NAPOLEON AT FONTAINEBLEAU AND ELBA. A Journal of Occurrences and Notes of Conversations. By SIR NEIL CAMPBELL, C.B. With a Memoir. By REV. A. N. C. MACLACHLAN, M.A. Portrait. 8vo. 15s.

NASMYTH AND CARPENTER. The Moon. Considered as a Planet, a World, and a Satellite. With Illustrations from Drawings made with the aid of Powerful Telescopes, Woodcuts, &c. 4to. 30s.

NAUTICAL ALMANAC (The). (*By Authority.*) 2s. 6d.

NAVY LIST. (Monthly and Quarterly.) Post 8vo.

NEW TESTAMENT. With Short Explanatory Commentary. By ARCHDEACON CHURTON, M.A., and ARCHDEACON BASIL JONES, M.A. With 110 authentic Views, &c. 2 Vols. Crown 8vo. 21s. *bound.*

NEWTH'S (SAMUEL) First Book of Natural Philosophy; an Introduction to the Study of Statics, Dynamics, Hydrostatics, Optics, and Acoustics, with numerous Examples. Small 8vo. 3s. 6d.

—————— Elements of Mechanics, including Hydrostatics, with numerous Examples. Small 8vo. 8s. 6d.

—————— Mathematical Examinations. A Graduated Series of Elementary Examples in Arithmetic, Algebra, Logarithms, Trigonometry, and Mechanics. Small 8vo. 8s. 6d.

NICHOLS' (J. G.) Pilgrimages to Walsingham and Canterbury. By ERASMUS. Translated, with Notes. With Illustrations. Post 8vo. 6s.

—————— (SIR GEORGE) History of the English, Irish and Scotch Poor Laws. 4 Vols. 8vo.

NICOLAS' (SIR HARRIS) Historic Peerage of England. Exhibiting the Origin, Descent, and Present State of every Title of Peerage which has existed in this Country since the Conquest. By WILLIAM COURTHOPE. 8vo. 30s.

NIMROD, On the Chace—Turf—and Road. With Portrait and Plates. Crown 8vo. 5s. Or with Coloured Plates, 7s. 6d.

NORDHOFF'S (CHAS.) Communistic Societies of the United States; including Detailed Accounts of the Shakers, The Amana, Oneida, Bethell, Aurora, Icarian and other existing Societies; with Particulars of their Religious Creeds, Industries, and Present Condition. With 40 Illustrations. 8vo. 15s.

OLD LONDON; Papers read at the Archæological Institute. By various Authors. 8vo. 12s.

ORMATHWAITE'S (LORD) Astronomy and Geology—Darwin and Buckle—Progress and Civilisation. Crown 8vo. 6s.

OWEN'S (LIEUT.-COL.) Principles and Practice of Modern Artillery, including Artillery Material, Gunnery, and Organisation and Use of Artillery in Warfare. With Illustrations. 8vo. 15s.

OXENHAM'S (REV. W.) English Notes for Latin Elegiacs; designed for early Proficients in the Art of Latin Versification, with Prefatory Rules of Composition in Elegiac Metre. 12mo. 3s. 6d.

PALGRAVE'S (R. H. I.) Local Taxation of Great Britain and Ireland. 8vo. 5s.

—————— NOTES ON BANKING IN GREAT BRITAIN AND IRELAND, SWEDEN, DENMARK, AND HAMBURG, with some Remarks on the amount of Bills in circulation, both Inland and Foreign. 8vo. 6s.

PALLISER'S (MRS.) Brittany and its Byeways, its Inhabitants, and Antiquities. With Illustrations. Post 8vo. 12s.

—————— Mottoes for Monuments, or Epitaphs selected for General Use and Study. With Illustrations. Crown 8vo. 7s. 6d.

PARIS' (DR.) Philosophy in Sport made Science in Earnest; or, the First Principles of Natural Philosophy inculcated by aid of the Toys and Sports of Youth. Woodcuts. Post 8vo. 7s. 6d.

PARKMAN'S (FRANCIS) Discovery of the Great West; or, The Valleys of the Mississippi and the Lakes of North America. An Historical Narrative. Map. 8vo. 10s. 6d.

PARKYNS' (MANSFIELD) Three Years' Residence in Abyssinia: with Travels in that Country. With Illustrations. Post 8vo. 7s. 6d.

PEEK PRIZE ESSAYS. The Maintenance of the Church of England as an Established Church. By REV. CHARLES HOLE—REV. R. WATSON DIXON—and REV. JULIUS LLOYD. 8vo. 10s. 6d.

PEEL'S (SIR ROBERT) Memoirs. 2 Vols. Post 8vo. 15s.

PENN'S (RICHARD) Maxims and Hints for an Angler and Chess-player. Woodcuts. Fcap. 8vo. 1s.

PERCY'S (JOHN, M.D.) Metallurgy. Vol. I., Part 1. FUEL, Wood, Peat, Coal, Charcoal, Coke, Refractory Materials, Fire-Clays, &c. With Illustrations. 8vo. 30s.

———— Vol. I., Part 2. Copper, Zinc, Brass. With Illustrations. 8vo. [*In the Press.*

———— Vol. II. Iron and Steel. With Illustrations. 8vo. [*In Preparation.*

———— Vol. III. Lead, including part of SILVER. With Illustrations. 8vo. 30s.

———— Vols. IV. and V. Gold, Silver, and Mercury, Platinum, Tin, Nickel, Cobalt, Antimony, Bismuth, Arsenic, and other Metals. With Illustrations. 8vo. [*In Preparation.*

PERSIA'S (SHAH OF) Diary during his Tour through Europe in 1873. Translated from the Original. By J. W. REDHOUSE. With Portrait and Coloured Title. Crown 8vo. 12s.

PHILLIPS' (JOHN) Memoirs of William Smith. 8vo. 7s. 6d.

———— Geology of Yorkshire, The Coast, and Limestone District. Plates. 2 Vols. 4to.

———— Rivers, Mountains, and Sea Coast of Yorkshire. With Essays on the Climate, Scenery, and Ancient Inhabitants. Plates. 8vo. 15s.

———— (SAMUEL) Literary Essays from "The Times." With Portrait. 2 Vols. Fcap. 8vo. 7s.

POPE'S (ALEXANDER) Works. With Introductions and Notes, by REV. WHITWELL ELWIN. Vols. I., II., VI., VII., VIII. With Portraits. 8vo. 10s. 6d. each.

PORTER'S (REV. J. L.) Damascus, Palmyra, and Lebanon. With Travels among the Giant Cities of Bashan and the Hauran. Map and Woodcuts. Post 8vo. 7s. 6d.

PRAYER-BOOK (ILLUSTRATED), with Borders, Initials, Vignettes, &c. Edited, with Notes, by REV. THOS. JAMES. Medium 8vo. 18s. cloth; 31s. 6d. calf; 36s. morocco.

PRINCESS CHARLOTTE OF WALES. A Brief Memoir. With Selections from her Correspondence and other unpublished Papers. By LADY ROSE WEIGALL. With Portrait. 8vo. 8s. 6d.

PUSS IN BOOTS. With 12 Illustrations. By OTTO SPECKTER. 16mo. 1s. 6d. Or coloured, 2s. 6d.

PRINCIPLES AT STAKE. Essays on Church Questions of the Day. 8vo. 12s. Contents:—

Ritualism and Uniformity.—Benjamin Shaw.	Scripture and Ritual.—Canon Bernard.
The Episcopate.—Bishop of Bath and Wells.	Church in South Africa.—Arthur Mills.
The Priesthood.—Dean of Canterbury.	Schismatical Tendency of Ritualism.—Rev. Dr. Salmon.
National Education.—Rev. Alexander R. Grant.	Revisions of the Liturgy.—Rev. W. G. Humphry.
Doctrine of the Eucharist.—Rev. G. H. Sumner.	Parties and Party Spirit.—Dean of Chester.

PRIVY COUNCIL JUDGMENTS in Ecclesiastical Cases relating to Doctrine and Discipline. With Historical Introduction, by G. C. BRODRICK and W. H. FREMANTLE. 8vo. 10s. 6d.

QUARTERLY REVIEW (THE). 8vo. 6s.

RAE'S (EDWARD) Land of the North Wind; or Travels among the Laplanders and Samoyedes, and along the Shores of the White Sea. With Map and Woodcuts. Post 8vo. 10s. 6d.

RAMBLES in the Syrian Deserts. Post 8vo. 10s. 6d.

RANKE'S (LEOPOLD) History of the Popes of Rome during the 16th and 17th Centuries. Translated from the German by SARAH AUSTIN. 3 Vols. 8vo. 30s.

RASSAM'S (HORMUZD) Narrative of the British Mission to Abyssinia. With Notices of the Countries Traversed from Massowah to Magdala. Illustrations. 2 Vols. 8vo. 28s.

RAWLINSON'S (CANON) Herodotus. A New English Version. Edited with Notes and Essays. Maps and Woodcut. 4 Vols. 8vo. 48s.

———— Five Great Monarchies of Chaldæa, Assyria, Media, Babylonia, and Persia. With Maps and Illustrations. 3 Vols. 8vo. 42s.

———— (SIR HENRY) England and Russia in the East; a Series of Papers on the Political and Geographical Condition of Central Asia. Map 8vo. 12s.

REED'S (E. J.) Shipbuilding in Iron and Steel; a Practical Treatise, giving full details of Construction, Processes of Manufacture, and Building Arrangements. With 5 Plans and 250 Woodcuts. 8vo.

———— Iron-Clad Ships; their Qualities, Performances, and Cost. With Chapters on Turret Ships, Iron-Clad Rams, &c. With Illustrations. 8vo. 12s.

REJECTED ADDRESSES (THE). By JAMES AND HORACE SMITH. Woodcuts. Post 8vo. 3s. 6d.; or *Popular Edition*, Fcap. 8vo. 1s.

RESIDENCE IN BULGARIA; or, Notes on the Resources and Administration of Turkey, &c. By S. G. B. ST. CLAIR and CHARLES A. BROPHY. 8vo. 12s.

REYNOLDS' (SIR JOSHUA) Life and Times. By C. R. LESLIE, R.A. and TOM TAYLOR. Portraits. 2 Vols. 8vo.

RICARDO'S (DAVID) Political Works. With a Notice of his Life and Writings. By J. R. M'CULLOCH. 8vo. 16s.

RIPA'S (FATHER) Thirteen Years' Residence at the Court of Peking. Post 8vo. 2s.

ROBERTSON'S (CANON) History of the Christian Church, from the Apostolic Age to the Reformation, 1517. *Library Edition*. 4 Vols. 8vo. *Cabinet Edition*. 8 Vols. Post 8vo. 6s. each.

———— How shall we Conform to the Liturgy. 12mo. 9s.

ROME. *See* LIDDELL and SMITH.

ROWLAND'S (DAVID) Manual of the English Constitution. Its Rise, Growth, and Present State. Post 8vo. 10s. 6d.

———— Laws of Nature the Foundation of Morals. Post 8vo. 6s.

ROBSON'S (E. R.) SCHOOL ARCHITECTURE. Being Practical Remarks on the Planning, Designing, Building, and Furnishing of School-houses. With 300 Illustrations. Medium 8vo. 31s. 6d.

RUNDELL'S (MRS.) Modern Domestic Cookery. Fcap. 8vo. 5s.

RUXTON'S (GEORGE F.) Travels in Mexico; with Adventures among the Wild Tribes and Animals of the Prairies and Rocky Mountains. Post 8vo. 3s. 6d.

ROBINSON'S (REV. DR.) Biblical Researches in Palestine and the Adjacent Regions, 1838—52. Maps. 3 Vols. 8vo. 42s.

———— Physical Geography of the Holy Land. Post 8vo. 10s. 6d.

———— (WM.) Alpine Flowers for English Gardens. With 70 Illustrations. Crown 8vo. 12s.

———— Wild Gardens; or, our Groves and Shrubberies made beautiful by the Naturalization of Hardy Exotic Plants. With Frontispiece. Small 8vo. 6s.

———— Sub-Tropical Gardens; or, Beauty of Form in the Flower Garden. With Illustrations. Small 8vo. 7s. 6d.

SALE'S (SIR ROBERT) Brigade in Affghanistan. With an Account of the Defence of Jellalabad. By REV. G. R. GLEIG. Post 8vo. 2s.

SCHLIEMANN'S (DR. HENRY) Troy and Its Remains. A Narrative of Researches and Discoveries made on the Site of Ilium, and in the Trojan Plain. Edited by PHILIP SMITH, B.A. With Maps, Views, and 500 Illustrations. Medium 8vo. 42s.

SCOTT'S (SIR G. G.) Secular and Domestic Architecture, Present and Future. 8vo. 9s.

——— (DEAN) University Sermons. Post 8vo. 8s. 6d.

SHADOWS OF A SICK ROOM. With a Preface by Canon LIDDON. 16mo. 2s 6d.

SCROPE'S (G. P.) Geology and Extinct Volcanoes of Central France. Illustrations. Medium 8vo. 30s.

SHAW'S (T. B.) Manual of English Literature. Post 8vo. 7s. 6d.

——— Specimens of English Literature. Selected from the Chief Writers. Post 8vo. 7s. 6d.

——— (ROBERT) Visit to High Tartary, Yarkand, and Kashgar (formerly Chinese Tartary), and Return Journey over the Karakorum Pass. With Map and Illustrations. 8vo. 16s.

SHIRLEY'S (EVELYN P.) Deer and Deer Parks; or some Account of English Parks, with Notes on the Management of Deer. Illustrations. 4to. 21s.

SIERRA LEONE; Described in Letters to Friends at Home. By A LADY. Post 8vo. 3s. 6d.

SINCLAIR'S (ARCHDEACON) Old Times and Distant Places. A Series of Sketches. Crown 8vo. 9s.

SMILES' (SAMUEL) British Engineers; from the Earliest Period to the death of the Stephensons. With Illustrations. 5 Vols. Crown 8vo. 7s. 6d. each.

——— George and Robert Stephenson. Illustrations. Medium 8vo. 21s.

——— Boulton and Watt. Illustrations. Medium 8vo. 21s.

——— Self-Help. With Illustrations of Conduct and Perseverance. Post 8vo. 6s. Or in French, 5s.

——— Character. A Sequel to "SELF-HELP." Post 8vo. 6s.

——— Thrift. A Companion Volume to "Self-Help" and "Character." Post 8vo. 6s.

——— Boy's Voyage round the World. With Illustrations. Post 8vo. 6s.

STANLEY'S (DEAN) Sinai and Palestine, in connexion with their History. 20th Thousand. Map. 8vo. 14s.

——— Bible in the Holy Land; Extracted from the above Work. Second Edition. Woodcuts. Fcap. 8vo. 2s. 6d.

——— Eastern Church. Fourth Edition. Plans. 8vo. 12s.

——— Jewish Church. 1st & 2nd Series. From the Earliest Times to the Captivity 8vo. 24s.

——— Third Series. From the Captivity to the Destruction of Jerusalem. 8vo.

——— Church of Scotland. 8vo. 7s. 6d.

——— Memorials of Canterbury Cathedral. Woodcuts. Post 8vo. 7s. 6d.

——— Westminster Abbey. With Illustrations. 8vo. 21s.

——— Sermons during a Tour in the East. 8vo. 9s.

——— ADDRESSES AND CHARGES OF THE LATE BISHOP STANLEY. With Memoir. 8vo. 10s. 6d.

——— Epistles of St. Paul to the Corinthians. 8vo. 18s.

LIST OF WORKS

SMITH'S (Dr. Wm.) Dictionary of the Bible; its Antiquities, Biography, Geography, and Natural History. Illustrations. 3 Vols. 8vo. 105s.

————— Concise Bible Dictionary. With 300 Illustrations. Medium 8vo. 21s.

————— Smaller Bible Dictionary. With Illustrations. Post 8vo. 7s. 6d.

————— Christian Antiquities. Comprising the History, Institutions, and Antiquities of the Christian Church. With Illustrations. Vol. I. 8vo. 31s. 6d.

————— Biography and Doctrines; from the Times of the Apostles to the Age of Charlemagne. 8vo. [*In Preparation.*

————— Atlas of Ancient Geography—Biblical and Classical. Folio. 6l. 6s.

————— Greek and Roman Antiquities. With 500 Illustrations. Medium 8vo. 28s.

————— Biography and Mythology. With 600 Illustrations. 3 Vols. Medium 8vo. 4l. 4s.

————— Geography. 2 Vols. With 500 Illustrations. Medium 8vo. 56s.

————— Classical Dictionary of Mythology, Biography, and Geography. 1 Vol. With 750 Woodcuts. 8vo. 18s.

————— Smaller Classical Dictionary. With 200 Woodcuts. Crown 8vo. 7s. 6d.

————— Greek and Roman Antiquities. With 200 Woodcuts. Crown 8vo. 7s. 6d.

————— Latin-English Dictionary. With Tables of the Roman Calendar, Measures, Weights, and Money. Medium 8vo. 21s.

————— Smaller Latin-English Dictionary. 12mo. 7s. 6d.

————— English-Latin Dictionary. Medium 8vo. 21s.

————— Smaller English-Latin Dictionary. 12mo. 7s. 6d.

————— School Manual of English Grammar, with Copious Exercises. Post 8vo. 3s. 6d.

————— Modern Geography. 12mo. [*Nearly ready.*

————— Primary English Grammar. 16mo. 1s.

————— History of Britain. 12mo. 2s. 6d.

————— French Principia. Part I. A First Course, containing a Grammar, Delectus, Exercises, and Vocabularies. 12mo. 3s. 6d.

————— Part II. A Reading Book, containing Fables, Stories, and Anecdotes, Natural History, and Scenes from the History of France. With Grammatical Questions, Notes and copious Etymological Dictionary. 12mo. 4s. 6d.

————— Part III. Prose Composition, containing a Systematic Course of Exercises on the Syntax, with the Principal Rules of Syntax. 12mo. [*In the Press.*

————— German Principia, Part I. A First German Course, containing a Grammar, Delectus, Exercise Book, and Vocabularies. 12mo. 3s. 6d.

————— Part II. A Reading Book; containing Fables, Stories, and Anecdotes, Natural History, and Scenes from the History of Germany. With Grammatical Questions, Notes, and Dictionary. 12mo. 3s. 6d.

————— Part III. An Introduction to German Prose Composition; containing a Systematic Course of Exercises on the Syntax, with the Principal Rules of Syntax. 12mo. [*In the Press.*

SMITH'S (Dr. Wm.) Principia Latina—Part I. First Latin Course, containing a Grammar, Delectus, and Exercise Book, with Vocabularies. 12mo. 3s. 6d.

In this Edition the Cases of the Nouns, Adjectives, and Pronouns are arranged both as in the ORDINARY GRAMMARS and as in the PUBLIC SCHOOL PRIMER, together with the corresponding Exercises.

———————— Part II. A Reading-book of Mythology, Geography, Roman Antiquities, and History. With Notes and Dictionary. 12mo. 3s. 6d.

———————— Part III. A Poetry Book. Hexameters and Pentameters; Eclog. Ovidianæ; Latin Prosody. 12mo. 3s. 6d.

———————— Part IV. Prose Composition. Rules of Syntax with Examples, Explanations of Synonyms, and Exercises on the Syntax. 12mo. 3s. 6d.

———————— Part V. Short Tales and Anecdotes for Translation into Latin. 12mo. 3s.

———— Latin-English Vocabulary and First Latin-English Dictionary for Phædrus, Cornelius Nepos, and Cæsar. 12mo. 3s. 6d.

———— Student's Latin Grammar. Post 8vo. 6s.

———— Smaller Latin Grammar. 12mo. 3s. 6d.

———— Tacitus, Germania, Agricola, &c. With English Notes. 12mo. 3s. 6d.

———— Initia Græca, Part I. A First Greek Course, containing a Grammar, Delectus, and Exercise-book. With Vocabularies. 12mo. 3s. 6d.

———————— Part II. A Reading Book. Containing Short Tales, Anecdotes, Fables, Mythology, and Grecian History. 12mo. 3s. 6d.

———————— Part III. Prose Composition. Containing the Rules of Syntax, with copious Examples and Exercises. 12mo. 3s. 6d.

———— Student's Greek Grammar. By PROFESSOR CURTIUS. Post 8vo. 6s.

———— Smaller Greek Grammar. 12mo. 3s. 6d.

———— Greek Accidence. Extracted from the above work. 12mo. 2s. 6d.

———— Plato. The Apology of Socrates, the Crito, and Part of the Phædo; with Notes in English from Stallbaum and Schleiermacher's Introductions. 12mo. 3s. 6d.

———— Smaller Scripture History. Woodcuts. 16mo. 3s. 6d

———————— Ancient History. Woodcuts. 16mo. 3s. 6d.

———————— Geography. Woodcuts. 16mo. 3s. 6d.

———————— Rome. Woodcuts. 16mo. 3s. 6d.

———————— Greece. Woodcuts. 16mo. 3s. 6d.

———————— Classical Mythology. Woodcuts 16mo. 3s. 6d.

———————— History of England. Woodcuts. 16mo. 3s. 6d.

———————— English Literature. 16mo. 3s. 6d.

———————— Specimens of English Literature. 16mo. 3s. 6d

———— (PHILIP) History of the Ancient World, from the Creation to the Fall of the Roman Empire, A.D. 455. *Fourth Edition.* 3 Vols. 8vo. 31s. 6d.

———— (REV. A. C.) Nile and its Banks. Woodcuts. 2 Vols. Post 8vo. 18s.

SIMMONS' (CAPT.) Constitution and Practice of Courts-Martial. *Seventh Edition.* 8vo. 15s.

STUDENT'S OLD TESTAMENT HISTORY; from the Creation to the Return of the Jews from Captivity. Maps and Woodcuts. Post 8vo. 7s. 6d.

——— NEW TESTAMENT HISTORY. With an Introduction connecting the History of the Old and New Testaments. Maps and Woodcuts. Post 8vo. 7s. 6d.

——— ECCLESIASTICAL HISTORY. A History of the Christian Church from its Foundation to the Eve of the Protestant Reformation. Post 8vo. 7s 6d.

——— ANCIENT HISTORY OF THE EAST; Egypt, Assyria, Babylonia, Media, Persia, Asia Minor, and Phœnicia. Woodcuts. Post 8vo. 7s. 6d.

——— GEOGRAPHY. By Rev. W. L. Bevan. Woodcuts. Post 8vo. 7s. 6d.

——— HISTORY OF GREECE; from the Earliest Times to the Roman Conquest. By Wm. Smith, D.C.L. Woodcuts. Crown 8vo. 7s. 6d.
*** Questions on the above Work, 12mo. 2s.

——— HISTORY OF ROME; from the Earliest Times to the Establishment of the Empire. By Dean Liddell. Woodcuts. Crown 8vo. 7s. 6d.

——— GIBBON'S Decline and Fall of the Roman Empire. Woodcuts. Post 8vo. 7s. 6d.

——— HALLAM'S HISTORY OF EUROPE during the Middle Ages. Post 8vo. 7s. 6d.

——— HALLAM'S HISTORY OF ENGLAND; from the Accession of Henry VII. to the Death of George II. Post 8vo. 7s. 6d.

——— HUME'S History of England from the Invasion of Julius Cæsar to the Revolution in 1688. Continued down to 1868. Woodcuts. Post 8vo. 7s. 6d.
*** Questions on the above Work, 12mo. 2s.

——— HISTORY OF FRANCE; from the Earliest Times to the Establishment of the Second Empire, 1852. By Rev. H. W. Jervis. Woodcuts. Post 8vo. 7s. 6d.

——— ENGLISH LANGUAGE. By Geo. P. Marsh. Post 8vo. 7s. 6d.

——— LITERATURE. By T. B. Shaw, M.A. Post 8vo. 7s. 6d.

——— SPECIMENS of English Literature from the Chief Writers. By T. B. Shaw. Post 8vo. 7s. 6d.

——— MODERN GEOGRAPHY; Mathematical, Physical, and Descriptive. By Rev. W. L. Bevan. Woodcuts. Post 8vo. 7s. 6d.

——— MORAL PHILOSOPHY. By William Fleming, D.D. Post 8vo. 7s. 6d.

——— BLACKSTONE'S Commentaries on the Laws of England. By R. Malcolm Kerr, LL.D. Post 8vo. 7s. 6d.

SPALDING'S (Captain) Tale of Frithiof. Translated from the Swedish of Esias Tegner. Post 8vo. 7s. 6d.

STEPHEN'S (Rev. W. R.) Life and Times of St. Chrysostom. With Portrait. 8vo. 15s.

ST. JAMES (The) LECTURES. Companions for the Devout Life. By the following authors. 8vo. 7s. 6d.
IMITATION OF CHRIST. Rev. Dr. Farrar.
PASCAL'S PENSEES. Dean Church.
S. François de Sales. Dean Goulburn.
Baxter's Saints' Rest. Archbishop Trench.
S. Augustine's Confessions. Bishop Alexander.
Jeremy Taylor's Holy Living and Dying. Rev. Dr Humphry

ST. JOHN'S (CHARLES) Wild Sports and Natural History of the Highlands. Post 8vo. 3s. 6d.
——— (BAYLE) Adventures in the Libyan Desert. Post 8vo. 2s.
STORIES FOR DARLINGS. With Illustrations. 16mo. 5s.
STREET'S (G. E.) Gothic Architecture in Spain. From Personal Observations made during several Journeys. With Illustrations. Royal 8vo. 30s.
——————————————— in Italy, chiefly in Brick and Marble. With Notes of Tours in the North of Italy. With 60 Illustrations. Royal 8vo. 26s.
STANHOPE'S (EARL) England during the Reign of Queen Anne, 1701—13. *Library Edition.* 8vo. 16s. *Cabinet Edition.* Portrait. 2 Vols. Post 8vo. 10s.
——————— from the Peace of Utrecht to the Peace of Versailles, 1713-83. *Library Edition.* 7 vols. 8vo. 93s. *Cabinet Edition,* 7 vols. Post 8vo. 5s. each.
——————— British India, from its Origin to 1783. 8vo. 3s. 6d.
——————— History of "Forty-Five." Post 8vo. 3s.
——————— Historical and Critical Essays. Post 8vo. 3s. 6d.
——————— Life of Belisarius. Post 8vo. 10s. 6d.
——————— Condé. Post 8vo. 3s. 6d.
——————— William Pitt. Portraits. 4 Vols. 8vo. 24s.
——————— Miscellanies. 2 Vols. Post 8vo. 13s.
——————— Story of Joan of Arc. Fcap. 8vo. 1s.
——————— Addresses Delivered on Various Occasions. 16mo. 1s.
STYFFE'S (KNUTT) Strength of Iron and Steel. Plates. 8vo. 12s.
SOMERVILLE'S (MARY) Personal Recollections from Early Life to Old Age. With Selections from her Correspondence. Portrait. Crown 8vo. 12s.
——————— Physical Geography. Portrait. Post 8vo.
——————— Connexion of the Physical Sciences. Portrait. Post 8vo.
——————— Molecular and Microscopic Science. Illustrations. 2 Vols. Post 8vo. 21s.
SOUTHEY'S (ROBERT) Book of the Church. Post 8vo. 7s. 6d.
——————— Lives of Bunyan and Cromwell. Post 8vo. 2s.
SWAINSON'S (CANON) Nicene and Apostles' Creeds; Their Literary History; together with some Account of "The Creed of St. Athanasius." 8vo.
SYBEL'S (VON) History of Europe during the French Revolution, 1789—1795. 4 Vols. 8vo. 48s.
SYMONDS' (REV. W.) Records of the Rocks; or Notes on the Geology, Natural History, and Antiquities of North and South Wales, Siluria, Devon, and Cornwall. With Illustrations. Crown 8vo. 12s.
TAYLOR'S (SIR HENRY) Notes from Life. Fcap. 8vo. 2s.
THIELMAN'S (BARON) Journey through the Caucasus to Tabreez, Kurdistan, down the Tigris and Euphrates to Nineveh and Babylon, and across the Desert to Palmyra. Translated by CHAS. HENEAGE. Illustrations. 2 Vols. Post 8vo. 18s.
THOMS' (W. J.) Longevity of Man; its Facts and its Fiction. Including Observations on the more Remarkable Instances. Post 8vo. 10s. 6d.
THOMSON'S (ARCHBISHOP) Lincoln's Inn Sermons. 8vo. 10s. 6d.
——————— Life in the Light of God's Word. Post 8vo. 5s.

TOCQUEVILLE'S State of Society in France before the Revolution, 1789, and on the Causes which led to that Event. Translated by HENRY REEVE. 8vo. 12s.

TOMLINSON (CHARLES); The Sonnet; Its Origin, Structure, and Place in Poetry. With translations from Dante, Petrarch, &c. Post 8vo. 9s.

TOZER'S (REV. H. F.) Highlands of Turkey, with Visits to Mounts Ida, Athos, Olympus, and Pelion. 2 Vols Crown 8vo. 24s.

—————— Lectures on the Geography of Greece. Map. Post 8vo. 9s.

TRISTRAM'S (CANON) Great Sahara. Illustrations. Crown 8vo. 15s.

—————— Land of Moab; Travels and Discoveries on the East Side of the Dead Sea and the Jordan. Illustrations. Crown 8vo. 15s.

TWISLETON (EDWARD). The Tongue not Essential to Speech, with Illustrations of the Power of Speech in the case of the African Confessors. Post 8vo. 6s.

TWISS' (HON. CE) Life of Lord Eldon. 2 Vols. Post 8vo. 21s.

TYLOR'S (E. B.) Early History of Mankind, and Development of Civilization. 8vo. 12s.

—————— Primitive Culture; the Development of Mythology, Philosophy, Religion, Art, and Custom. 2 Vols. 8vo. 24s.

VAMBERY'S (ARMINIUS) Travels from Teheran across the Turkoman Desert on the Eastern Shore of the Caspian. Illustrations. 8vo. 21s.

VAN LENNEP'S (HENRY J.) Travels in Asia Minor. With Illustrations of Biblical Literature, and Archæology. With Woodcuts. 2 Vols. Post 8vo. 24s.

—————— Modern Customs and Manners of Bible Lands, in illustration of Scripture. With Maps and 300 Illustrations. 2 Vols. 8vo. 21s.

WELLINGTON'S Despatches during his Campaigns in India, Denmark, Portugal, Spain, the Low Countries, and France. Edited by COLONEL GURWOOD. 8 Vols. 8vo. 20s. each.

—————— Supplementary Despatches, relating to India, Ireland, Denmark, Spanish America, Spain, Portugal, France, Congress of Vienna, Waterloo and Paris. Edited by his SON. 14 Vols. 8vo. 20s. each. ** An Index. 8vo. 20s.

—————— Civil and Political Correspondence. Edited by his SON. Vols. I. to V. 8vo. 20s. each.

—————— Despatches (Selections from). 8vo. 18s.

—————— Speeches in Parliament. 2 Vols. 8vo. 42s.

WHEELER'S (G.) Choice of a Dwelling; a Practical Handbook of Useful Information on Building a House. Plans. Post 8vo. 7s. 6d.

WHYMPER'S (FREDERICK) Travels and Adventures in Alaska. Illustrations. 8vo. 16s.

WILBERFORCE'S (BISHOP) Essays on Various Subjects. 2 vols. 8vo. 21s.

—————— Life of William Wilberforce. Portrait. Crown 8vo. 6s.

WILKINSON'S (SIR J. G.) Popular Account of the Ancient Egyptians. With 500 Woodcuts. 2 Vols. Post 8vo. 12s.

WOOD'S (CAPTAIN) Source of the Oxus. With the Geography of the Valley of the Oxus. By COL. YULE. Map. 8vo. 12s.

WORDS OF HUMAN WISDOM. Collected and Arranged by E. S. With a Preface by CANON LIDDON. Fcap. 8vo. 3s. 6d.

WORDSWORTH'S (BISHOP) Athens and Attica. Plates. 8vo. 5s.

—————— Greece. With 600 Woodcuts. Royal 8vo.

YULE'S (COLONEL) Book of Marco Polo. Illustrated by the Light of Oriental Writers and Modern Travels. With Maps and 80 Plates 2 Vols. Medium 8vo. 63s.

www.ingramcontent.com/pod-product-compliance
Lightning Source LLC
Chambersburg PA
CBHW032102230426
43672CB00009B/1613